A COMPACT FOR HIGHER EDUCATION

A Compact for Higher Education

Edited by
K. MOTI GOKULSING and CORNEL DaCOSTA
University of East London

Routledge
Taylor & Francis Group

LONDON AND NEW YORK

First published 2000 by Ashgate Publishing

Reissued 2018 by Routledge
2 Park Square, Milton Park, Abingdon, Oxon OX14 4RN
711 Third Avenue, New York, NY 10017, USA

Routledge is an imprint of the Taylor & Francis Group, an informa business

Publisher's Note
The publisher has gone to great lengths to ensure the quality of this reprint but points out that some imperfections in the original copies may be apparent.

Disclaimer
The publisher has made every effort to trace copyright holders and welcomes correspondence from those they have been unable to contact.

A Library of Congress record exists under LC control number: 00013525

ISBN 13: 978-1-138-73816-4 (hbk)
ISBN 13: 978-1-138-73813-3 (pbk)
ISBN 13: 978-1-315-18497-5 (ebk)

Contents

List of Figures

List of Tables

List of Contributors

Patrick Ainley is Reader in Learning Policy at the University of Greenwich School of Post-Compulsory Education and Training. His latest book is *Learning Policy, Towards the Certified Society* (Macmillan, 1999) and he is co-editor with Helen Rainbird of *Apprenticeship, Towards a New Paradigm of Learning* (Kogan Page, 1999). He is co-author with Bill Bailey of *The Business of Learning, Staff and Student Experiences of Further Education in the 1990s* (Cassell, 1997), a companion to *Degrees of Difference: higher education in the 1990s* (Lawrence and Wishart, 1994), *Class and Skill, Changing divisions of knowledge and labour* (Cassell, 1993) and, with Mark Corney, *Training for the Future: The rise and fall of the Manpower Services Commission* (Cassell, 1990).

Ronald Barnett is Dean of Professional Development and Professor of Higher Education, Institute of Education, University of London. He is an institutional leader, with an informed insight into the challenging nature of higher education in the modern world and has edited, co-authored and authored a number of books some of which have been national prizewinners. His most recent book *Realizing the University in an Age of Supercomplexity*, was published by Open University Press. He was a team leader in the Dearing Report (1997), and has been consultant to a significant number of committees, including Higher Education Funding Councils for England and Wales (the Barnett Report), Committee of Vice-Chancellors and Principals and the Institute for Learning and Teaching in Higher Education.

Michael Bassey is Emeritus Professor of Education at Nottingham Trent University and Academic Secretary of the British Educational Research Association (BERA). Of his eight books the latest is *Case Study Research in Educational Settings*. For BERA he edits *Research Intelligence* and his contribution to this volume draws on some of his recent editorials. He was active in setting up the new Academy of Learned Societies for the Social Sciences and draws on this experience. He is currently working on the philosophical concept of fuzzy prediction and, in a different dimension, the empowerment of school children to tackle global warming.

Richard Brown became Director of the Council for Industry and Higher Education (CIHE) in July 1996 and Chief Executive in 1999. He is also Chairman of the Executive Board of The National Centre for Work Experience (NCWE) a subsidiary of CIHE, funded by government to develop the agenda on quality work experience. He has held senior positions in both the public and private sectors. In the Department of Trade and Industry he dealt, among other matters, with European policy and inward investment. At Meyer International, and then at the National Grid Company he was General Manager in charge of business strategy and new business development. He became Chief Executive in a partnership-based development agency in 1993 before joining CIHE early in 1996.

Phil Cohen is Professor of Applied Cultural Studies at the University of East London where he currently directs the centre for New Ethnicities Research. His recent publications include *New Ethnicities, Old racisms* (Zed Books, 1999) and *Rethinking the Youth Question: Education, labour and cultural studies* (Duke University, 1998).

Cornel DaCosta is Deputy Head in the Department of Education and Community Studies at the University of East London. He has had substantial experience of course development and teaching in schools, further and higher education. His research and scholarly work has been in the areas of higher education, multicultural education, and teacher education/training. He has published extensively and is the coauthor and coeditor of *Usable Knowledges as the Goal of Higher Education, and A selected Bibliography of Competence-Based Education and Training.* In 1981, he founded with Colin Mably, the International Society for Teacher Education which today has a worldwide membership and publishes an international journal. The society promotes international research and individual and institutional collaboration.

Meghnad Desai (Lord Desai of St Clement Danes) is Professor of Economics at the London School of Economics and Political Science, and is currently the Director of the Centre for the Study of Global Governance, LSE. Born in July 1940, he was educated at the University of Bombay. He secured his PhD, from the University of Pennsylvania, USA. He has written extensively on a wide range of subjects. From 1984–1991, he was co-editor of the *Journal of Applied Econometrics.* He has been both Chair and President of Islington South and Finsbury Constituency Labour Party in London and was made a peer in April 1991. He is currently Chairman of the Trustee's Board for Training for Life, Chairman of the Management Board of City Roads and on the Board of Tribune magazine.

K. Moti Gokulsing is Reader in Education and Director of the Centre for South Asian Studies at the University of East London. He is the author of a number of articles and books on Education and the Media including the following: *Sociology – a user friendly guide*; *Beyond Competence* (co-authored); *Usable Knowledges as the Goal of University Education* (co-edited); and *Indian Popular Cinema – a narrative of cultural change* (co-authored).

Norman Jackson currently holds the positions of Senior Research Fellow in the Centre for Policy and Change in Higher Education at the University of Surrey, Assistant Director in the Development Directorate of the Quality Assurance for Higher Education, where he is responsible for developing policy on programme specifications and progress files, and HE Advisor to Ufi Ltd. He was a member of the Higher Education Quality Council's Graduate Standards Programme research team which provided evidence to the Dearing Committee on standards-related issues in HE.

Ian Johnston is Principal and Vice-Chancellor of Glasgow Caledonian University (1998–) and Board Member of the University for Industry: Learn direct (1999–) where he was transition Chief Executive in 1998. He became interested in virtual education and training through the Opentech and Open College initiatives of the Manpower Services Commission and its successors where he was eventually Director General Training Enterprise and Education at DfEE. For three years (1995–98) he was Deputy Principal at Sheffield Hallam where heavy investment has been made in networked learning. He is currently a member of the Council for Industry and Higher Education.

Louise Morley is Senior Lecturer in Higher Education Studies and Assistant Dean of Professional Studies at the University of London Institute of Education. She was previously at the University of Sussex and the University of Reading. Her research and publication interests focus on equity, gender, power and empowerment in higher and professional education. Her recent publications include *Organising Feminisms: The Micropolitics of the Academy* (Macmillan, 1999), *School Effectiveness: Fracturing the Discourse* (The Falmer Press, 1999) (co-authored with Naz Rassool), *Breaking Boundaries: Women in Higher Education,* (1996) and *Feminist Academics: Creative Agents for Change* (1995) both edited with Val Walsh and published by Taylor and Francis.

Martin O'Donovan worked in NUS's Public Affairs Unit from 1997–April 2000, having previously worked for Ann Keen MP and the Socialist Group of the European Parliament. A graduate in French and Russian from the University of Westminster, Martin is now the Director of the trade union pressure group, Unions 21.

Andrew Pakes was, until recently, the 47th president of the National Union of Students (NUS). A graduate in politics from Hull University, Andrew took on the lead role in the student movement at a very difficult time with so many fundamental changes in education. He encapsulates much of the progressiveness of the student movement today, with a firm belief in Green issues, a commitment to the various liberation campaigns and NUS ability to make a difference for the future.

Viv Parker is Reader in Educational Development (Learning Support) and the University Co-ordinator for Students with Disabilities at the University of East London. She has managed three HEFCE funded projects to promote access to the university for students with disabilities and specific learning difficulties (dyslexia). Her 1996–99 project was to set up a centre for the assessment of the study support needs of students with disabilities and dyslexia from the East London region as part of the National Federation of Access Centres in the UK. She has researched several aspects of disability and HE including Disability Statements and developing a code of practice for co-ordinators.

Glenn Rikowski is Senior Research Fellow in Lifelong Learning in the Faculty of Education, University of Central England, Birmingham. From 1994–99, he was a Research Fellow in the School of Education, University of Birmingham. Prior to that, Dr Rikowski taught in further education colleges and in schools. His latest book (co-edited with Dave Hill, Peter McLaren and Mike Cole) is *Postmodernism in Educational Theory: Education and the Politics of Human Resistance* (Tufnell Press, 1999).

Judith Watson is a partner in Sustainable Findings, the research agency for sustainable economic development. Until recently she was also Senior Research Fellow in the School for Post-Compulsory Education and Training at the University of Greenwich. She has recently conducted an 'Education Audit for London' (for Focus Central London TEC) and was principal researcher on the ESRC-funded study 'Learning Pathways: Patterns of Progression in Post-16 Education and Training'.

Tom Wilson is head of the Universities Department at NATFHE, the National Association of Teachers in Further and Higher Education. Prior to that he was Assistant General Secretary at the Association of University Teachers (AUT). Between 1986 and 1989 he worked as national Trade Union Liaison Officer for the Labour Party and before that in the research department of the GMB, Britain's general trade union, which organises university manual workers. He is a Fellow of the Institute of Personnel and Development, has an MA in Industrial Relations and has written widely on various aspects of trade unionism and higher education.

Acknowledgements

We wish to thank our contributors for their patience in meeting the tight deadlines for their contributions and for making this project an exciting and valuable experience for us.

In dealing with such a variety of themes, we have been helped by a number of people, too many to name individually. We do, however, owe a special debt of gratitude to the following: Patrick Ainley, for steadfast support and help with the drafts; Ron Barnett, for his encouraging advice and valuable suggestions throughout the project; Lord Dearing, for his enthusiasm about the book and for privileging us with a foreword; Ms Katherine Hodkinson and her team at Ashgate Publishing Ltd for ensuring the publication of the book by December 2000; and Pat Silverlock and Pat FitzGerald for help with the compilation of the chapters prior to publication.

We also wish to thank our respective families, Seetah, Shishana, Nishani Ramphul Gokulsing, and Nancy, Joanna and Jessica DaCosta, for their patience and understanding while we were working on this book. Seetah Ramphul Gokulsing helped substantially with the chapters and their bibliographies, wordprocessing, and coping with the frequent glitches of the computer, particularly when strict deadlines had to be met.

The publication of this book was made possible through the University of East London funding arising out of the 1996 Research Assessment Exercise.

Finally, we, the named editors, take full responsibility for any errors or omissions which may remain in this book.

Prefatory Note

All the contributions to this volume were commissioned, except for chapter 8, What Kind of Place is This?, which drew upon a paper the author gave at a conference in Homerton College, Cambridge in May 1998.

The acronyms and abbreviations used in the chapters in this volume are common and widespread in writings about education. The following, however, have been used interchangeably by the contributors:

CIT/ICT Information and Communication Technology

The Dearing Report (1997), aka National Committee of Inquiry into Higher Education (NCIHE).

Foreword

A Compact for Higher Education

I welcome this collection of papers. I welcome it because the National Committee of Inquiry into Higher Education, which reported in 1997, had a vision of higher education purposively engaged with society, rather than standing apart from it, and seeking to identify explicitly what it has to contribute and what it should seek to achieve through purposive engagement. But in the time we had, we could only sketch out our thinking in broad outline.

In my own mind, the advantage of expressing what is implicit and seeking to give form to the relationship between the institutions of higher education, and all who have an actual or potential relationship with them lay first in the conviction that the only secure basis for maintaining and enhancing living standards in the United Kingdom lies in a knowledge and research based economy. This meant that the development of our people through education at its highest levels, and the pursuit of knowledge through research, were of the most direct relevance to their well being. It meant that while the distancing of the university from the insistent demands of today's preoccupations was fundamental to maintaining the quality of what they have to offer, at the same time there was clear advantage for society and the institutions themselves in recognising and seeking to develop to their mutual advantage what each had to offer the other, and in developing that potential through a series of compacts. All this seemed obvious to me in principle but, it was much less obvious how the compacts could be developed and expressed. That is why we need this publication. The concept we outlined is far too important to lie only within the covers of our Report.

I have discussed the concept so far only in terms of the institutions and communities whether at local, regional or national levels. But we also had in mind the relationship between the institutions and their staff and between the institutions and their students. The former are the prime assets of the institutions and yet we felt that on the one hand staff identified with their discipline or department rather than with the institution, and on the other hand the institutions did too little to develop the capabilities and the careers of staff. There would be gain to both sides from addressing these issues through a compact expressing how each might respond, to their mutual benefit.

Turning finally and arguably most importantly to the student, it is relevant to refer to my Committee's development of the statement of the purposes of higher education as formulated by the Robbins Committee thirty years previously. That Committee had drawn a distinction between the purpose of promoting the general powers of the mind and the purpose of providing instruction in skills for employment. While understanding the distinction made in Robbins, we thought it unnecessary and at least in my mind, an echo of those debates in the nineteenth century, in which strong arguments were advanced for distancing the universities from 'instruction in skills'. While we probably would not have chosen to use the word 'instruction' in any context, we chose not to make these separate purposes, and in that we were implicitly positioning the universities and their service to students in society.

The extent to which universities and colleges of higher education are today dependent on funding from central government is not in the best interests of the institutions or in the best interests of society itself. This dependence is analogous in a commercial context – and nowadays universities have to be thought of as businesses as well as centres of learning – to being almost wholly dependent on one customer. Although the state is a benevolent customer, it has a wider loyalty than to education. The pressures on the public purse of healthcare, social security and the provision for old age are likely to be great. It is therefore in the interest of institutions to broaden their funding base. The compact provides a framework within which they can develop a broader base. It offers a framework within which society can realise the full potential contribution of higher education to its own well-being.

R.E. Dearing
Chairman of the National Committee of Inquiry

Introduction

K. MOTI GOKULSING AND CORNEL DaCOSTA

The present volume brings together a series of contributions about the idea of a compact for higher education as it confronts a new millennium. A compact for higher education was proposed by the Dearing Report (1997). This book focuses on the idea of a compact from several different perspectives. But what is a compact and is it really possible to formulate one in a rapidly changing world?

The dictionary definition of a compact is 'an agreement or contract between two or more parties'. Our use of the term derives from this dictionary definition, but builds on the Report of Lord Dearing (hereinafter referred to as the Dearing Report, 1997) whose vision of higher education was underpinned by the following 'big' ideas, according to Watson and Taylor (1998, p. 151):

• the contribution of higher education to lifelong learning;
• a vision for learning in the twenty-first century;
• funding research according to its intended outcomes;
• a new compact between the state, the institutions and their students.

The Dearing Report (1997), however, was constrained by the government's political agenda and this has been discussed by a number of writers (Barnett, 1999; Watson and Taylor, 1998). Barnett (1999, p. 301), in particular, has drawn our attention to how the Dearing Report (1997) 'is the product of the state and its dominant client group – the corporate sector – concerned to ensure that higher education is playing its part in the positioning of the UK within a globalised and fast-changing economy and world order'. While there are some shortcomings in the Dearing Report (1997) such as its failure to address the structure of higher education itself, and the idea of a curriculum in higher education and associated pedagogical matters, one of its strengths lies in its emphasis to address multiple audiences as the fundamental aims of higher education and its character have become problematic. It thus strove to strike a compact among its varied stakeholders.

However, reflecting critically on the state of higher education two years after his Report, Lord Dearing himself acknowledged that 'despite much

1

promising work and some real achievement, the debate (on higher education) never materialised' (Dearing 1999, p. 11). Focusing on the contemporary situation in higher education in Britain, Lord Dearing (ibid.) continued:

> of course universities have enduring purposes that transcend changes in time and circumstance, but times and circumstance have never been changing more speedily, and the needs of society with them. The institutions need continually to be reassessing their strengths and opportunities as well as the challenges deriving from the development of the global economy, the creation of a society committed to learning for life, the unfolding implications of communications and information technology, and from such reassessments, judging how best to equip students to be effective in a world of such rapid change.

These reassessments need to take place periodically if we wish to obviate the need for another Dearing Report (1997) in the near future. The massification of higher education, the acceleration of the technological revolution, the global economy, the government's prioritisation of stronger links with industry and students contributing to their higher education mean that the providers – the academics and their institutions – are increasingly saddled with obligations and the consumers – students and employers – are increasingly empowered with rights.

These dramatic changes, which are taking place in higher education in Britain as a result of serial reforms in a short space of time, are on the whole impacting negatively on the universities and their staff. Thus, the announcement in December 1999 of the third and final year of the present comprehensive spending review of the New Labour government gives the major share of post-16 funding to further education colleges rather than to the universities, thus confirming the latter's funding reductions (although this could be said to go some little way towards redressing the imbalance between funding for the two sectors). As the *Times Higher Educational Supplement* (*THES*) (1999, p. 1) reported '… the year-on-year cuts are unsustainable and pose serious problems for infrastructure and pay' (in higher education).

But government policies initiated in the Thatcher years of the late 1970s and the 1980s and continued by the present New Labour government remind us of Theodore Zeldin's apt observation 30 years ago that the modern anti-clericalism is not against the clergyman but against the 'clerc', the privileged and arrogant academic. This accusation is still being levelled at academics, particularly at social scientists. Writing in the *THES* David Blunkett (2000, pp. 36–7), the Secretary of State for Education and Employment, supports the view that too much social science is inward-looking, irrelevant to key social issues and he calls for more cooperation, understanding and partnership between researchers and policy makers for the benefit of the government and society. In this new climate, we feel it is crucial that not only the voices of the researchers and policy makers but also those of others with roles in higher education should be heard. It is in this sense that we believe this book is innovative since, in one volume, it articulates the voices of some important stakeholders in higher education, thus aiming to implement Lord Dearing's suggestion of 'a compact which in certain respects could with advantage be made explicit' (Dearing Report 1997, 1.27).

Consequently, we are using the notion of a compact as the organising principle of this book in order to identify and examine the separate responsibilities or contributions that each stakeholder e.g. students, the state, employers, unions, academics commits to the compact. To what extent are the different agendas of stakeholders compatible and can they be realised in a consensual way that will carry the widest support of the greatest number of parties?

Such a notion of a compact generates a number of themes which provide coherence and a structure to the various contributions of the stakeholders. In Part 1, the idea of a compact is explored. Focusing on the Dearing concept of a compact, Ron Barnett teases out the implications of a compact for higher education and highlights the ambiguities which are embedded in such a notion. He argues that as we live in an age of supercomplexity, such a compact based on familiar ideas of the university is an illusion. The university is dead, he argued in the *THES* (Barnett 2000, p. 14), but we need an idea of the university more than ever with multiple frames of understanding; he suggests, therefore, that the compact should be seen as a process rather than an outcome.

The view of the present British government, however, is more focused on outcome than on process, as a number of government policy statements show. In a recent article Baroness Blackstone (1999) the Minister of State for Higher Education, identified the forces of change in higher education which will meet the new millennium. Drawing attention to the joined-up thinking that think tanks supply to political decision makers, Blackstone (1999, p. 14) suggests that the 'space occupied by think tanks – between academia, the media, civil society and government – is likely to expand in coming years'. One important consequence of this is that 'the pivotal role of higher education in knowledge development is being transformed' (Blackstone, 1999) Furthermore:

> New Technologies make the provision of learning in real time anywhere in the globe a reality for whoever can access it. This means that different institutions

can operate across previously geographically distinct markets, and that new
providers of skills and learning can compete with higher education institutions
in terrains previously considered sacrosanct (Blackstone 1999, p. 14).

Lord Desai's views for a forthright and radical agenda for higher education
are in line with the government's thinking. Arguing, in chapter 2, that the
higher education system as at present financed is inequitable and inadequate,
Lord Desai suggests that we need to establish a set of contracts in line with
the American higher education system. This suggestion is likely to be widely
supported in some higher education institutions. In like manner, commenting
on university performance indicators published in the press in the first week
of December 1999, Alan Smithers (1999, p. 2) argued that universities should
be allowed:

> to develop courses of different lengths to meet different needs and, crucially,
> they should be permitted to price their courses to generate income. The
> government could secure the state's interest through, say, merit scholarships
> and grants for the socially disadvantaged.

Consequently, in Part 1, two different agendas are set: Barnett's arguments
favour a notion of an entrepreneurial university operating in a society of
supercomplexity while the government and Lord Desai would appear to
promote greater privatisation of the universities.

In Part 2 a number of themes address the possibilities of how a compact
in higher education can be brought off in practice. Taking his cue from the
Dearing Report's (1997) call for a new compact between institutions and their
staff, students, government, employers and society in general, Norman Jackson,
in chapter 3, focuses on the important role of quality assurance. This issue
has now assumed national significance since the confrontation between the
Quality Assurance Agency (QAA) and the universities represented by the
Committee of Vice-Chancellors and Principals (CVCP) and the Standing
Conference of Principals (SCOP) ended in January 2000 with the QAA
rejecting the majority of the proposals of the CVCP and SCOP and imposing
their own codes of practice. This strengthens Jackson's argument that a
collective commitment to rigorous assurance of quality and standards would
be in the interests of all stakeholders by providing rigorously assured awards
of national and international standing and a high quality learning experience.
Consequently, his chapter examines how the contribution of a national quality
assurance policy can help create the conditions within which a compact
between stakeholders can be arrived at. This is in stark contrast to the arguments

made elsewhere by Smithers (1999, p. 2) who says that the universities should be left 'to concentrate on identifying and developing talents, free from the silliness of the Quality Assurance Agency'.

In chapter 4 Louise Morley considers how discourses of quality and equality interact or collide in the context of massification and the changing demography of higher education. Part of her argument relates to how human capital theory has been increasingly applied to higher education in relation to global competitiveness and national prosperity, a point made in the Dearing Report (1997).

Using a Foucauldian framework, she scrutinises a range of arguments to show how the quality discourse has achieved hegemonic authority. She raises questions about the appropriateness of applying quality assurance systems from industry to the complex social and intellectual processes of higher education. On the one hand she finds some of the arguments oppressive while on the other hand she states that quality audits represent a form of consumer empowerment. The scrutiny of organisations/institutions is seen as a refreshing challenge to elitism and to disciplinary authority, reinforcing a point made by Luke (1997), according to Morley.

But clearly one of the most important points of the Dearing Report (1997) is that by addressing multiple stakeholders, it attempted to reposition higher education as a force for continuing economic regeneration (Barnett 1999, p. 293). In the last decade, according to Atkins et al. (1999, p. 99), there has been an increase in the potential roles that higher education institutions can play in the economies of their immediate region. Indeed, during 1995–96 a team from Newcastle University carried out a detailed study of the North East and West Midlands for the DfEE 'in an effort to identify factors that would either promote or inhibit the engagement of universities in the economic development agendas'. In chapter 5, Judith Watson uses the Thames Gateway as a case study of the largest economic development project in South East England. She singles out 'academic services' as a key industry in economic development. Focusing on five universities – three new and two old ones – Watson identifies their strengths and weaknesses in terms of their response to economic development imperatives. The three new universities are enthusiastic participants in economic development but their involvement is hindered by bureaucratic regulations and they lose out when it comes to the allocation of research funds. The two old universities thus have fewer incentives to participate in economic development. The allocation of research funds identified by Watson as one of the reasons why new universities 'lose out' brings to the fore the vexed question of the role of teaching and research in higher education.

Next, in chapter 6 Michael Bassey draws attention to the role of government agencies such as the HEFCs in funding research through the Research Assessment Exercise (RAE). He deplores the quick fixes that the pressure to publish is engendering. This point was also made by Rosamond McKitterick (1999, p. 23) who stated that despite the RAE's claims to be assessing quality rather than quantity, some university departments encourage their staff to produce a number of articles on the basis of making a greater contribution to the arithmetical calculation of the RAE. She deplored the reactive marketing policies of many publishers which damage the promotion of pioneering research. Using as his starting point the mission statement of the recently formed Academy of the Social Sciences, which seeks to advance the social sciences in terms of understanding today and shaping tomorrow, Bassey argues particularly for a compact between various stakeholders in the social sciences in the hope that this could lift the siege and enable the social sciences to flourish. For the social sciences have been under a threat since the 1970s, particularly following the election of Margaret Thatcher as Prime Minister in 1979 and her notorious statement that there is no such thing as society. The New Labour government have created a more promising environment for research but are more in favour of evidence-based research to guide policy making. Consequently, Bassey's arguments are timely, since social scientists do not have an umbrella body such as the Royal Society to speak for them.

The last chapter in Part 2 links up with the Dearing Report's (1997) emphasis on the role of communications and information technology (CIT). However, Ian Johnston's chapter goes much further and argues strongly for what is virtually a new paradigm: the virtual university. In his chapter he adduces valid reasons for applying CIT to the delivery of higher education, following the well-known argument that this is the third major revolution in human vocational behaviour after the agricultural and industrial revolutions. The implications of the virtual university could be staggering – it will change the needs and expectations of on-campus students, including expected learning outcomes. It will permit hugely widened access to off-campus students, through virtual delivery with consequent changes to concepts of tutoring, mentoring and assessment.

Some observers of this new phenomenon, however, see great danger and significant social loss in such a scenario. As Mason (1998, p. 9) put it:

> the essence of our education system has been the community of a classroom and the physical reality of the textbook. It has changed relatively little over the past few hundred years.

But, Mason (ibid.) continues:

> What we will have in the next few years is an education system that is part of
> computer culture. It is not just the physical environment that will be transformed.
> Whereas books have encouraged us to think in terms of a stable body of
> knowledge, a form of content that we can read, digest, learn and know, computers
> dispose us to think differently – to be engaged in a constantly changing process
> where information is not stable or fixed.

Consequently, new areas of research such as the cognitive effects of
computerisation and screen-based learning will develop and probably the most
significant effect could be to challenge both how universities are organised
and the fundamental reasons why they need to continue to exist.

The implications of such a scenario for a compact need to be explored. It
is part of what Blackstone, quoted earlier, meant when she said 'that new
providers of skills and learning can compete with higher education institutions
in terrains previously considered sacrosanct'. Recent reports suggest that this
is already happening. Thus, Currie (2000, p. 17) states that British academics
will be advisers to Regent's College, America's leading 'virtual university'.
The Department of Trade and Industry (DTI) has set up a Foresight taskforce
to find out how new technology and new organisations will alter teaching and
learning by 2020 (ibid.). As the leader in the *THES* (2000, p. 18) states:

> New technology and new organisations are opening options, and universities
> are under threat from competitors. This is forcing a re-examination not only of
> universities' organisation and structure, but also of their essential purposes.

Consequently, a new kind of compact in which higher education might play a
lesser role than hitherto will have to be worked out.

In Part 3, we explore how a compact for higher education could work out
in practice. The issues addressed in this section have been largely ignored or
are under-researched in higher education. To start with, Phil Cohen makes a
strong case for a multicultural university. As he says, multicultural societies
require multicultural universities. 'It is as simple and as complicated as that.
It is simple because it embodies a clear statement of principle: the university
should draw its students and staff from every section of society....'

It is complicated because such a proposal for multicultural universities is
fraught with difficulties. It challenges the very model of the Western university
by the counterflow of populations and ideas from South to North and East to
West. Cohen investigates the claim that higher education institutions dispense

universalistic forms of knowledge. The knowledge is based on classical or Biblical foundations and has a long history going back to the middle ages as far as the universities are concerned. This history reveals the following, although not in a linear fashion:

> an archaeology of Western Reason in its successive transformations, from the medieval community of scholars, and the institutions of Renaissance humanism, through the 18th century Enlightenment, the so-called Age of Reason, followed by the Victorian Age of belief in Science, Progress and Modernity and thence on to the twentieth century megastructures modelled on corporate capitalism.

In dealing with issues of equal opportunity to account for the diverse student body of higher education, Cohen emphasises issues of diversity, difference and de-differentiation or the breaking down of boundaries and norms. Most of the providers and the consumers of higher education would subscribe to a compact which builds on such issues.

Cohen's chapter provides an umbrella for the discussion of the next two chapters in this section. The New Labour government's commitment to education and training is underpinned by their attempt to provide a coherent political philosophy. This philosophy relates to the role that learning now plays in providing an enabling framework to tackle issues of poor levels of literacy and numeracy which lead to increased social exclusion. It was Gordon Brown, the Chancellor of the Exchequer, who spelt out in some detail the political philosophy of the New Labour government. He sees education and training as mechanisms:

> to improve individuals' access to the labour market and enhance their job security. Rather than alleviate poverty and reduce income differentials through increased taxation and redistributive welfare spending, Brown argued that the most effective means of tackling inequality and social exclusion was to provide recurrent equality of opportunity for individuals to learn ... (Hodgson and Spours, 1999, pp. 10–11).

In chapter 9, Viv Parker examines precisely the issue of how higher education can be fully inclusive. She asks whether the principles of universal design developed by architects, product designers, engineers and environmental design researchers could be applied to higher education. If this is feasible, what are the implications for innovations in teaching strategies, learning environments and extending the role of communication and information technology to students with disabilities? Recommendation 6 of the Dearing

Report (1997) states:

> We recommend to the Institute for Learning and Teaching that it includes the learning needs of students with disabilities in its research, programme accreditation and advisory activities.

The implementation of the above recommendation and the extension of the scope of the Disabled Students Allowance to students in higher education also recommended in the Dearing Report (1997) are steps in the right direction. They will help remove many of the barriers identified by Parker in her chapter. But disability, as a number of writers have reminded us, is also a form of oppression and the difficulties encountered by disabled people intersect with age, race and class.

In the final chapter in this section, Cornel DaCosta deals with another form of oppression, that suffered by lower socioeconomic groups. This is the term used in the Dearing Report (1997), which is more inclusive than social class differences, probably the most researched theme in the sociology of education in Britain. Although in the words of Reid (1999, p. xix):

> social class differences and inequalities have become less central concerns both politically and socially and within social science, perhaps because of developing interest in these features of gender and ethnicity, and/or because the popularity of class has declined owing to its intransigence ...

the New Labour government's emphasis on widening participation in higher education makes socioeconomic disadvantage a central plank of its social justice agenda, referred to earlier on in this introduction.

However, comparatively little work has been done on the participation of lower socioéconomic groups in higher education. It is perhaps the Robbins Report (1963) which provides the most comprehensive, though now dated, research in this area. As Reid (1999, p. 181) states, the Robbins Report documents the very separate ways in which:

> the social classes, based on father's occupation at the time the sample left school, were in terms of entry to higher and further education ... the situation did not change with the expansion of universities and other forms of education following the recommendations of the Robbins Report (1963).

DaCosta draws our attention to the fact that socioeconomic differences and inequalities in higher education are alive and flourishing and that these have to be addressed through a compact.

In the final part, we try to identify and examine the contributions that the consumers of higher education may make to the compact. Patrick Ainley, in chapter 11, situates the new public management of higher education within the 'contracting state'. Looking ahead, he examines the new unified system of further education and training that will be introduced under the Learning and Skills Council on 1 April 2001. Arguing for a reversal of the marketisation of the state and society, Ainley proposes a democratic compact for higher education instead of the commercial contract described by Meghnad Desai in Part 1.

However, one of the fundamental changes any compact has to take into account concerns the lack of sufficient progress being made by university employees in equal opportunities. MacLeod (2000, p. 9) reports the result of a survey which concludes that as far as the employment of women and minority groups is concerned, universities were far from being bastions of liberal employment policies and that they were no better than companies and organisations in the country at large. The Equal Opportunities Advisory Service as well as NATFHE is now involved in addressing such issues.

Next, in chapter 12, Tom Wilson, Head of Education at NATFHE puts the case for NATFHE's approach to higher education and argues against the narrow focus of higher education serving the needs of the economy. He distances himself from the government policy of student fees and removal of grants. Rejecting performance pay for academics, even at a minimal level, Wilson welcomes the Bett Report (1999) and draws attention to the casualisation of higher education employees. Thus, Swain (1999, p. 3) reported that the proportion of all academic/research staff on fixed-term contracts had increased from 9 per cent for females and 12 per cent for males pre-1970 to 80 per cent for females and 77 per cent for males in 1997–98. This situation is now characterising higher education in most advanced industrial countries. According to the US Department of Education (1990), in the United States about a quarter of academic staff are on part-time appointments. In France, Cazenave and Zahn (1989) state that twenty thousand academic positions are part-time and in Canada more than a third of academic staff are on part-time appointment according to Rajagopal and Farr (1992).

Most of the arguments Wilson makes are in line with a trade union approach: protecting pay, conditions and contracts, dealing with discrimination and the improvement of the quality of lecturers' working lives and students learning experience. A compact would therefore have to incorporate these fundamental issues.

In the next chapter, Andrew Pakes, until recently the President of the NUS, and his colleague, Martin O'Donovan, currently director of the trade union pressure group, Unions 21, assess the implications of the changed culture and concerns of the NUS in the light of the changing higher education scene. They emphasise the importance of the learning age, particularly the advantages of Internet learning and CIT. They approve of the government plan to expand higher and further education in order to develop a highly skilled workforce and draw attention to the immense funding implications resulting from the increased participation rate in higher education. They agree that a new age of learning cannot be funded by the methods of the past and that 'students and their representatives must embrace change and move on'. In their view a compact for higher education will evolve as lifelong and distance learning expands.

An issue raised by Pakes and O'Donovan concerns the impact on students' learning of part-time work in which full-time students are now increasingly engaged. In chapter 14, 'The Rise of the Student-Worker', Glenn Rikowski draws upon his research to provide an analysis of the student-worker as a full-time student and explores the risks, stresses and role conflicts that this increasingly important dimension in the lives of full-time students poses. This new situation raises fundamental questions not only for the student worker but also for Higher Education Institutions (HEIs). Should students take longer to complete a degree and should HEIs revisit their structures to accommodate full-time student workers'? There is no doubt that a new compact for higher education needs to consider this.

Finally, Richard Brown of the Council for Industry and Higher Education gives the views of industry. He insists that:

> UK business wants and needs a higher education system that is pre-eminent. It needs the highest quality from all institutions as they pursue through partnerships their own distinctive missions.

According to Jary and Parker (1998, p. 64) The Council for Industry and Higher Education (CIHE) is an independent body made up of heads of large companies, universities and colleges whose views have some influence on government policies. CIHE has consistently promoted the concept of a partnership between government, higher education and industry working together to develop a different kind of higher education system altogether (CIHE, 1987 – quoted in Jary and Parker 1998, p. 54).

However, the relationship between higher education and business has not always been smooth and productive. Consequently, Brown states that higher education has to respond and meet the challenges of the knowledge economy. But business too has to change. If organisations want:

graduates with more employability skills that can better hit the ground running, then they have to engage more with institutions ... they need to communicate their ideas clearly and consistently enough.

Brown makes the interesting point that 'organisations are not always best at thinking of their long-term rather than short-term needs and a dialogue with academia (that tends to have the opposite trait!)' can be particularly useful. A compact would, in Brown's view, involve a closer partnership between higher education, organisations and the government.

Whether such a compact will be politically or organisationally feasible remains to be seen. Other versions of a compact between higher education and society, such as those suggested by the contributors to this volume, offer alternative models. Or it may be that Lord Dearing's idea of a compact may be lost in the move to full contractual relations between higher education, its students and other clients or customers, as suggested by other contributors. Whatever actually occurs, the notion of a compact should not be lost from the legacy of the Dearing Report. It affords a conceptual space within which discussion can take place over the future of higher education in relation to the society of which it is a part and over the practical organisational forms that that relationship can take. This collection is a contribution to that debate.

References

Atkins, M., Dersley, J. and Tomlin, R. (1999), 'The Engagement of Universities in Regional Economic Regeneration and Development: a Case Study of Perspectives', *Higher Education Management*, March, Vol. 11, No. 1, pp. 97–115.

Barnett, R. (1999), 'The Coming of the Global village: a tale of two inquiries', *Oxford Review of Education*, Vol. 25, No. 3, pp. 293–306.

Barnett, R. (2000), 'The University is Dead, Long Live the University', *THES*, 11 February.

Bett Report (1999), *The Independent Review of HE pay and conditions: Report of a Committee chaired by M. Bett*, London: HMSO.

Blackstone, T. (1999), 'Twin Forces of Change Set to Meet the Millennium', *THES* 15 January.

Blunkett, D. (2000), 'Influence or irrelevance?', *THES*, 4 February.

Cazenave, P. and Zahn, J.F. (1989), *Evolution in the Modes of Financing Higher Education: National Report*, France: OECD.

Currie, J. (2000), 'Virtual Faculty recruits in the UK', *THES*, 28 January.

Dearing, R. (1999), 'Higher Education: Dearing: Regrets, I've had a few', *The Guardian*, 13 July.

Hodgson, A. and Spours, K. (1999), *New Labour's Educational Agenda*, London: Kogan Page.

Jary, D. and Parker, M. (eds) (1998), *The New Higher Education: Issues and Directions for the Post-Dearing University*, Staffordshire: Staffordshire University Press.

Luke, C. (1997), 'Quality Assurance and Women in Higher Education', *Higher Education*, 33, pp. 433–51.

MacLeod, D. (2000), 'Colour of Money', *The Guardian*, 21 March.

Mason, R. (1998), *Globalising Education Trends and Applications*, London: Routledge.

McKitterick, R. (1999), 'Rumours of a Death that May be True', *THES*, 9 December.

National Committee of Inquiry into Higher Education (Dearing Report) (1997), *Higher Education in the Learning Society*, London: HMSO.

Rajagopal, I. and Farr, W.D, (1992), 'Hidden Academics: The Part-Time Faculty in Canada', *Higher Education*, 24, pp. 317–31.

Reid, I. (1999), *Class in Britain*, Cambridge: Polity Press.

Robbins Report (1963), *Report of the Committee on Higher Education*, London: HMSO.

Smithers, A. (1999), 'Comment', *The Independent*, 9 December.

Swain, H. (1999), 'Jobs Insecurity Spreads', *THES*, 10 December.

THES (1999), 'Universities lose out as FE scoops cash', 26 November.

THES (2000), 'Leader', 28 January.

Watson, D. and Taylor, R. (1998), *Lifelong Learning and the University A Post-Dearing Agenda*, London: Falmer Press.

PART I
THE IDEA OF A COMPACT

1 Realizing a Compact for Higher Education

RONALD BARNETT

Introduction

> We think in terms of a compact between higher education and society which reflects their strong bond of mutual interdependence: a compact which in certain respects could with advantage be made explicit. A compact which is based on an interpretation of the needs of both sides at national, regional and local level requires continuing dialogue and a framework within which it takes place (NCIHE, 1997, 1.27).

The notion of a 'compact' runs throughout the report of the National Committee of Inquiry into Higher Education (1997); it forms a key idea in the 'vision' (1.22) of higher education offered by the report. Through the development of such a compact, higher education – as we see from the lead-in quotation – is to come into a set of known and productive interrelationships with the wider society, to their *mutual* benefit.

If such a compact could be brought about, much happiness would ensue, presumably. We would be in the presence of a win-win situation. All parties would gain and their mutual interests would be strengthened. The idea of compact, accordingly, invites attention.

The Key Issues

I suggest that there are six key issues:

1 In general, what is meant by 'compact'? What criteria do arrangements have to satisfy in order to warrant the title of 'compact'?

2 Who are the parties to the compact?

3   How can the idea of 'compact' be properly interpreted in the context of higher education?

4   What are the features of mutuality in this context?

5   Can the ends that the compact is intended to serve be specified?

6   What are the conditions under which a compact for higher education might be realised? Could it work? How might it best work?

These questions – respectively questions of concept, composition, characteristics, process, goals, and prognosis – await us. In addressing these questions, we shall take our point of departure from the report of the National Committee of Inquiry. (The report is commonly known as the 'Dearing Report' after the Chair of the National Committee, then Sir Ron – now Lord – Dearing, and I shall refer to it in that way.)

The Idea of Compact

Crucially, there is a voluntary character to a compact. The parties each sign up willingly because they perceive that their own interests are likely to be advanced more than if they were each to go it alone. The parties are witting subscribers. They sign up deliberately but without duress. However, the signing up is informal in character. Compare 'compact' with 'contract': the latter has much more the sense of a formal arrangement, possibly even underpinned in law.

Even though the arrangements are relatively informal in character, the parties to a compact recognise obligations on each of their parts; as Dearing noted, there is a definite sense of mutuality to the relationships. The parties recognise that they have a responsibility in fulfilling their part of the compact even if there is little in the way of formal sanctions should one party default. Two points are worth drawing out here.

Firstly, the mutuality in question contains a degree of double mutuality. That is to say, not only does A recognise obligations to B and also B to A; but A and B both expect and understand that the other party is undertaking to meet its particular obligations.

Secondly, there would be likely to be set in hand at least a minimal set of processes or arrangements by which those mutual obligations might be sustained. For instance, there might be processes of intercommunication put in place (again, as our opening quotation from Dearing implies).

Note that there is an inevitable equivocation in the notion of 'mutual obligations' here. Those obligations might be direct or indirect. Party A may bestow resources directly on one Party B; or Party B may benefit indirectly from the contribution that Party A is making; or Party B may just stand neutrally in the matter. Minimally, Party B is not disadvantaged by the 'contribution' being made by Party A to the compact. In the first place, therefore, the obligations of parties to a compact are just that: that the parties meet their obligations to the compact. It may be that, in particular areas, an obligation is met by one of the parties being directly in receipt of some provision by another party; but, strictly speaking, that need not be the case.

We may conclude, therefore, that the minimal necessary conditions by which we might understand and recognise a compact are those of:

1   a quasi-informal agreement between two or more parties;

2   obligations placed on each party towards the compact;

3   each of the parties playing their parts voluntarily;

4   there being identified benefits for each party that could not otherwise be secured outside such a compact;

5   interaction among the parties.

In practice, these necessary conditions would be unlikely to be sufficient. A facilitative condition – as we might term it – that would aid the likely success of any compact would be:

6   a set of arrangements for encouraging interaction between the parties (that is, some minimal infrastructure).

It will be noted that this formal specification of the idea of compact omits mention of agreed goals. That may be a hope of a compact and, indeed, references to the Dearing 'compact' are sometimes set out in just that way, as a list of the goals that the Dearing compact is expected to deliver. A set of agreed goals, however, cannot form one of the necessary criteria for a compact to be properly working. Even so, such hopes of there being a consensus as to the goals that might be achieved can still be invested in a compact.

The Parties to a Compact in Higher Education

So far as higher education is concerned, it might be thought that the first issue is that of the ends that the compact is intended to serve: what are the agreed goals of the compact? This, however, is not the first issue since the answers to this question are likely to be, in part, a function of the interest groups involved. Different 'stakeholders' might have different hopes of such a compact.

Accordingly, the first question is: who might form the parties concerned? Within the section that introduces the idea of a compact (1.22–1.28), Dearing identifies:

- higher education institutions;
- students;
- industry and commerce;
- public bodies;
- 'the world of work';
- 'the state itself';
- society.

This may seem an uncontroversial list of participants but a number of problems are immediately apparent. Firstly, Dearing himself equivocates on the matter. A later table (18.1) specifying certain components of the compact substitutes for 'students' the phrase 'students and graduates'; it distinguishes higher education staff from their institutions; it adds (as a separate interest group) 'the families of students'; it puts together society and the state in the phrase 'society and taxpayers, as represented by the Government'; and it omits 'public bodies'. In other words, even within Dearing, the parties to the compact are not precisely clear.

Secondly, these interest groups are far from unitary. A part-time 40-year old 'student' with a family is unlikely to have the same expectations of her higher education as her 18-year old counterpart; social class, ethnicity, gender, knowledge field and country of origin are also likely to lead to wide variations of expectation within the student population. Correspondingly, there are likely to be large differences within 'industry and commerce' as to its hopes from higher education: compare the views towards higher education of a major transnational company (whose turnover exceeds that of a small country) with a small specialist company, just starting up. It is not just the size and even reach of the company that is at issue, but the character of its products and the ways in which it calls upon higher order capacities and the extent to which it itself is in the business of knowledge production (compare a specialist firm involved in the creative arts with a global pharmaceutical company).

Each potential party to the Dearing compact is, therefore, susceptible to disaggregation: there are parties within the parties. Higher education institutions and society are further candidates for such treatment; does 'higher education institution' include non-academic staff? Does 'society' include taxpayers who have no immediate interest in higher education? Even 'the state' itself is far from unitary, being a coalition of interests. It follows that unless, in some way, Dearing's higher education compact can be operationalised so as to be sensitive to perhaps major differences within the parties, the dominant interests within those parties will emerge to shape the compact. In short, we might conjecture that, without countervailing measures, the agenda of the compact will be defined by the state (especially the Treasury), large-scale corporations (especially those involved in the dynamic parts of the economy), research-led universities, and younger students (who have a lifetime of 'employability' ahead of them).

Since the process of disaggregation may go on infinitely, it follows that what might seem to be a limited number of parties to a higher education compact may turn out to be a very large number of parties. The image, if it was beginning to form, of the parties sitting round a table to deliver the compact, is at best misleading and, at worst, dangerous, since it is liable to rule out legitimate interests. It also follows that what is to count as a legitimate party to the compact is open, fluid and contestable. There can be no certitude at any one time that all the legitimate parties have even been identified. Are schools, for instance, a legitimate party to the compact? Are all the professional bodies to be included in its composition?

Two ways forward suggest themselves so far as the composition of the compact is concerned. Firstly, different levels of interest in the compact might be distinguished. However, determining the criteria by which levels of interest might be distinguished is not straightforward. For example, parties could be distinguished by their immediate involvement in the delivery of the compact. Such a move, we should note, would arguably place 'the world of work' outside the inner circle since – although it may be increasing and the government may wish to see it further increased – the actual extent of the involvement of the private sector in framing the student experience remains limited. That such a move would prove controversial indicates that the idea of 'compact' in higher education in practice has a political import: the compact is intended to fulfil interests of the state, especially those concerned with improving competitiveness in a global economy.

If distinguishing levels of interest in the compact is problematic, another tack in giving structure to the composition would be to think less in terms of a single compact and more in terms of a set of interlocking compacts: each compact would frame a set of cognate goals, the parties to which would be appropriate to the issues and goals in question. It may be observed that there exists, in the UK, the makings of such a set of compacts: each arm of the relevant departments (Education and Employment; Health and Social Security; International Development and so on and each quasi-state body such as the Funding Councils and the Quality Assurance Agency) typically engage in consultations with organisations within their immediate constituency. The compact for higher education would involve two further key elements: firstly, the key large issues would be identified as the hub of the compact (the core compact) and, secondly, there would be some infrastructure so that there would be established a continuing means of communication among the parties.

A fuller examination of the challenges and possibilities in relation to the composition of the compact must await another occasion. What can be said, in summary, is that the composition should remain fluid, that no major party should feel excluded, and that imaginative design solutions will need to be found of achieving these ends, while imparting some structure and focus to the compact. 'Compact' may turn out to be, in part, a metaphor for a series of interlocking circles, albeit with a particular strong circle containing the major players at its core. Even then, there will need to be fluidity in the definition of the players in that inner circle.

The Character of the Dearing Compact

In Dearing, we see terms such as 'interdependence', 'mutual interdependence', 'the needs of both sides' and 'each ... looking for much from the other': this is a language of mutuality that we can expect to be associated with the idea of a compact. And something of this mutuality is conveyed in relation to certain of the university's functions. Students, for example, in return for high quality services, 'will invest time, effort and money'. The state, too, 'will gain from ensuring the well-being of higher education'. Further, 'higher education must be able to look to society for respect for its purposes' (1.26), again in return for its services which here are bound up with its 'contribution to national competitiveness'.

All this is a picture of some balance with the different parties committed to and investing in the compact. However, already, we sense something of a skew developing: higher education on the one hand, and the remaining parties on the other hand. The compact is a matter of higher education offering services on the one hand and receiving goods (such as resources and respect) on the other hand. In relation to the role of higher education in research and scholarship, this skew is enhanced. There, higher education is urged 'to take a more active role in relating the outcomes ... to the wider needs of society'. On the other side, so to speak, Dearing looks to 'industry and commerce, and a wide range of public bodies ... to make greater use of [that] knowledge and expertise ...' (1.24). Although the paragraph continues and includes reference to 'how much each has to offer the other', it is by no means clear what it is that industry and commerce and those public bodies are expected to offer higher education as such. Certainly, for example, there is no mention of those bodies being a source of funds for higher education institutions.

We may judge, therefore, that, in Dearing, the dominant conception of the compact – though by no means the only conception – is that of higher education producing and offering useable goods and services to consumers of various kinds which they in turn find useable and which have some kind of productive power. There are two points here.

Firstly, the degree of mutuality is limited. We are not quite being offered a situation of higher education providing and the wider society taking; but there are definite signs of the embryo of such a relationship in the Dearing depiction of the compact. Implicit in this concept of the relationship is a consumer-purchaser model: the provider produces goods and services that are consumed by the purchasers *and* the character of those goods and services are to be determined by the purchasers.

Secondly, the services that higher education is to provide are to have a use value in society. That higher education might have more internal value seems not to be on the cards, in this definition of 'compact'. The implication is that, unless higher education comes up with the goods and services that have payoff beyond itself in the wider society, support for higher education from the other parties will be withdrawn.

A first, albeit tentative, conclusion that we may draw, therefore, is that the discourse of compact in Dearing is being deployed to convey a sense of mutuality, in which the parties stand in a position of more or less equality, but that that 'script' (van Dijk, 1999, p. 60) overlies an intended reshaping of the relationship between higher education and the wider society, such that the former is subservient to the latter. For our purposes here, this would be a disappointing conclusion to reach, however tentative; and it could divert us into a detailed examination of all the instances of 'compact' in the Dearing

Report to assess their character – intended or implicit – in relation to these initially critical comments. A key issue here would be whether there is scope within the Dearing Report for higher education itself to become an independent variable within the relationship to the compact; whether there is scope for higher education to contribute to the shaping of the agenda which is to be delivered. I shall come back to this issue as a substantive matter in its own right.

The Idea of a Compact in Higher Education

Dearing's idea of a compact for higher education is summarised in a table within a chapter on 'Who should pay for higher education?' (reproduced in Fig 1.1). Set out under different stakeholders, it identifies the separate contributions that they might make to higher education and the benefits that might accrue to them (presumably as a result of making their contributions). Although the table appears in a chapter on the financing of higher education, it ranges wider than financial matters. The table should be seen in the context of the many references to the idea of a compact that appear in the body of the Report in relation to different matters, such as student participation, institutions' regional role, quality and resourcing. There a number of observations to be made about that table that bear upon the idea of a compact.

The first point is simply that, since the idea of 'a compact' is arguably the key concept within the Report, is perhaps the Report's distinctive contribution to higher education policy debate, and is pivotal to the whole Report, *this table* – which pulls together and amplifies the references to 'compact' in the Report and lays out its component parts – *is the most important part of the whole Report*. That it has not been seen in this way, and that attention has focused on other, more particular parts of the Report (such as on student finance; on staff's teaching competence), suggests perhaps that different groups will seize on those matters that particularly appear to have implications for them. The concept of compact, involving as it does all the parties in higher education, has a more abstract character and appears to have a less immediate impact. Such thinking needs to be abandoned. Dearing is surely right to hope that this idea of compact will be given serious attention; and, therefore, this table should be the object of some detailed examination.

Secondly, there is an issue as to the relationship between contribution and benefits. A feature of the relationships embodied in that table is that the relationship appears to be non-linear. The underlying reasoning appears to be that, in this compact, the separate parties will make their contributions and, as a result of being a fully participating member of the compact, a number of benefits are likely to accrue. There is no necessary relationship between any one contribution and any one benefit: putting it crudely, one cannot read across the table in a straightforward way. No attempt is made to identify, for each contribution, a reciprocal benefit. This feature is immediately apparent in relation to students and graduates. They are to invest money, time and effort; in return, they are to receive a large number of benefits. There is no logical relationship between contribution and benefit. The benefits, somehow, simply accrue (or, at least, it is to be hoped that they will do so).

For example, one of the benefits that are to accrue to students and graduates is that of 'better support for part-time study'. It is not immediately obvious how this benefit is to occur. It is surely apparent that there is no cause-and-effect relationship at work here. What appears to be happening, and revealing of the character of Dearing's compact, is that the relationship between contributions made by the parties to the compact and the benefits that each receives appears to be indirect. Nor is it even the case, necessarily, that any particular benefit can be ascribed to any one contributor: 'better support for part-time study', for instance, is likely to be the result of a combination of contributions from the state and from employers and possibly even from institutions themselves. In this compact, the parties subscribe to the compact, make certain contributions and, as a result, certain benefits accrue, in some kind of mysterious way.

This point about the nature of the relationships in this compact, their non-linearity, raises two issues in particular: firstly, to what extent is it necessary for the source of any benefit accruing to one of the parties to be attributed to one or more of the other parties? In other words, does there need to be an acceptance of a 'responsibility' on the part of each of the parties to contribute their share in delivering the benefits that the other parties are to derive? Secondly, how is the compact to be orchestrated such that these non-linear relationships might be developed and sustained? We shall revisit the second matter later. The first matter we can explore further here.

If relationships between contributions and benefits are non-linear, if a benefit to a party in the compact does not flow simply as a result of that party making its contributions, then attention needs to be paid to benefits as such. There are two possibilities: (1) that a benefit can be traced to a particular party within the contract; and (2) that a benefit accrues as a result of a combination of contributions made by the other parties to the compact. A third scenario beckons in which benefits are conferred by actions by parties outwith the compact but, in that case, by definition, those parties would not

	Contribution	Benefits
Society and taxpayers, as represented by the Government	• A fair proportion of public spending and national income devoted to higher education • Greater stability in the public funding and framework for higher education	• A highly skilled, adaptable workforce • Research findings to underpin a knowledge-based economy • Informed, flexible, effective citizens • A greater share of higher education costs met by individual beneficiaries
Students and graduates	• A greater financial contribution than now to the costs of tuition and living costs (especially for those from richer backgrounds • Time and effort applied to learning	• More chances to participate in a larger system • Better information and guidance to inform choices • A higher quality learning experience • A clear statement of learning outcomes • Rigorously assured awards which have standing across the UK and overseas • Fairer income contingent arrangements for making a financial contribution when in work • Better support for part-time study • Larger Access funds
Institutions	• Collective commitment to rigorous assurance of quality and standards • New approaches to learning and teaching • Continual search for more cost-effective approaches to the delivery of higher education • Commitment to developing and supporting staff	• A new source of funding for teaching and the possibility of resumed expansion • New funding streams for research which recognise different purposes • Greater recognition from society of the value of higher education • Greater stability in funding

Higher education staff	• Commitment to excellence • Willingness to seek and adopt new ways of doing things	• Greater recognition (financial and non-financial) of the value of all their work, not just research • Proper recognition of their profession • Access to training and development opportunities • Fair pay
Employers	• More investment in training of employees • Increased contribution to infrastructure of research • More work experience opportunities for students • Greater support for employees serving on institutions' governing bodies	• More highly education people in the workforce • Clearer understanding of what higher education is offering • More opportunities for collaborative working with higher education • Better accessibility to higher education resources for small and medium size enterprises • Outcomes of research
The families of students	• Possible contribution to costs	• Better higher education opportunities for their children • Better, more flexible, higher education opportunities for mature students

Figure 1.1 Higher education: a new compact

Source: NCIHE, 1997, p. 283.

be part of the compact. In that case, we would not be in the domain of a compact and so that scenario does not require our attention here. We are left, therefore, with our first two possibilities. Responsibility for delivering a benefit is relatively easy to attribute in the first case (the one-donor situation) but much more difficult in the second case (of multiple donors towards a benefit). This reflection in turn raises issues of mutuality.

On Mutuality

Mutuality within a compact comprises six elements:

1   a joint determination of the agenda – or joint goals – that the compact is intended to meet;

2   a reasonable level of equality in the resources that each party agrees to commit to the compact;

3   an equality of process in implementing the compact: no one party shall have a dominant influence;

4   a reasonable balance between contribution and benefit for each party;

5   an acceptance of 'responsibility' by each party in making its contribution to the compact;

6   an equivalence of status in monitoring and evaluating the working out of the compact and, thereby, of any redefinition of the agenda that it is intended to meet.

Together, these six elements:

• embrace inputs, process and outputs;
• presume a cycle of agenda-setting, implementation, evaluation and agenda-refinements;
• look to a *collective understanding of* and agreement on the ends of the compact and the ways in which its operation is to deliver the benefits identified for each party.

The logic of such a conception of a compact is twofold. Firstly, the compact is dynamic: its ends are being kept under review and developed on a continuing basis but through mutual agreement. Secondly, the compact has to be 'lived' by the parties as a collective process. (We shall come on more specifically to the conditions of that collective process in the next section.) Mutuality, accordingly, is not secured simply by each party understanding its contribution in isolation, as it were: rather, each party's understanding of its contribution will be informed by an increasing *collective* understanding of the ends that the compact is intended to fulfil and actually fulfils.

Once set in motion, therefore, a compact of the kind envisaged here is open-ended. As it takes off, new joint goals might be identified and new ways of interacting might be developed. Implicit in this reflection about open-endedness is the additional consideration that, over time, the compact might change its character from one in which the separate parties were seeing in the compact a vehicle to secure their own ends (provided that they made a commensurate contribution) to one in which the parties were identifying broad societal goals that transcended their own individual agendas. In this way, the nature of the mutuality within the compact could change its identity from a matter of 'each party being provided with a framework to meet its own ends' to a matter of 'a pooled effort in fulfilment of public goods'. Admittedly, the extent to which there might be public goods in relation to higher education as distinct from a collection of separate aspirations held by different interest groups is a further matter; but, at least, the possibility can be held out of there being at least goods that the compact might deliver that transcend the interests of any one party.

A key element in the working out of any compact and especially the extent of its mutuality lies in trust. In short, a compact is a set of trust relationships. Each party trusts that the others will deliver on their part in the compact. Insofar as a party believes that it is going to benefit from the compact, doubtless that trust takes on an added element of partiality: we trust that you will meet your obligations if we meet ours.

The Ends of a Compact in Higher Education

There has developed a view that there are definite ends written into the Dearing compact. Newby (1999) cites these ends as the following:

• lifelong learning;

- creation of a learning society;
- regional economic regeneration and development;
- pure research and scholarship across and within disciplines;
- technological innovation;
- social cohesion;
- public accountability.

Newby adds that 'This, I should emphasise, is my summary of the Dearing "compact"' (ibid., p. 111). It is true that the matters picked out by Newby figure in Dearing but they figure, surely, more as general ends that higher education should serve rather than as particular ends of the compact as envisaged by Dearing. We may note, for example, that phrases such as 'a learning society', regional economic regeneration, technological innovation and social cohesion do not appear in the table (18.1) that summarises the Dearing compact. It might be said that the Newby list is exactly as mentioned, a 'shorthand' and that the many specific matters mentioned in the table presume these more general ends. That may be so but consider another list:

> We suggest that there are four 'big' ideas which underpin [Dearing's] vision in practical terms:
>
> 1 *The contribution of higher education to lifelong learning*, as embedded in ...
> 2 *A vision for learning in the twenty-first century*, as embodied in ...
> 3 *Funding research according to its intended outcomes*, as set out in the multi-stranded model ...
> 4 *A new compact between the state, the institutions and their students*, involving especially a 'deal' whereby institutions retain their independence and gain increasing security in return for clearer accountability (especially on standards) and greater responsiveness to a wide range of legitimate stakeholders. Governance and collaboration are also relevant here, as is the notion that a greater student contribution is matched by assured outcomes (Watson and Taylor, 1998, pp. 151–2).

Here, we may note, the compact (4) is separate from large societal goals such as lifelong learning and a vision for learning in the twenty-first century (1, 2). In other words, the compact, as envisaged by Dearing, is unconnected with agreed societal goals: it has no rationale other than meeting the separate needs of interested parties. Some common goods may fall out of its operation but that appears to be happenstance. The compact is not set up actually to assist the identification of large societal or even global issues, still less to assist in their being addressed in a coherent fashion by the key agencies working in concert. As such, the title of the Report, 'Higher Education in the Learning Society' appears somewhat misleading. Properly worked out, a compact could be an excellent vehicle for helping to realise the learning society. Admittedly, any such common agenda would be contentious; it would need to be kept under review and open to change. The compact, in other words, could be a vehicle for helping to identify on a continuing basis the challenges facing society – and the world 'in a global age' – and for developing a coherent strategy for tackling issues, with each party being clear as to its role in that shared venture.

Secondly, and coming directly to the table itself, on another occasion, a different schema might suggest itself. For example, one axis could have consisted of different knowledge and educational functions that need to be developed within a modern society in the twenty-first century while the other axis might show the different contributions that the separate parties might make. This would be a different kind of compact, where weight is thrown on the different parties jointly contributing to fulfilling an agreed social and public agenda. Characteristic of its components (and constitutive of that axis in any such new table) might be functions such as:

- knowledge production;
- the development of professional competence;
- social access to learning opportunities;
- the advancement of citizenship through an enhanced understanding and competence within society in key domains (science, the polity itself, the environment);
- capacities for 'supercomplexity' (Barnett, 2000) on both a personal and a social level, to facilitate a more relaxed and reflexive stance towards a world of change, uncertain and radical contestation.

The university would be a key institution in addressing all of these challenges of late modernity but it would not be the only institution. All of the parties to the Dearing compact would be present here, higher education being positioned in terms of its contribution to that common agenda which, in turn, would serve as the basis for the compact.

Conditions of a Compact

From our analysis, the conditions under which a compact might be realised are beginning to suggest themselves. Minimally, the conditions would have to provide for:

1   continuing dialogue between the parties: this point would suggest that there should be a standing forum of some kind that would provide a framework for and a spur to such a dialogue;

2   an equality of positioning among the parties: the dialogue could not be dominated by the voice of one or more of the parties;

3   the parties to the compact being kept fluid: there should be no sense of a closed 'inner circle'. However, it might be judged that there could be – perhaps in relation to different issues – parties having differing statuses;

4   an openness as to the agenda: the agreed goals that the compact is intended to bring off should be kept under review and changed as felt desirable;

5   a capacity that allowed for progress in achieving the agreed goals to be monitored and evaluated.

Implicit in these conditions is the supposition that forming, maintaining and developing a compact requires effort, resources and a collective will. A genuine compact will not just occur of its own accord: it has to be created. Nor is its creation simply a matter of setting in place a bureaucratic infrastructure, important though that is. The challenge of forming a compact that draws together different parties having differing interests and located amid differing discourses is fundamentally one of language and communication: can the parties come to so understand each other that they can bridge the multiple discourses which such a compact must contain? A compact for higher education cannot be realised, accordingly, as a purely technical matter. It cannot be a matter of providing a set of means on the assumption that the ends will follow. Ultimately, a compact in higher education is a form of conversation; or, at least, it has to allow for conversation. Here, too, the conditions of such a conversation flourishing are that understanding between the parties should develop and that there should develop accommodation between the parties. Such understanding and preparedness to adjust is unlikely to be present on day one: mutuality has to be formed over time.

A fundamental difficulty standing in the way of such a conversation developing is precisely one of language: the parties to the compact may not speak the same language. Their basic values, assumptions and approaches may not just differ but may conflict. Translation services and bridging devices may be required. For example, quite apart from the specific projects and reports that bear its name, the UK Council for Industry and Higher Education has acted as just such a forum in which individuals from the different sectors could engage with each other in a non-threatening environment conducive to developing mutual understanding across what are, in effect, cultural barriers.

However, as implied, the formation of a compact for higher education cannot just be a matter of establishing lines of communication: a common agenda has to be formed, there would have to be developed a general understanding of the challenging context facing higher education, goals would have to be agreed and the responsibilities of each party towards sustaining the compact would have to be identified and accepted. These large challenges point, as we have now glimpsed, to there being:

1 some kind of standing means of providing an organisational basis for interactions between the parties to be developed and sustained over time. There needs, in other words, to be at least a minimal infrastructure;

2 a will on the part of the parties to the compact that it should succeed. In reality, both the will and the compact would be likely to develop together. As the parties came more to understand each other's position, so both a will towards success and the necessary mutuality would strengthen. In the process, the compact – now understood as mutual ties of communication, understanding and obligation – would be formed;

3 an intelligence arm both to enable the parties to monitor the achievement of their agreed goals and to furnish the parties with pertinent new contextual information that, for example, might even suggest new goals that the compact might strive to achieve.

The model sketched out here, it will be observed, is dual in character, both parts being necessary to the success of the compact. On the one hand, there would be a bureaucratic component, dedicated to developing and sustaining the compact. Even though there could well be large elements of *virtuality* to the interactions, and many parties would be 'at a distance', some organisational capability would be required with a physical presence. The gathering of data and intelligence and the monitoring of goals also point to an organisational presence. On the other hand, the compact is primarily understood as the formation and development of mutual understanding between parties. There is a virtuality here too. Unless mutual respect, understanding and agreements develop, with all the adjustment, negotiation and compromise that that entails, the compact would not and could not be realised. The human dimension, as it were, is crucial. But it can be aided by the infrastructure: if the parties can be brought together, can form goals, and have a way of monitoring their achievement, then the necessary will is likely to be generated.

Realizing a Compact

What are the prospects of such a compact being realised? In a global age, and in a 'supercomplex' age, governments are less and less able to achieve things by themselves. They can, though, assist in establishing the conditions in which things might happen. The responsibility for establishing such a framework within which a compact for higher education might take off lies, accordingly, with the Government. No one party in itself would command legitimacy if it sought to establish such a framework. Dearing pleaded for an inquiry into higher education to be mounted at relatively frequent intervals, on a five-yearly cycle. But Dearing also pleaded for there being more intelligence on higher education itself. It is clear that a five-yearly cycle of review and report would be inadequate. Both because the world is moving much more rapidly than such a timeframe would imply and because the formation of the necessary levels of understanding, agreement and will are bound to take time, a more continuing and more durable framework is necessary.

The realisation of the kind of compact sketched out here – dialogical, open-ended, consensual, and systematically reflective – requires the kind of resource and commitment from the centre that only the government can provide. In effect, what is surely required is the establishment of a standing Council for Higher Education which was charged with the remit of establishing, developing and driving forward a compact for higher education. A council, after all, is a deliberative body but one which is intended to set and to realise some goals and a name such as 'Council for Higher Education' would signify the significance of such a forum. As well as giving life to Dearing's idea of a compact, such a body, too, could also fulfil Dearing's other hopes of keeping higher education under review and of developing the intelligence base to inform planning and national policy making in higher education.

To recall points made in our discussion, a Council such as this should not be thought of simply as a physical forum for a limited number of representatives of interested parties to assemble round a table periodically. That would doubtless be an ingredient but even there, the parties might vary according to issues under discussion. Such a Council would be a forum in which a number of discussions and inquiries were set in hand, pursued by large assemblies and small intensive task groups. It would not be a decision-making body per se but it would attempt to map out areas of agreement and goals shared by the different parties. It would also build up databases of pertinent networks (of different employers, of professional bodies and so forth) and facilitate electronic networking and Web-based access to emerging ideas and intelligence. In this way, the Council would also act to enhance the general level of understanding of all of the parties – which would themselves be expanding over time – and, in this more indirect way, views of the different parties would be likely to become less partisan or, at least, more nuanced, over time.

A compact for higher education offers a prospect of developing higher education in an even more enlightened way through integrating the hopes of the many interested parties. A compact will not exist of its own volition, however: it requires nurturing and sustaining over time. A standing national body, independent of current funding and quality arrangements, is surely required. A 'Council for Higher Education' would just perhaps signify the status and desired authority of the new body and enable Dearing's idea of a compact to be realised.

References

Barnett, R. (2000), *Realizing the University in an Age of Supercomplexity*, Buckingham: Open University Press.

National Committee of Inquiry into Higher Education (Dearing Report) (1997), *Higher Education in the Learning Society*, London: HMSO.

Newby, H. (1999), 'Higher Education in the Twenty-first Century – Some Possible Futures', *Perspectives*, 3 (4), pp. 106–13.

van Dijk, T.A. (1999), *Ideology: a multidisciplinary approach*, London: Sage.

Watson, D. and Taylor, R. (1998), *Lifelong Learning and the University: A post-Dearing Agenda*, London: Falmer.

2   British Higher Education: Compacts or Contracts?

MEGHNAD DESAI

British higher education is in a curious state. It has never been more accessible than now. But precisely for that reason the system of financing it has become unsustainable. The choice is between continuing with the present system – in which the government becomes increasingly niggardly with deteriorating quality and a serious erosion of research capacity – or breaking out of the mould and opting for a radical shift to a privatised system, with government offering generous scholarships rather than 75 per cent tuition support at the minimum. Many others in this collection argue for a compact between government and higher education. I am sceptical of that path.

Compacts are not unknown in UK public policy. I am old enough to remember that at the worst time of inflation and high unemployment, there was a constant search for some corporatist consensual bargain to which all the parties – unions, employers, government – could sign up. It is a hopeful way of saying there are common interests rather than conflicts between the parties and that the commonality will prevail. It all ended in tears.

Why then a compact for higher education? My chapter will pinpoint the tensions and contradictions in the higher education system and warn against any simple argument that compacts will work. Harsh truths have to be faced about the nature of higher education and its financing, about the political economy of class and inequality, about the perennial evasions of governments of all parties, as to who bears the burden of higher education and of course the pathetic leadership of higher education institutions.

History

Let me begin with a caricature history of higher education in the UK. In the 1950s education at all levels was severely unequal and class biased. The 11+ and grammar schools creamed off the better and the cleverer and then a small proportion of them – about 10 per cent – went into higher education at the older universities, which were few. There were other forms of education, mainly vocational and technical, for a minority of the rest in technical colleges of various types. Most young people had no education beyond the age of 15.

Lord Robbins chaired a Committee of Higher Education in the 1960s (education does not rate a Royal Commission; the English are anti-education). This Committee – much hailed – expanded university education for the middle class elite and made it virtually free and widely available. Redbrick colleges became universities in their own right and new plate glass universities opened up – Essex, Sussex, Warwick and elsewhere. There was an entry barrier in terms of academic qualifications, which given the secondary education system, was sufficient to filter the poor out. Anthony Crosland as Secretary of State for Higher Education in a famous Minute in 1965 upgraded the technical colleges to polytechnics. The distance between the two sectors remained, but each expanded.

Attempts to improve the secondary education system were much beset by political wranglings. But between 1965 and 1979 there was a bipartisan attempt to make the comprehensive education system work. The school leaving age was raised but at 16 it still required a heroic effort on the part of the young and their parents to stay on for another two years before they could have access to higher education. So while secondary education improved, higher education remained privileged. It was free for those who could access it but only a few could. So while free, it was not universal or democratic.

Then came Government Education Reform Bill (GERBIL) and the enormous expansion in higher education at the end of the 1980s. Student numbers in higher education went up from roughly 400,000 in 1970 to 800,000 by 1985 and doubled again in the next 12 years. In the meantime, high unemployment and deindustrialisation had wrecked the comprehensive system. Baker, as Secretary of State for Education, added parental choice and reproduced within the comprehensive system the pre-1965 divided education system.[1] But on the higher education side there was a massive expansion. Once again the middle classes – now a larger constituency than in the 1950s since there has been a process of class recomposition since the 1950s – got their subsidised higher education. But alas, there were problems.

Structural Problems in Higher Education

An elitist higher education system based on privilege had high costs and restricted units. Small colleges were considered better than large ones, tutorials *a deux* better than large classes; universities better than polytechnics, old universities better than new universities. But above all there was free tuition – not for everyone, but for those who jumped through the secondary school hoops at the right age and opted to do higher education. There was also a grant which was universally available. That was the first to go and became means tested. Cries of student poverty went up as parents reckoned they did not like paying for their children's higher education. There was no reason why they should, since in every other way a person is an adult at 18 and should be financially responsible. Only middle classes of the A/B level paid, because that was a way of transferring wealth *intra vivos*.

Then the burden of free tuition for nearly a third of the cohort of university age population became 'too much' for British governments. The crisis is of their own making. If one has canonised tax cuts then public spending priorities bite harder. Since there is a total bipartisan agreement on fiscal policy – tight expenditure control, lots of tax cuts and no borrowing – there is a resource constraint. Higher education's rank in the list of spending priorities shows up as rather low. But politicians seldom want to face the truth or even tell it to the public when they see it. Thus the financing of higher education was left to drift, with a steady cut in the unit of resources year after year under the guise of productivity gains. From £7,000 per student in 1990/1, the unit of resource came down to £4,000 in 1998/9. Politicians were, and still are, too cowardly to tell the students to pay for their own education. So the deterioration of the quality of higher education, the relative loss of earnings of higher education staff and the exodus of talent continues.[2] The leadership of the higher education sector is craven and will be the last to protest lest they lose their hoped-for baubles.

The Major government saw the crisis in funding but flunked the challenge. Instead of legislating or even discussing fees it appointed a Committee under Dearing. It was an evasive strategy. The intellectual case of a fee based higher education system with income contingent financing had been made cogently by my colleagues Nicholas Barr, John Barnes and Iain Crawford (Barr, 1991). An income contingent loan, even with a mildly progressive income tax system, makes a lot of sense. A student pays for higher education as s/he would pay for food or housing or clothes out of either current or future income. For durables such as housing, people, even working class people, take out mortgages. So why can't they do so for education? Higher education is not a necessity like health. It is an income-enhancing investment. The subsidy for higher education goes largely, if not exclusively, to the better-off of today and (if not today) certainly of tomorrow. So adults should pay for higher education from their future life time income and this alone makes any sense.

Denials and Defences

This is, of course, denied. Grown up people – politicians and educationists – argue that we have had a system of 'universal' free higher education. It has not been universal and, except for the students coming down the High Road after A levels at 18 into full-time higher education, it has not been free. The barrier at 16 in our education system makes it impossible for the many poorer children to aspire to free higher education. If they come after a delay they are charged as mature students or as part-time students. It is the cowardice of politicians and sheer dishonesty on the parts of those who should know better to pretend that we have a free system. People tell me working class students will be discouraged by the fee or the debt that they will have to incur. But when education was free, there were few working class students. The barrier, as I said, is not fees but the chance of staying on after 16 in our schools. And as far as debt is concerned, as I said above, if they can get mortgages up to three times their income, how come they don't want to borrow for education? What is going on here is that working class myths are being used as a fig leaf by the middle classes to protect their subsidies. Governments are too scared to take on these middle classes and impose the proper cost of higher education on their children. So they invent excuses to pass on the cost of underfunding to those who have to work in the sector. And like donkeys we accept these costs. So what can be done?

Education ought to be widely available. We have reached a good figure of about 30 per cent of the cohort, but there is no reason why it should not increase. But what cannot be done is to keep the system uniform in its administrative and financial aspects such as fees and salaries and maintain the de facto differences in quality. A good example here is the USA, where education is widely available, universities are diverse and of varying quality but uniformity is avoided and students finance their education by a combination of loans and fees and scholarships. A high percentage, more than a third, of the cohort goes on to higher education in the USA. The British system mistakes uniformity for equality and pretends that charging the same fee across the sector or paying similar salaries achieves equity or equality. All it does is keep higher education a political football, starved of funds.

A New Contract

So the compact I would like would be a straightforward market contract. Universities should be free to charge whatever fees they can think they need to provide a decent education. Fees can vary by subjects and of course by universities. Salaries too will vary by subjects and by universities. It costs more to have a Professor of Accounting than of English Literature; you either have third rate accountants as professors and first rate English literature ones and pay them the same salaries, or you get smart. Universities will make their money from fees and any other research income they can earn. They will also be able to charge extra for facilities.[3]

Government ought to leverage its entire higher education budget as scholarships for students who, either by merit or other circumstances, deserve support. Perhaps a part of this money can be used to support loan schemes that universities can join in to provide self-financing students access to income contingent payment collection via the Inland Revenue. The present scheme was a shoddy compromise of the Dearing Committee recommendations. The New Labour government flunked the courage test. It should have put up student fees by their full amount with an income contingent scheme. Instead of which only £1,000 was charged and that too was means tested by parental income. Grants were made subject of a loan, reversing the Dearing recommendations.

Foreign (non-EU) students pay £9,000 fees per annum. That is a true measure of the costs of higher education. You only have to recall that the unit of resource was £7,000 and add inflation on to that to arrive at the figure of £9,000. By not charging full costs the government is passing on the burden to students in terms of shoddy facilities, bad equipment, and to teachers in terms of low salaries. Undercharging without topping up from general funds is ruining the higher education system. Consider therefore the following radical alternative. Students pay £10,000 per annum on average for their degrees though different universities may charge differently by subjects. Loan schemes can be devised by the government as of now allowing for an income contingent loan covering the costs including tuition and maintenance. But universities should be encouraged to set up scholarship funds from the tuition income. This is the point of charging a little more above the average costs so that a kitty can be built up for scholarships. But the government can also help. It spends roughly £3 billion for student tuition support. All this money can be ploughed into creating scholarships for students. The money can fund up to 300,000 students at full tuition fee level scholarships. This works out at one in five of all students – part-time and full-time, mature and standard age. So a transition to a fully privatised system should be aided by government funds being used to leverage student finances. Those who can will pay and those who deserve either on merit or on need basis will get full funding.

Universities can then respond creatively by offering a diversity of courses, at different levels – degrees, diplomas, certificates. There could be flexible terms so that students could study round the year or spread their education over many years and many universities through credit transfers. Universities would sign contracts with their students to deliver specific types of education, with guaranteed tutorial supervision and pastoral care. They would reward their staff by the merit of their performance and the number of students they were attracting.

The government would maintain research funding at a high level. But above all it would improve the staying on rate at the schools to enable students from poorer backgrounds to access higher education. Universities could even link up with schools at 16 plus levels and offer students pre-university preparatory courses. That may break up the tyranny of A levels.

A Radical Contract

There is an even more radical alternative but it takes us beyond the narrow confines of higher education finances. The present system is inherently biased towards the middle classes who rip off the welfare state in any case. We have to look after those not present in the higher education sector, those who never make it because the system is skewed against them. Government should offer a contract to all 16-year olds that it would try its best to provide higher education or other skills to them over the next seven years of their lives. The spending on each youth would be roughly similar but more may come via merit scholarships to those who try harder. But everyone, and not only 18-year olds who do well at A levels, should have the same amount per capita spent on them. Even today a student paying £1,000 per each of three years at university will walk away with a subsidy of £9,000 (three years at £4,000 each less £1,000 per each year paid). A third of the cohort get it. Why not give everyone at 16 a voucher of £2,000 to £3,000 to cash as educational provision wherever s/he chooses? This may relieve the 16 plus barrier for staying on. Once this barrier is cleared, the field is open to everyone to enter higher education.

I am sure that a wide ranging cost benefit analysis would support such a contract. At present we consign many young people to a lifetime of poverty by crippling them at 16. We subsidise the well-off who then complain that they don't have enough. Many middle class benefit scroungers are at universities and they are applauded, while poorer people are derided for benefit dependency. It is time to redress this inequity.

Conclusion

The higher education system as at present financed is inequitable, inadequate and inefficient. It is also unsustainable. It puts enormous pressure on universities in terms of staff retention, morale and quality. It will kill our best universities and not even achieve equity the way it is going on. Governments cannot be relied on to charge the true cost of higher education. What the system needs is a new set of contracts, rather like the American system. But in the place of charitable giving which the USA has, the government ought to leverage its revenues currently spent on tuition subsidies to finance scholarships for one in every five students. Universities then should provide diverse high quality education with flexible features. The government ought to have a contract with the young in or out of higher education. That alone will overcome the class ridden nature of the British education system.

Notes

1   This process was brilliantly described by Nick Davies in his series of articles in *The Guardian*, 14–16 September 1999.
2   See for example Machin and Oswald, 1999. There are similar stories in the natural sciences, in Accounting and Finance and the Humanities.
3   Martin Woolf wrote two articles in the *Financial Times* on 9 and 21 June which also argue for a similar approach. They provoked an interesting correspondence in the columns of the *FT*. See Woolf, 1999.

References

Barr, N. (1991), 'Income-Contingent Student Loans: An idea whose time has come', in Shaw, G.K. (ed.), *Economics, Culture and Education: Essays in honour of Mark Blaug*, Cheltenham: Edward Elgar.
Barr, N. and Crawford, I. (1998), 'Funding Higher Education in an Age of Expansion', *Education Economics*, Vol. 6, No. 1 pp. 45–70.

Machin, S.J. and Oswald, A.J. (1999), 'Signs of Disintegration: a Report on UK Economics Ph.Ds and ESRC studentship Demand', Report of the ESRC, Bank of England and Government Economic Service, June.

Woolf, M. (1999), 'More Meant Worse: Privatising UK Universities', *Financial Times*, 21 June; 'Empty Chairs', *Financial Times*, 9 June.

PART II
THE POLITICAL ECONOMY
OF A COMPACT

3 Quality Assurance: Champion or Servant of the Dearing Compact?

NORMAN JACKSON

Introduction

This chapter examines the Dearing *compact* (Dearing Report, 1997) from the perspective of quality assurance policies that were intended to help bind the parties into the *non-negotiated public agreement.*

In higher education, quality assurance (QA) encompasses all the policies, systems, processes and practices directed to ensuring the maintenance and enhancement of the quality of educational provision and the standards achieved by students' (definition adapted from Hannah, 1996). The application of policy is intended to guarantee to the state (politicians and funding bodies), to students, employers (and society at large), or professional and statutory regulatory bodies that certain expectations or conditions pertaining to quality and standards have been satisfied.

QA is used by institutions to protect their reputation, through the checks and safeguards they operate to ensure that the quality and standards of education they provide are appropriate and satisfy public accountability (are we providing good value for the public investment). Institutional QA also protects the interests of students (are they getting a good education) and staff (can we demonstrate that we are providing good quality education and that our standards are appropriate). When problems arise, as they inevitably do during times of rapid expansion, innovation and reducing unit resources, QA policies are there to understand what went wrong and to make sure that the various interest groups are not disadvantaged. At a national level QA policies are designed to protect and promote the reputation of the system as a whole (including international perceptions of the system), the public purse (is the state getting good value for money) and the interests of students, employers, professions and other interest groups. National QA policies also serve the interests of the agencies that promote them as without them they would not exist. The agencies themselves (and other regulators like professional bodies and statutory regulators) have a vested interest in developing and maintaining policies that keep them in business!

The UK has always tried to balance the accountability function of national QA policy with the enhancement function (Jackson, 1997b, 1997c and 1998). This provides opportunities for the identification and dissemination of what practitioners and administrators believe to be 'good' practice (best practice is probably not an appropriate concept for HE). Through the production of good practice guidelines and survey reports, reinforced by external review mechanisms, the system as a whole can be encouraged to adopt or abandon certain practices and beliefs. The enhancement function also provides opportunities for collaborative research and development relating to curriculum design, teaching, learning and assessment and academic management. It also provides a focus for issues-led debate within the academic community (see for example the national debate created through the Graduate Standards Programme – HEQC, 1995a, 1996a and 1997 and the current policy development activity of QAA) and a framework within which different 'stakeholder' views can be represented. Institutional and national QA policies and public debate around their development have made higher education more publicly accountable for its educational, pedagogic, academic management and administrative practices, and encouraged academics to think about the broader and longer term social implications of the education they are providing.

Over the last 35 years a succession of national QA policies managed by a range of agencies have been used to underpin, support and publicly validate the quality and standards of UK higher education provided initially by the polytechnics and colleges and, since 1992, the universities as well. The systemic application and evolution of national QA policy in the 1990s has become a distinctive feature of the UK system: one that is recognised globally judging by the number of international visitors coming to witness the phenomenon. A central tenet of this chapter is that QA policy and practice has been a necessary adjunct to the creation of a mass system. Along with funding mechanisms, strategic reviews and Department for Education and Employment (DfEE) sponsored development initiatives QA has been one of the levers used to create the conditions and promote the changes necessary to achieve this political objective.

The Dearing Report (1997) used the notion of a compact in the sense of a moral or social agreement that set out the obligations and responsibilities of different parties in a publicly accessible way. As such it provided a vehicle for making all those with an interest in higher education accountable for their actions and future performance. As far as the HE community was concerned it was tied to a carrot (follow this line and there will be less need for tight external controls) and a stick (if you don't follow this line then the state will have every right to intervene to ensure that these things happen).

National QA policies have been instrumental in creating the discourse for quality and standards that has made the system as a whole, institutions and the individuals in it more accountable to society and the state. It might be argued that this is a necessary precondition for the creation of a compact involving institutions and their staff, students, government, employers and society since without the mechanisms for accountability universities and colleges are unlikely to embrace such obligations voluntarily (see for example the reluctance of the universities to establish effective QA mechanisms in the 1980s). Such a compact was seen by the Dearing Report (1997), as important to achieving its vision of a *learning society* (Dearing Report, 1997, pp. 9–10, summary report).

> We see the historic boundaries between vocational and academic education breaking down, with increasingly active partnerships between higher education institutions and the worlds of industry, commerce and public service. In such a compact, each party should recognise its obligation to others ... There is a growing interdependence between students, institutions, the economy, employers and the state. We believe that this bond needs to be more clearly recognised by each party, as a compact which makes clear what each contributes and what each gains.

The compact is intended to place the package of recommendations in the Dearing Report (1997) in a social context. It thus provides a framework within which the effectiveness of policies can be referenced – do they work together to deliver the overall social contract?

The contributions made by each party in the compact are outlined in Table 1 (p. 10) of the Dearing summary report and it is clear that QA policy is pivotal to the contributions made by institutions '*a collective commitment to rigorous assurance of quality and standards*'. The perceived benefits derived from this commitment are given as: (1) rigorously assured awards which have standing across the UK and overseas; (2) a clear statement of learning outcomes; and (3) a high quality learning experience.

This chapter considers the new public policy framework that will give meaning and substance to key parts of the compact regardless of whether it is explicitly defined and agreed by the parties concerned. The key recommendations relating to this QA framework and an indication of policy derived from these recommendations are given in Table 3.1. The views and interpretations expressed are those of the author; they do not represent the views of the Quality Assurance Agency for Higher Education.

Creating the Conditions for a New Compact

The key events in the creation of national QA policy over the last decade are summarised in Figure 3.1. The most striking feature is the sheer scale and energy of policy development, QA-related activities, public debate and incorporation of QA policy into national strategic review. It can been argued that the net effect of QA policy and practice over the last decade has been to progressively shift the university system from one founded on the notion of autonomous self-regulation (the right of institutions *and people* to decide freely

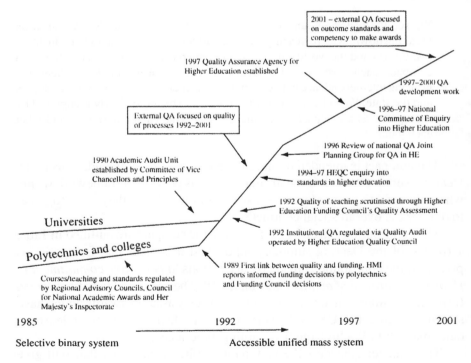

Figure 3.1   Evolution of national QA agencies and policies in UK higher education 1985–2001

and independently how to perform their tasks, Johnson, 1994), to a notion of institutional self-regulation that is founded on a set of expectations promoted through the quality review activities of national QA bodies and in future through a national code of practice for the assurance of quality and standards (Alderman, 1996a and b; Jackson 1997b and c).

Effective regulation in professional communities has both a formal (explicit) component and an informal (implicit) component. Regulatory regimes that are based on informal/implicit approaches rely on unwritten rules and operate in a climate of trust that works on the principle that professionals are, first and foremost, accountable to themselves and their immediate peers. It assumes that responsibilities will be discharged, in spite of mutual self-interests within the professional community. Such an approach works best when there is a single common purpose (e.g. a collaborative research effort) but perhaps works less well when there are a number of competing interests and demands (e.g. teaching, administration, research and consultancy) and as competition for diminishing resources or markets increases.

The progressive shift away from informal conditions to more formal conditions, as concerns for public accountability have increased, suggests that there is a political belief that regulation, in contemporary HE (and elsewhere in the education system and other public services) must be underpinned by explicit rules and specifications. Such beliefs are reinforced and legitimised by the DfEE Charter for HE (DfE, 1993), the recommendations of the Graduate Standards Programme (HEQC, 1997b) and the Dearing Report (1997).

But there is another reason for the emphasis on explicitness and specification that relates to the shift in public policy management (seen elsewhere in Europe as well) in which central control of inputs is displaced by centralised strategic control that focuses on performance and outcomes (Maassen, 1997). The idea of the 'evaluative state,' in which a variety of funding mechanisms and policy levers are used to promote the assessment of teaching, research, management and administration in order to evaluate the extent to which performance contracts are being delivered, is central to this strategy (Henkel, 1991; Dill, 1998). One of the core obligations that Dearing placed on the QAA is to provide public information about the quality and outcomes of higher education. So another reason for placing so much emphasis on specifications in the new public policy framework is to satisfy the demand for information by the 'evaluative state'. A compact is another tool in the management of public services by the evaluative state.

UK higher education institutions are now operating within an increasingly specified framework of expectations contained in guidelines, codes of practice and review processes that effectively comprise a non-statutory regulatory framework. Compliance with the expectations of this framework is required as a condition of funding. Because of this, it has been argued (Jackson, 1997b) that the idea of QA has been superseded by the idea of non-statutory regulation. Regulation is a difficult and emotive concept for academic communities that value, above all other values, personal and institutional autonomy and academic freedom (the absence of outside interference, censure or obstacles to academic practice). But in a world where public services have become increasingly accountable for their quality and performance, the interests and values of the academic community must be positioned against the interests, values and needs of society. The idea of regulation is more readily understood by a public that expects the interests and values of society as a whole, as well as those of the academic community, to be respected and protected.

The Dearing Compact and the Regulation of HE

The compact must be seen in the light of the contexts outlined above. Its location at the very front of the Dearing Report (1997) (first mentioned in paragraph 3 of the summary report) and its link to the committee's vision of HE in the future suggests that it might provide the key organising principle and explanatory framework for the report. Yet it is barely mentioned after this suggesting that it is not really central to the committees deliberative process. Parry (1999 and personal communication) believes that the compact was probably a concept that was introduced very late in the genesis of the Dearing Report (1997) in response to political imperatives to frame policy in terms of the stakeholder society.

The framework for the compact provided in Table 1 of the summary report appears to be inclusive, the ideas and relationships are clearly expressed and the language and tone is reasonable and non-threatening. It captures within it the key dimensions of funding, quality, standards, development/change, participation and partnership. From a drafting perspective the compact is a clever device. It is: 'operationally functional, ideologically neutral and intellectually vacuous ... and like all good condensation symbols, absorbed and collapsed underlying contradictions' (Gareth Parry, personal communication). It provides a unifying, non-divisive framework that deliberately avoids the contractual language of responsibilities and outcomes: something that the recommendations which the compact is designed to embrace, cannot do (Table 3.1).

An anonymous source inside the National Committee of Inquiry into Higher Education (personal communication) confirmed that the compact did emerge at a late state in the committee's deliberations and that it was championed by a small number of HE members. The idea originated in discussions relating to the evidence and thinking around the social benefits and rates of return from a higher education (evidence that was only provided late in the proceedings). The idea of the compact was to create a 'social contract' that would bind the parties together in recognition of the benefits that accrued to all concerned. The late emergence of the idea meant that it had little influence on the main body of the report and therefore did not constitute a foundation principle on which the recommendations and new quality assurance policies were constructed.

If you believe that these observations reflect the circumstances in which the compact evolved then it is easy to relegate the idea to a piece of window dressing and argue that the compact is of little consequence in the strategic policy framework presented in the Dearing Report (1997). An alternative view (one held by the author) is that it is of cardinal importance in locating QA policy in the public policy domain and it is this conceptualisation that will be used as the test of 'fitness for purpose' of the QA policies that are evolved.

National QA Policy and the Compact

The Dearing Report's (1997) vision of how standards and quality in a publicly accountable mass HE system would be maintained are contained in recommendations 20, 21 (chapter 9) and 22, 23, 24, 25 (chapter 10) of the Dearing Report (1997). Table 3.1 summarises these recommendations and explains the progress made since 1997 in creating policy. Since the Dearing Report (1997) was published in mid-1997 the QAA has led policy development work through working groups, expert panels, officer papers, public debate and consultation exercises, trials and field testing of ideas. Aspects of the evolving QA policy framework are described in QAA (1997, 1998a, b and c, 1999a, b, c, d and e), Jackson (1998 and 1999a) and Brown (1998). In developing policy the HE system and QAA have responded in one of three ways. The first type of response is where policy has been developed more or less in line with the recommendation and any associated guidance e.g. recommendations 20 and 23. The second type of response has been to develop policy in a different way to that envisaged in recommendation 21. The third type of response has been to reject the recommendation most notably the call

Table 3.1 Main recommendations of the Dearing Report relating to quality assurance and the subsequent development of national quality assurance policy by QAA

Dearing Report Recommendations	QA Policy Development
Chapter 9 We recommend that institutions of higher education: **Rec 20. Develop a progress file**. The File should consist of two elements: • a transcript recording student achievement which should follow a common format devised by institutions collectively through their representative bodies; • a means by which students can monitor, build and reflect upon their personal development.	• Joint QAA/CVCP/SCoP Discussion Paper March 1999 http://www.qaa.ac.uk/public.htm. • Joint QAA/CVCP/SCoP/CoSHEP Consultation Paper issued September 1999 http://www.qaa.ac.uk/public.htm. • Joint QAA/CVCP/SCoP/CoSHEP report of the consultation exercise April 2000 http://www.qaa.ac.uk/public.htm. • Joint CVCP/SCoP/CoSHEP/QAA policy statement published May 2000 http://www.cvcp.ac.uk/CVCPPublications/Consultation/consultation.html. • Joint CVCP/SCoP/CoSHEP/QAA Guidelines for an HE Progress File expected Autumn 2000.
Rec 21. Develop a 'programme specification' which identifies potential stopping off points and gives the intending outcomes of a programme in terms of: • the knowledge and understanding that a student will be expected to have upon completion; • key skills: communication, numeracy, the use of information technology and learning how to learn; • cognitive skills, such as an understanding methodologies or ability in critical analysis; • subject specific skills, such as laboratory skills.	• QAA led development work on Programme Specification 1997–2000 involved hundreds of academic staff in many HE institutions. • Development process catalogued in:Higher Quality (QAA 1998a and b, QAA 1999a and b) and Jackson (1999 and 2000). • Guidance on Programme Specifications published June 2000 (QAA 2000a).
Chapter 10 We recommend that: **Rec 22** the Government, the representative bodies, the Quality Assurance Agency, other awarding bodies and the organisations which oversee them, should endorse immediately the framework for higher education qualifications that we have proposed.	• QAA led process. Two committees established to develop qualification frameworks for (Scotland and rest of UK). • Consultation Paper October 1999 (QAA 1999d and http://www.qaa.ac.uk/public.htm). • Feedback report and further consultation April 2000.
Rec 23 the Quality Assurance Agency should specify criteria for franchising arrangements…after 2001, no franchising should take place in the UK or abroad except where compliance with the criteria has been certified by the Quality Assurance Agency.	Code of Practice for the assurance of quality and standards in higher education: collaborative provision prepared and published (QAA 1999e). HEI practice will be reviewed against the precepts in the code.
Rec 24 the representative bodies and Funding Bodies amend the remit of the Quality Assurance Agency to include: • quality assurance and public information; • standards verification; • the maintenance of the qualifications framework;	• Quality Assurance Agency established during 1997. Role developed in line with Dearing remit. • New public policy framework (Code of Practice and related Guidance) developed between July 1997 and July 2000. HEI practice will be reviewed against the precepts in the Code. (see QAA web site for published sections of Code).

Table 3.1 cont'd

the requirement that the arrangements for these are encompassed in a code of practice which every institution should be required formally to adopt by 2001/02 as a condition of public funding.

Rec 25 the Quality Assurance Agency should:
• work with institutions to establish small, expert teams to provide benchmark information on standards, operating within the framework of qualifications, and completing the task by 2000;
• work with universities and other degree awarding institutions to create, within three years, a UK-wide pool of academic staff recognised by the QAA, from which institutions must select external examiners;
• develop fair and robust system for complaints relating to educational provision;
• review the arrangements in place for granting degree-awarding powers.

• New process of peer review, focused on Avademic Standards developed and tested (QAA 2000b). Academic Review Handbook – published May 2000 http://www.qaa.ac.uk/AcRevHbook/contents.htm describes new method of review for use in Scotland (2000–2001) and England, Wales & N.Ireland (2001–2002).
• 42 Subject Benchmark Groups established and first 22 subject benchmarking statements published http://www.qaa.ac.uk.benchmark/index.htm.
• The idea that external examiners could serve HEIs and provide independent public assurance was rejected by HE system. New Academic Reviewers have been created.
• Code of Practice – External Examining http://www.qaa.ac.uk/COPee/contents.htm.
• Code of Practice for Academic appears and student complains published March 2000 (QAA 2000c).
• New criteria developed for degree awarding powers.

Source: NCIHE, 1997.

for the immediate adoption of the qualifications framework proposed in the report and the idea that external examiners could fulfil the dual functions of external examining and independent quality assurance for the HE system. This is a complicated policy framework requiring the wholesale shift of an education system to an outcomes-model of learning and it will be some years before national policy is fully developed and deployed and the consequences understood. Policy intentions are however sufficiently advanced to be able to relate these to the Dearing Report (1997) proposals for a compact and illustrate how national QA policy and the likely responses of institutions to these policies will help secure the delivery of the compact. The items in the compact that relate to QA can be used as the basis for an analytical tool to show how they translate in detail into policies and activities at both the national and local level (Table 3.2).

Discussion

The Dearing compact is a clever and apparently innocuous device to connect

Table 3.2   Relationship between key statements in compact that relate to QA, the policies that are being created in the new QA framework and the likely responses of HEIs to national policy

QA statements in compact	National QA policies	Institutional policies and responses
'collective commitment to rigorous assurance of quality and standards'	Comprehensive code of practice for the assurance of quality and standards covering: qualification/credit; framework; programme specification; subject benchmarking; academic review.	Adoption of the code as a condition of funding. Where necessary, adjustment of own policies in line with precepts in the code. New policy and practice relating to subject benchmarking and programme specification.
'rigorously assured awards which have standing across the UK and overseas'	Qualification/credit framework supported by policies on programme specification, subject benchmarking and academic review. Code of practice for external examining.	Adoption of qualification and credit framework and where necessary retitling of awards. Greater focus on QA to support the awarding function. Revision of external examiners role to a) meet expectations in code; b) underpin institutional practice relating to the use of programme specifications and subject benchmarking.
'a clear statement of learning outcomes'	Programme specification and subject benchmarking which steer the HE system to an outcomes model of learning. Transcript element of a progress file that provides a consistent public record of learning and achievement.	Adoption of an outcomes model of learning and use of programme specifications to provide clear statements of outcomes for student programmes. Provision of information on learning and achievement through a consistent national transcript.
'a high quality learning experience'	Part of the Academic Review process is focused on the quality of student experience. It evaluates: teaching and learning; student progression; and learning resources. Subject benchmarking – information is primarily focused on intended outcomes and guidance on the characteristics of standards but some statements describe teaching and learning methods. Personal development planning element of progress file – has the potential to improve institutional monitoring of student progress and to encourage students to appreciate the methods used to support learning.	Institutions are already geared to showing how they meet the expectations of a high quality learning experience contained in the QAA Handbook for Quality Assessors. Institutions have a variety of policies to assure the quality of the students' learning experience e.g.: validation of programmes/modules; annual review of programme/modules; periodic review of student support services. student feedback mechanisms; staff appointment, development and appraisal.

society, HE providers, funding bodies, staff, students and employers through their respective contributions and derivative benefits. In doing so it locates QA policy in the public policy domain rather than restricting it to HE interests. This obliges HE to involve interest groups other than the HE community in the policy making process. This has to date been achieved mainly through the national consultation exercises undertaken when policy ideas are proposed (e.g. QAA, 1998a, 1998b and 1999; CVCP et al., 1999). But there are also examples of students and employers being actively engaged in the policy shaping process through discussion groups and conferences and there is a student representative on the QAA Board which ultimately endorses all policy statements that emanate from the Agency.

To a casual observer it might appear that the QA recommendations made in the Dearing Report (1997) were entirely the product of the fertile minds of the committee members. It must however be recognised that the origins of many of the recommendations relating to QA grew out of a complex debate during the mid-1990s. This debate took place in the academic, public and political arenas in response to: (1) the massive expansion of HE; and the growing political imperative to make HE more accountable for its academic standards; (2) concerns to protect the international reputation of UK HE in the increasingly competitive global market; and (3) the concerns of the HE community to reduce the overall burden of external scrutiny and the effort and bureaucracy required to meet the expectations of different external review processes. It is also important to realise that the subsequent interpretation of the recommendations and development of policy by QAA has been conditioned by other factors, the most important of which are: (1) the need to be able to relate an outcomes model to academic practice; and (2) to ensure that the Funding Councils have sufficient information to enable them to fulfil their statutory responsibilities for the quality of provision.

The Dearing Report's (1997) recommendations relating to quality assurance and outcome standards grew out of the substantial public debate (1994–97) led by the Higher Education Quality Council and the system-level research that was undertaken (HEQC, 1997). The changes associated with the transformation of UK HE fundamentally modified the institutional environments within which standards are created. It taxed the external examiner system and led to substantial changes in the way it operated in different institutions. The rapid expansion of the student population and the number of universities reduced public credibility in the idea that standards can be comparable across a large, diverse, multipurpose HE system. Furthermore, the apparent upward drift in the proportion of first class and upper second class honours degrees since the mid-1980s (MacFarlene, 1992; Chapman in HEQC, 1996c) questioned the capacity of the HE system as a whole to regulate its outcome standards. The public did not understand how universities could teach many more students, at lower unit costs and apparently achieve better results. Neither did they understand how some universities could award a much higher proportion of 'good' degrees than others with a broadly similar student population. The final report (HEQC, 1997) listed 19 recommendations aimed at strengthening the capacity of HE to assure its academic standards and these recommendations were an important influence on the thinking and recommendations of the Dearing Report (1997). It is however noticeable that in some areas of policy (notably programme specification) the QAA has drawn on the earlier thinking of HEQC to create policy that serves a broader range of purposes than the original intention.

The two most significant changes in the UK's approach to quality assurance proposed in the Dearing Report (1997) are embedded in recommendations 21 (outcomes-based learning) and 24 (Code of Practice). Programme specifications and subject benchmarking (rec 25) contain within them the imperative to adopt an outcomes model of learning in order to support an outcomes-based quality assurance model. The assumption that the whole of HE will be able to adopt an outcomes model of learning remains to be tested. Development work on the feasibility of an outcomes-based approach in UK HE was undertaken in the early 1990s (Otter, 1992). The main conclusions of this study (involving the subjects of engineering, design, English, environmental science and social science) were that:

- it is possible to describe the outcomes of higher education more explicitly, although they cannot be expressed in simple 'can do' statements, and, in a complex and changing environment, such definitions will never be complete or fixed;
- descriptions of learning outcomes in higher education cannot be expressed as a single set of 'national standards' of the kind developed for national vocational qualifications, since higher education exists to meet the needs of a variety of client groups and a range of social, economic, scientific and actual needs, and properly embodies a range of different cultures and value systems;
- it is necessary to develop processes within each institution to link outcome definitions with quality assurance, since the authority to define the purposes of degree programmes rests with the chartered institution, rather than with any national agency;

• an outcomes led approach requires staff to develop and use methods of assessment which measure achievements directly, but current assessment practice tends to neglect these questions of validity in favour of reliability, and many academic staff lack experience of appropriate approaches to assessment.

It is unlikely that programme specification alone would by itself promote a system-wide move to an outcomes approach to learning. However, the introduction of subject benchmarking (QAA 1998a and b, 1999a and b), in which subjects like history, chemistry and engineering will create a set of generic learning outcome statements (see for example on-line at http://www.qaa.ac.uk/public.htm) for the achievement of a particular award like an honours degree. When coupled to the academic review process (independent peer review of subjects/programmes) these policies and the activities they promote will be powerful agents for change.

The second significant change in the UK's approach to quality assurance resulting from the Dearing review relates to the development of a national Code of Practice for the assurance of quality and standards (recommendation 24). When complete the Code will identify a series of system-wide expectations covering all matters relating to the management of quality and standards in higher education. In so doing, it will provide an authoritative reference point for institutions as they assure, consciously, actively and systematically, the academic quality and standards of their programmes and awards. The Code will assume that, taking into account nationally agreed principles and practices, each institution will have its own systems for independent verification both of their quality and standards and of the effectiveness of their own quality assurance systems. The extent to which individual institutions are meeting the expectations contained in the component parts of the code will be taken into account by QAA during the course of its quality assurance reviews. The Agency will report regularly on the extent to which higher education institutions individually are meeting these expectations and are discharging their responsibilities for the academic standards and quality of their programmes and awards. (Note: the above description is contained in the foreword to all sections of the Code, e.g. QAA, 1999d, p. 3.)

The overarching Code will provide a set of reference points against which institutions will review their own practice and external review will be conducted. This approach to the regulation of institutional practice is fundamentally different to the non-prescriptive good practice guidelines approach that pertained in the previous QA regime and was promoted through

Quality Assurance Guidelines (HEQC, 1996d). It is anticipated that an approach based on a Code of Practice will result in institutions: (1) adjusting their current practices to comply with the expectations contained in the Code; and (2) developing their capacity to check that they are meeting the expectations of the Code. The thrust of outcomes-focused QA is to increase the level of specification in all aspects of academic management practice. This will create an environment that is more amenable to audit methodologies. It might also be anticipated that HEIs will have performance measures linked to the Codes in order to help them demonstrate to themselves (and third parties) that they are complying with the Codes.

Modification of the Dearing Agenda

Although the Dearing Report (1997) replaced the existing process-focused QA model (endorsed by the Joint Planning Group for Quality Assurance in Higher Education, CVCP, 1996) a compound model is actually emerging. There are two main reasons for this. Firstly, in order to apply an outcomes approach model of learning, it is necessary to be able to relate outcomes to the process by which the outcomes are achieved. Consequently key QA policies like programme specification, subject benchmarking and academic review have to be framed in ways that enable process to be considered as well as outcomes. In an outcomes model of QA it is probably inevitable that 'quality' will be redefined (for QA purposes) in terms of the fitness for purpose (or other notion of quality) of the learning opportunities that enable the outcomes to be achieved. The second reason why the Dearing model of QA does not entirely satisfy the needs of the UK HE system relates to the need to provide the Funding Councils with information that will enable them to fulfil their statutory responsibilities for ensuring that the quality of education is satisfactory. This requires judgements to be made through the academic review process informed by information provided by HEIs themselves. The new academic review process will therefore contain within it an evaluation of the quality of learning opportunities in terms of three of the current aspects of provision that are scrutinised through the Quality Assessment process namely, teaching and learning; student progression and learning resources. This hybrid model reflects the current set of political imperatives in the HE system and illustrates well how policy ideas conceived within the mindset of a national committee are reshaped when they are developed in the real world.

Conclusions

The story of the compact is instructive because it reveals how a committee charged with reforming a higher education system sought to bind the parties together in an acceptable and non-threatening set of moral obligations and relationships. It is argued that the compact fulfilled a number of purposes although none were central to the Committee's thinking as recommendations were formulated. Firstly, it created a framework within which different sets of recommendations could be positioned and the main audiences for the report and the reforms it promoted could be located and related, i.e. it was a presentational device. Secondly, it located policy that affected higher education in the public domain rather than being entirely a concern of HE interests. This has been important in the development of QA policy as evidenced by the strategies and consultations that have included all those with an interest in higher education (not just the providers). Thirdly, it provided a means of measuring (in a very general sense) the future actions and performance of a system and its constituent parts. As such it provides a weak analytical tool for the evaluative state. The QA policies that have been developed however provide more detailed and explicit frameworks and mechanisms for the measurement of system actions and performance. Collectively, they constitute a dynamic and more effective analytical tool for the evaluative state. The net effect has been to shift from a compact that was rooted in the domain of unenforceable moral obligations to a set of policies that form part of the government's performance contract with HE institutions.

History will show that HE responded magnificently to most of the Dearing recommendations (hopefully this is recognised by government) but this would have happened without the idea of the compact as it has not been a primary motivator for change or featured prominently in public debate. QAA has carried forward the Dearing recommendations for QA (following their endorsement by government, the HE system and many different interest groups outside HE) and tried to balance the various political agendas affecting the education system (e.g. accountability for quality and standards; skills for employability and lifelong learning) in formulating policy. But the idea of the compact has been an implicit rather than explicit feature of the policy development process and it must be concluded that the new QA policy framework is a champion rather than a servant of the compact.

Acknowledgements

I would like to thank Gareth Parry for helpful insights into the genesis of the Dearing Report (1997) compact and for constructive criticism of the arguments assembled in this chapter. I would also like to thank an anonymous member of the Dearing Committee for insights into the origin of the idea of the compact. The views expressed are my own, they do not represent in any way the views of the Quality Assurance Agency.

References

Alderman, G. (1996a), 'Audit, Assessment and Academic Autonomy', *Higher Education Quarterly*, 50, No. 3, pp. 178–92.
Alderman, G. (1996b), 'Self-Regulation versus Inspection: The quality debate in British higher education', *Quality World Technical Supplement*, September, pp. 73–6.
Brown, R. (1998), *The Post-Dearing Agenda for Quality and Standards in Higher Education*, Monograph Institute of Education University of London.
Committee of Vice Chancellors and Principals (CVCP) (1996), *Final Report Executive Summary. Joint Planning Group for Quality Assurance in Higher Education*, December.
CVCP (1999), Joint CVCP, SCoP and QAA consultation paper on an HE Progress File, 11 September, on-line at http://www/cvcp.ac.uk/CVCPPublications/Consultation/consultation.html.
CVCP (2000), Joint CVCP, CoSHEP, SCoP and QAA policy statement on a Progress File for HE. Information for members 1/00/80. Committee of Vice-Chancellors and Principals, 17 May.
Dill, D. (1998), 'Evaluating the "Evaluative State": Implications for research in higher education', *European Journal of Education*, Vol. 33, No. 3, pp. 361–77.
Hannah, I. (1996), 'The Management of Quality on Higher Education: A perspective from Scotland', *Quality World Technical Supplement*, Institute of Quality Assurance, pp. 84–9.
Henkel, M. (1991), *Government, Evaluation and Change*, London: Jessica Kingsley.
Kettl, D. (1997), 'The Global Revolution in Public Management: Driving themes, missing links', *Journal of Public Policy Analysis and Management*, 16, pp. 446–62.
Higher Education Quality Council (HEQC) (1995a), *Graduate Standards Programme Interim Report*, London: Higher Education Quality Council.
HEQC (1996a), *Graduate Standards Programme, Draft Final Report*, London: Higher Education Quality Council.
HEQC (1996b), *Guidelines on Quality Assurance*, London: Higher Education Quality Council.
HEQC (1996c), *Inter-institutional Variability of Degree Results, an Analysis of Selected Subjects*, London: Higher Education Quality Council.
HEQC (1997), *Graduate Standards Programme Final Report*, 2 vols, London: Higher Education Quality Council.
Jackson, N.J. (1997a), 'Role of Self-Evaluation in the Self-Regulating UK Higher Education System', in Jackson, N. (ed.), *Managing Quality and Standards in UK Higher Education*,

Approaches to Self-Evaluation & Self-Regulation, London: Higher Education Quality Council, pp. 71–85.

Jackson, N.J. (1997b), 'Regulation in UK Higher Education: Part I – the Concept of Collaborative Regulation', *Quality Assurance in Education*, Vol. 5, pp. 120–35.

Jackson, N.J. (1997c), 'Academic Regulation in UK Higher Education: Part II – Typologies and frameworks for discourse and strategic change', *Quality Assurance in Education*, Vol. 5, pp. 165–79.

Jackson, N.J. (1998a), 'Understanding Standards-based Quality Assurance Part I: Rationale and conceptual basis', *Quality Assurance in Education*, Vol. 6, pp. 132–40.

Jackson, N.J. (1998b), 'Understanding Standards-based Quality Assurance Part II: Nuts and bolts of the Dearing policy framework', *Quality Assurance in Education*, Vol. 6, pp. 220–31.

Jackson, N.J. (1999), 'Programme Specifications and Their Role in Creating a More Explicit Environment for Demonstrating and Recording Achievement', *Journal of Further and Higher Education*, Vol. 23, No, 2, pp. 197–210.

Jackson, N.J. (forthcoming), 'Programme Specification and its role in promoting an outcomes model of learning', *Active Learning, Journal of the Institute of Learning and Teaching*.

Johnson, N. (1994), 'Dons in Decline', *Twentieth Century British History*, pp. 370–85.

Maassen, P.A.M. (1997), 'Quality in European Higher Education: Recent trandes and their historical roots', *European Journal of Higher Education*, 32, pp. 111–27.

MacFarlene, B. (1992), 'The Results of Recession: Students and university degree performance during the 1980s', *Research in Education*, 49, pp. 1–10.

National Committee of Inquiry into Higher Education (Dearing Report) (1997), *Higher Education in the Learning Society*, London: HMSO.

Otter, S. (1992), *Learning Outcomes in Higher Education*, Unit for the Development of Adult and Continuing Education (UDACE): Employment Department.

Parry, G. (1999), 'Education Research and Policy Making in Higher Education: The case of Dearing', *Journal of Education Policy*, Vol 14, No. 3, pp. 225–41.

Quality Asssurance Agency (QAA) (1997), 'Progress on the Dearing Quality Agenda', *Higher Quality, Bulletin of the Quality Assurance Agency for Higher Education*, No. 3, November.

QAA (1998a), 'An Agenda for Quality', consultation issue of *Higher Quality, Bulletin of the Quality Assurance Agency for Higher Education*, No. 3 March.

QAA (1998b), 'An Agenda for Quality', *Higher Quality, Bulletin of the Quality Assurance Agency for Higher Education*, No. 4, October.

QAA (1998c), consultation paper on the Qualifications Frameworks: Postgraduate Qualifications, Quality Assurance Agency for Higher Education, November.

QAA (1999a), 'The New Quality Assurance Framework: Update', *Higher Quality, Bulletin of the Quality Assurance Agency for Higher Education*, No. 5, May.

QAA (1999b), *Higher Quality, Bulletin of the Quality Assurance Agency for Higher Education*, October, No. 6, 1999.

QAA (1999c), consultation paper on the Qualifications Frameworks: Postgraduate Qualifications, Quality Assurance Agency for Higher Education, October.

QAA (1999d), *Code of Practice for the Assurance of Academic Quality and Standards in Higher Education: Collaborative provision*, Gloucester: Quality Assurance Agency for Higher Education.

QAA (2000a), *Guidelines for preparing Programme Specifications. April 2000*, Gloucester: Quality Assurance Agency for Higher Education.

QAA (2000b), *Handbook for Academic Review. April 2000*, Gloucester: Quality Assurance Agency for Higher Education.

QAA (2000c), *Code of Practice for the Assurance of Academic Quality and Standards in Higher Education. Section 5 Academic appeals and student complaints on academic matters*, Quality Assurance Agency for Higher Education, March.

4   Regulating the Masses: Quality and Equality in Higher Education

LOUISE MORLEY

Held to Account

This chapter will consider how discourses of quality and equality interact or collide in the context of massification and the changing demography of higher education. Questions will be raised about the appropriateness of applying quality assurance systems from industry to the complex social and intellectual processes of the academy. Attention will be paid to the current moral panic over standards and inflation of certification in higher education.

The juxtaposition of political and intellectual authority means that public service institutions over the last two decades, have been subject to 'human accounting' (Strathern, 1997). New structures, new rationalities and new regimes of regulation were introduced largely from the corporate context of the private sector ostensibly to promote efficiency, productivity, quality and cost-effectiveness in the public services. Values, as well as technologies and drive systems from the cultural world of business and commerce, have been imported into higher education, bringing with them new meanings, priorities and truths (Morley and Rassool, 1999).

In the context of the new compact between the state, higher education institutions, students and employers, the quality discourse has achieved hegemonic authority whereas the equality discourse has not. Ironically, New Right educational reform was able to effect more significant changes in the quantity and composition of the student body in higher education than two decades of equality legislation and organisational policies. The Dearing Report (1997) noted that only one third of higher education institutions with equal opportunities policies had plans directed towards their achievement (Watson and Taylor, 1998). However, there could be an equity paradox (Morley, 1997) in so far as the transition from an elite to a mass system has produced considerable concerns about the quality of the higher education product. Just as under-represented groups begin to access higher education, the quality of the education product is called into question. This is reminiscent of Bourdieu's notion of distinction which allows the elite to constantly define and denote new forms of differentiation (Bourdieu, 1984).

After the 1992 FHE Act, the number of universities in Britain increased from 46 to 112. There was a rise in the number of students from 900,000 to 1,800,000 (from 15 to 33 per cent). The 'industrialisation' of higher education seemed to suggest that new systems of quality assurance needed to be introduced. Quality had previously been assured via the system of peer review and external examiners (Silver, 1993). This was increasingly regarded as imprecise, ad hoc and archaic by the modernisers. As Evans (1999, p. 147) indicates 'peer review is clearly not an exact science' (and quality assurance is?). In my experience, the notion of 'peer' frequently excludes considerations of exclusionary and discriminatory practices. It is often based on gendered networks and comradeship.

Massification raised questions about how to ensure quality and standards. Concerns also related to value for money and public accountability. Within the new compact, the requirement for reference points and benchmarks has steadily evolved. The new mass system represented a type of chaos that had to be managed via interventions associated with objective measurement. There has been an attempt to secure calculators of value, encoded in performance indicators and league tables (Cave et al., 1997). In the 1985 Green Paper (DES), the government saw the development of performance indicators as the key to demonstrate value for money. As Laurillard (1980, p. 187) observed, performance indicators 'reduce a complexity of subjective judgements to a single objective measure'. However, I wish to argue that the quality discourse in higher education is a technology masking an ideology, with values, priorities, panics and prejudices thinly disguised in the language of standards and excellence.

Human capital theory has also been more overtly applied to higher education in relation to global competitiveness and national prosperity (Dearing, 1997). Within the context of the changing relations between the state and universities, there is now an input/output mindset. Members of the new compact want reassurance and a common language relating to standards. The state wants a return on its investment, and this is linked to the three Es of new managerialism – economy, efficiency and effectiveness.

There is an implied relationship between accountability and improvement. Quality has become a vast industry which dominates organisational culture in the academy today. To some, quality assurance represents a form of consumer empowerment, introducing accountability into dominant organisations of knowledge production. Quality relates to 'fitness for purpose' and measurement of outcomes in relation to product specifications, 'zero defect', effectiveness in achieving institutional goals and success in meeting customers' stated or implied needs (Green, 1995). Quality indicators are assumed to provide information which allows consumers to make informed choices. This notion assumes that choice, decision-making and consumption are rational processes open to reason.

However, quality audits are sometimes perceived as transformational devices. The scrutiny of organisations is seen as a refreshing challenge to elitism and to disciplinary authority (Luke, 1997). For others, quality in general, and total quality management (TQM) in particular, represent an example of surveillance and regulation, with a primary aim to render employees more docile, compliant and governmentable (Ball, 1997). The technology of quality assurance is seen as process of impression management and performativity, with performance indicators socially and politically constructed.

The Genesis of the Discourse

Quality became an issue with the advent of industrialisation, relating to elimination of waste (time, materials, money) and safety. Quality gained currency in Japanese industry in the 1940s and 1950s and was applied specifically to the public services in the USA and UK in the 1980s. Japan appeared to have made a significant economic recovery after the second world war. The West attempted to decode Japanese economic success. Japanese work practices were imported into different sectors of British manufacturing production – and at first – in the car manufacturing industry. According to Imai (1986) the key to the overall success of Japanese business and industry lies first in the philosophical concept of *kaizen*. *Kaizen*, literally translated, means continuous improvement 'involving everyone, including both managers and workers' (Imai, 1986, p. 3). Imai (ibid.) states that '[t]he *kaizen* philosophy assumes that our way of life – be it our working life, our social life, or our home life – deserves to be constantly improved'. There is never an endpoint. This is now strongly associated with neo-Fordist employment regimes, lifelong learning, continuous professional development and the politics of flexibility (Jessop et al., 1991).

In a period of rapid technological and social change, the world has become a riskier place (Beck, 1992). Skill requirements are constantly in flux. Power

(1997) argues that quality assurance is about seeking comfort and certainties. Quality was originally associated with quality control, and was part of Fordist production processes. It consisted of the detection and elimination of components or final products which were not up to standard. It was invariably undertaken by inspectors/controllers, rather than by the workers themselves. In education, this translated into external inspections consisting of observations and judgements. The emphasis gradually moved away from control and towards quality assurance. Systems were put in place throughout the production process, with a quest for zero defect. In education, this is often represented as the quest for excellence (DfEE, 1997). Institutions are not just evaluated on the students' performance, but the provision that is made for getting them to that point.

In 1991 the Further Education Unit (FEU) published what was to be become a highly influential document in the framing of the quality debate in British education. *Quality Matters* (FEU, 1991, p. 2) positioned the concept of quality in education within the framework of manufacturing industry's definition of 'fitness for purpose' which, it argued, is 'arrived at through conformance to specification'. The document emphasised 'the search for opportunities for improvement rather than maintaining current performance' (ibid.). Organisations are required constantly to evaluate, research, analyse and measure needs, results and effectiveness as part of the process of continuous improvement (FEU, 1991). The emphasis is increasingly on the tangible. For example, between 1992–98, it is estimated that about 30 per cent of UK HEIs adopted an outcomes-based curriculum (Jackson, 1999).

Managing Quality

The regulation and management of quality in higher education has been a fairly fragmented affair. In 1990 the CVCP set up an Academic Audit Unit (which lasted for two years). In 1992 the Higher Education Quality Council was established. In 1997 the Quality Assurance Agency (QAA) was set up (after the Dearing Report). It is important to stress that there are now at least two accounting systems for academics. Just as the workforce was acclimatising to research audit, teaching became highlighted as a signifier of excellence and productivity. Subject reviews have been introduced and the Institute for Learning and Teaching opened in 1999 to provide professional development for university teachers. While the two accounting systems could be seen as an example of multiskilling, this often results in academics experiencing split focusing (Coate et al., 2000), with oppositional relationships developing between teaching and research and publication (Morley, 1995).

Managing quality represents a considerable financial and temporal investment. A criticism of quality in relation to higher education is that quality is being promoted at a time when public funding is decreasing. For example, public funding per student in higher education has fallen by more than 40 per cent since 1976. The student:staff ratios moved from 9.3:1 in the old universities and 8.4:1 in the former polytechnics to an overall figure of 16.5:1 (Watson and Bowden, 1999). There is also an increasing casualisation of labour and decreasing employment conditions in higher education. However, the quality discourse attempts to demonstrate how standards can rise even when investments and employment rights drop, thus demonstrating the profligacy of pre-managerialist regimes.

The euphemism 'efficiency gains' for the cuts in higher education asserts that cuts in unit costs have not lowered the quality of the education provided by British universities (Trow, 1998). Hence quality may be being audited in conditions of funding and employment that could be eroding it. The well-being of the work force is not perceived as a quality issue. There is little attention given to occupational stress, intensification and longer working hours (AUT, 1996).

Quality could well be seen as a massive displacement activity, distracting attention away from under-resourcing and focusing on naming and shaming of individual organisations (Carvel, 1999). However, it is extremely effective, as naming is a significant aspect in the constitution of identity. As Butler (1997, p. 2) observed: 'to be called a name is one of the first forms of injury that one learns'. The labelling of universities iterates and inscribes the discourses in a complex chain of signification. Audit and the ensuing certification and grading means that private in-house matters are now in the public domain. The results of audit provide a reified reading, which becomes a truth. For universities at the bottom of the league tables, identity is a form of negative equity. The damage to reputation becomes an attack on the competence of every organisational member. For those at the top, there is an artificial halo effect which invites the projection of a range of positive attributes on to their services. These identities have cash value in the market place. What is frequently undertheorised is how this labelling corresponds with the social class of the different constituencies. Elitism is reinforced and quality accolades are socially decontextualised. Some of the universities with high RAE scores have the lowest percentage of working class students. For example, between 1972 and 1993 the independent school proportion of the entry at

Oxbridge increased from 38 to 57 per cent (McCrum, 1998). Major (1999) cited how the London School of Economics has more applications from the top socioeconomic classes, with just under 70 per cent of UK admitted students from professional and managerial backgrounds in 1997–98, whereas some of the new universities with lower research assessment exercise (RAE) scores, such as Wolverhampton, Central Lancashire and Thames Valley have less than one third from that social group.

The Quality Gaze

Quality is a messy business. It has its product champions and raging critics. The insertion of the quality discourse into higher education represents a challenge to the Medieval achievement of separating the idea of intellectual authority from political authority (Finch, 1997). For some, this is perceived as an intrusion into academic freedom. Peters (1992, p. 128) argues that quality assurance 'will effectively cut across entrenched values of institutional autonomy, academic freedom, collegiality, peer review, cooperation and support which are at the heart of both local and international (academic) communities'. However, Luke (1997, p. 436) asks whether the 'Golden Age of Academic Autonomy Prior to Managerialism' was, in fact 'an epoch of access, equity and enfranchisement for women and people of colour?'. In this context, quality assurance can be seen as a long overdue attempt to make dominant organisations of knowledge production more accountable and transparent in their procedures.

Set in a broader analytical framework, the obsession with quality assurance is also a by-product of the risk society in which there has been a major decline in trust (Beck, 1992; Kramer and Tyler, 1996). Untrustworthy behaviour in the professions is perceived as costly, dangerous and wasteful. The failing university is as much a threat to public safety as the engine falling off an aeroplane. As Power (1997, p. 103) suggests: 'The performance culture of rewards and penalties is a refusal to trust.'

As suggested by Sitkin and Roth (1993), escalating cycles of distrust are frequently misunderstood as being rooted in details associated with reliability and competence. Trust, accountability and competence have been discursively linked. There is now a mania for classifying competencies in professional and higher education. There is also considerable preoccupation with reliable organisations (Slee et al., 1998). Predictability offers some indemnity against risk. Scores in the RAE and the subject review operate as performative utterances signifying a ritualistic movement from one state to another, similar to sentencing in the judicial service. It has both cognitive and emotional power, reassuring consumers of safety and classifying areas of strength and weakness. However, a further irony is how we are invited to place total trust in the auditors, many of whom are drawn from the profession on trial in the first place. The compilers and executors of taxonomies of effectiveness are left unproblematised. The audited are knowable agents, and a central criticism of the quality discourse is that it is a one-way gaze.

On Edge

Similar to the notion of original sin in Christianity, the construction of the individual and the organisation as being in deficit and in need of continuous improvement can be a powerful regulatory device. The mindset of never being satisfied can create an urgency and compliance that shifts attention away from values and ideologies and towards technologies and competencies. Hence, vast amounts of energy are invested in enhancing effectiveness, quality, learning and productivity rather than questioning whose interests are being served. Indeed, the endpoint of continuous improvement clearly is unclear. Strathern (1997, p. 307) argues that this lack of closure brings with it a 'morality of attainment'.

> 'Improvement' is wonderfully open-ended, for it at once describes effort and results. And it invites one to make both ever more effective – a process from which the tests themselves are not immune; measuring the improvement leads to improving the measures.

Quality is riven with ironies and discontinuities. Ball (1999, p. 197) identifies how Labour's education policies can be understood and analysed as a 'synthesis between market and social democratic values'. Started by the New Right, but continued by New Labour, quality now contains a mixture of democratic and economic imperatives. Sallis (1996) argues that there are four imperatives embedded in the quality discourse: moral, professional, competitive, and accountability. The multi-layering of imperatives, alongside the command economy, where funding is linked to external assessments, means that quality is difficult to contest and resist. Continuous improvement can represent opportunity for personal development and consumer empowerment. It challenges routinisation and staleness in the workplace. By calling professionals to account and producing codified signifiers of value, it also purports to challenge expert power and the mystification of professional processes. However, value is socially constructed, with judgements and interpretations of worth politically situated.

For many, interpretative academic freedom in education was causally linked to low standards. Indeed, by the time that the Conservative Government came to power in 1979:

> Education had come to epitomize much that was seen to be wrong with burgeoning state power. It was construed as expensive, not self-evidently adequately productive, insufficiently accountable, monopolistic, producer-dominated, a bastion of an entrenched professional elite, resistant to consumer demand and, at worst, self-generating and self-serving (Fergusson, 1994, p. 93).

In many respects, the higher education system needed to be opened up to scrutiny. It is debatable whether scrutinising quality and standards have promoted or eclipsed equity issues.

Within the standards approach to quality there is an emphasis on organisations and individuals regulating themselves. The auditing gaze is both internal and external, as educational institutions are subjected to inspection. Hierarchical observation often results in the self-surveillance of the observed. This self-regulation is an example of how power can be capillary, rather than monolithic. A capillary notion of power suggests that power operates everywhere in everyday transactions. It is totalising in so far as it is rehearsed in inter and intrapersonal relations, as well as in structures (Morley, 1999). Brown (1998) argues that the most critical aspect of the new quality framework is the relationship between external and internal assessments. For example, providers of subjects now compile a self-assessment document that reflects the areas open to external assessment. Power (1994, pp. 36–7) notes:

> What is audited is whether there is a system which embodies standards and the standards of performance themselves are shaped by the need to be auditable ... audit becomes a formal 'loop' by which the system observes itself.

The feedback loop and customer care have been important features of quality assurance in higher education, with the introduction of: handbooks, guidelines, codes of practice, student opinion surveys, a students' charter and staff development. The customer, however, remains a universal subject, without gender, social class or ethnicity.

Quality as a Regulatory Device

I wish to argue that quality is not a neutral notion; rather, it is a subjective category of description and its meaning derives from its point of articulation. Hoppers (1994, p. 175) reminds us that:

> Quality is a multi-dimensional concept and its interpretation is dependent on the interests of the different actors in the process and outcomes in the enterprise.

There are questions about who defines quality, and indeed, whose interests it represents. There is also the question whether standards are absolute or relative. The measures themselves are questionable. For example, Elton (1998) notes that there is a higher proportion of firsts in 'hard' subjects such as engineering and mathematics, than in 'soft' subjects such as history and French. He believes that this is more to do with assessment procedures than the ability of students.

There is little sociology in quality assurance. Quality assurance can be technicist and reductive in focus. Quality is often socially decontextualised. For example, in the context of subject review, the segment of student experience that is audited is predominantly their role as learners (Haselgrove, 1994). There are complex areas of higher education that are difficult to measure, quantify and capture e.g. processes, the affective domain, attitudes and values. In this framework, a sexist, racist tutor who gets good completion rates is deemed to be effective. The gaps and silences in taxonomies of effectiveness are often where equity issues constellate (Morley and Rassool, 1999). Discursive technologies of power produce, reproduce, marginalise and resist particular knowledges. Ball (1997) argues that quality is a technology for cultural engineering, with strong normative connotations. TQM is merely a way of ensuring the achievement of state policies, through a 'combination of micro-disciplinary practices and steering at a distance' (Ball, 1997, p. 322). TQM is also perceived as a system of government of employees. Tacit professional practices are bureaucratised and a panopticon culture is promoted (Foucault, 1979a and b). The quality discourse is an effective way of ensuring compliance and docility of employees by establishing a set of goals and objectives that are not always negotiable. For example, how much linguistic agency do universities have in the quality assurance framework?

Quality audits could also be perceived as positivistic. There is a notion that organisations are knowable via the appropriate instruments, checklists and taxonomies. The complexities of teaching and learning, for example have been reduced to six categories. Epistemological questions about these variables and methods are left unexamined. This approach inevitably only addresses a surface organisational rationality, and yet this becomes a truth. In quality assurance procedures, organisations have to represent their identities discursively. As Luke argues (1997, p. 440) 'a document of narrative prose suggests a textual version of the Foucauldian confessional' (Foucault (1979a and b). Quality audits encourage performativity (Lyotard, 1984), as organisations tend give aspirational accounts of themselves within certain prescribed parameters.

Quality as Consumer Empowerment

An argument in favour of quality is that it condenses complex professional processes into easily identifiable information for consumers. The use of league tables, grades for teaching quality and RAE scores can be indicators to assist choice-making processes. Similarly, benchmarking is often seen as a type of classification and framing exercise in the midst of the potential chaos of expansion in higher and further education. This can be seen as elite organisations being forced to become more user-friendly, particularly to those users who lack the cultural capital and social advantages often required for educational decision-making. Voice discourse is also a potent aspect of consumer empowerment (Morley, 1998). The reconstruction of students as consumers and clients gives the appearance of changing power relationships between purchasers and providers of the educational product. Quality audits could be said to privilege users' voices by measuring customer satisfaction via the use of evaluation instruments and consumer surveys.

In terms of equity, greater transparency of procedures can sometimes make discriminatory and exclusionary practices more visible. One view is that quality audits can be used by women as a mechanism for what Yeatman (1990) calls 'equity-oriented change management' (Luke, 1997, p. 437). The 'panoptic' gaze of audit can bring marginalised groups into the light. The emphasis on continuing professional development and on accountability can challenge expert power and routinisation. There is the potential for organisational reflexivity as preparation for quality audits can provide some discursive space for reflecting on practices, assumptions, and procedures. Quality audits are also perceived as transformational devices, allowing questions to be posed about whether equity provisions are measures of excellence, e.g. arrangements for students with special needs. If one takes a Foucauldian analysis of power, quality can be both oppressive and creative. Quality is a complex and contradictory affair. While I am critical of many of the stress-inducing regulatory functions, I have to admit to having experienced some delight several years ago, when some non-functioning, inactive colleagues who put most of their energies into making life a misery for more competent female colleagues, were flushed out and publicly graded 'unsatisfactory' by inspectors!

Conclusion

The standardisation implied in quality assurance can suggest normalisation. In the context of the new compact, there are dangers of homogenising teachers and learners and creating a universal subject and organisational isomorphism. Currently, very diverse organisations are placed on the same continuum for research excellence, for example. This automatically disadvantages those organisations with diverse populations, as Wagner (1989, p. 36) points out: 'It is those who restrict access by accepting only students with the highest traditional qualifications which receive status, privilege, honours and resources.'

The technology of quality assurance is perceived as a reductive input/output model. It is seen as a process of impression management and performativity, with performance indicators socially and politically constructed. It implies solutions, best practice, orthodoxies and consensus. The technology masks the ideology and value base of what is considered excellent at this particular political and historical moment (Ball, 1997).

As part of the modernisation programme, the current government has invested large sums of money in quality assurance. There is an implied relationship between accountability and improvement. Accountability has been linked to public information. The rhetoric of improvement is related to organisational development and continuous professional development. However, in spite of this vast machinery, there is little evidence to suggest that the quality of student or staff experiences has been enhanced, or whether the role that higher education plays in social reproduction has been interrupted. There has been an intensification of bureaucracy for staff which inevitably impacts on the amount of time and good attention available for students. Quality audits can both expose inequalities and reinforce them, by sealing staff into rigid hierarchies of accountability, and by creating a sense of fear and instability.

It is doubtful whether the evidence collected via quality audits reflects wider social transformations and shifting student demographics. Many of these concerns have crystallised around the issue of value-added i.e. ensuring that people exit with better characteristics than they possessed at the point of input (Brennan et al., 1997). However, issues of diversity and equity are only superficially addressed. Multifaceted qualitative processes such as pedagogical relations and barriers to participation are reduced to quantitative indicators (Morley, 2000). Vexed political questions relating to power and knowledge are condensed into concerns about course documentation, waiting time for essay feedback etc. It is dubious whether audit detects complex microprocesses of power in organisations (Morley, 1999). Meanwhile, the rhetoric of continuous improvement is a powerful message system to students and staff, informing them of their lack and deficit, in an attempt to make them more governmentable. Concerns about the authenticity of the exercise abound. Yet auditors and auditees perform a type of comedy of manners. We speak the discourse and the discourse speaks us. Quality audits are textual and grammatocentric, relying on reported practices within predetermined criteria. Complicity in this performance is partly because quality ratings play a pivotal role in capitalist modes of exchange. In the new compact, there is almost a form of contract compliance at work.

Quality in higher education offers normalising judgements that compare, differentiate, categorise, homogenise, correct and exclude. Discursive performaties not only act to constitute organisational realities they appear to describe, they simultaneously position these realities as existing prior to the description and intervention, e.g. falling standards. Quality assurance interventions actively produce the contexts in which they operate. In preparing for quality audits, organisations focus their attention and resources on the areas to be audited. While there is a claim to report realities, the quality discourse is actually responsible for constructing them in the first place.

References

AUT (1996), *Efficiency gains or quality losses?*, London: AUT.
Ball, S.J. (1999), 'Labour, Learning and the Economy: A "policy sociology" perspective', *Cambridge Journal Of Education*, 29(2), pp. 195–206.
Ball, S.J. (1997), 'Good School/Bad School: Paradox and fabrication', *British Journal of Sociology of Education*, 18 (3), pp. 317–36.
Beck, U. (1992), *Risk Society*, London: Sage.
Bourdieu, P. (1984), *Distinction*, London: Routledge and Paul.
Brennan, J., De Vries, P. and Williams, R. (eds) (1997), *Standards and Quality in Higher Education*, London: Jessica Kingsley.

Brown, R. (1998), *The Post-Dearing Agenda for Quality and Standards in Higher Education*, London: University of London Institute of Education.

Butler, J. (1997), *Excitable Speech: A Politics of the Performative*, London: Routledge.

Carvel, J. (1999), 'Thames Valley: The inside story', *The Guardian Higher Education*, 20 July, pp. ii–iii.

Cave, M., Hanney, S., Henkel, M. and Kogan, M. (1997), *The Use of Performance Indicators in Higher Education: The Challenge of the Quality Movement*, 3rd edn, London: Jessica Kingsley.

Coate, K., Court, S., Gillon, E., Morley, L. and Williams, G. (2000), *Academic and Academic Related Staff Involvement in the Local, Regional and National Economy*, London: AUT.

DES (1985), Green Paper, *The Development of Higher Education*, London: DES.

DfEE (1997), *Excellence in Schools*, London: HMSO.

Elton, L. (1998), 'Are UK Degree Standards Going Up, Down or Sideways?', *Studies in Higher Education*, 23(1), pp. 35–42.

Evans, G.R. (1999), *Calling Academia to Account: Rights and Responsibilities*, Buckingham: SRHE/Open University Press.

Fergusson, R. (1994), 'Managerialism in Education', in Clarke, J., Cochrane, A. and McLaughlin, E. (eds), *Managing Social Policy*, London: Sage Publications, pp. 93–114.

FEU (1991), *Quality Matters: Business and Industry Quality Models and Further Education*, London: FEU, August.

Finch, J. (1997), 'Power, Legitimacy and Academic Standards', in Brennan, J., De Vries, P. and Williams, R. (eds), *Standards and Quality in Higher Education*, London: Jessica Kingsley, pp. 146–56.

Foucault, M. (1979a), *Discipline and Punish*, trans. A. Sheridan, New York: Vintage.

Foucault, M. (1979b), 'Governmentability', *Ideology and Consciousness*, 6, pp. 5–22.

Green, D. (ed.) (1995), *What is Quality in Higher Education?*, Buckingham: SRHE/Open University.

Haselgrove, S. (ed.) (1994), *The Student Experience*, Open University Press/SRHE.

Hoppers, W. (1994), 'Learning the Lessons: A thematic review of project experiences', in Little, A., Hoppers, W. and Gardner, R. (eds), *Beyond Jomtien: Implementing Primary Education for All*, London: Macmillan, pp. 163–86.

Imai, M. (1986), *Kaizen (Ky'zen): The key to Japan's competitiveness*, New York: Random House.

Jackson, N. (1999), 'Modelling Change in a National HE System using the Concept of Unification', *Journal of Education Policy*, Vol. 14, No. 4, pp. 411–34.

Jessop, B., Kastendiek, H., Nielsen, K. and Pedersen, O. (eds) (1991), *The Politics of Flexibility*, Aldershot: Edward Elgar.

Kramer, R. and Tyler, T. (eds) (1996), *Trust in Organizations*, London: Sage.

Laurillard, D. (1980), 'Validity of Indicators of Performance', in Billing, D. (ed.), *Indicators of Performance*, Guildford: SRHE.

Luke, C. (1997), 'Quality Assurance and Women in Higher Education', *Higher Education*, 33, pp. 433–51.

Lyotard, J. (1984), *The Postmodern Condition*, Manchester: Manchester University Press.

Major, L. (1999), 'A Class Apart?', *The Guardian Higher Education*, 16 November, pp. 1–3.

McCrum, N.G. (1998), 'Gender and Social Inequality at Oxbridge: Measures and remedies', *Oxford Review of Education*, 24 (3), pp. 261–77.

Morley, L. (1995), 'Measuring the Muse: Creativity, eriting and career development', in Morley, L. and Walsh, V. (eds), *Feminist Academics: Creative Agents for Change*, London: Taylor and Francis.

Morley, L. (1997), 'Change and Equity in Higher Education', *British Journal of Sociology of Education*, 18 (2), pp. 231–42.

Morley, L. (1998), 'All You Need is Love: Feminist pedagogy for empowerment and emotional labour in the academy', *International Journal of Inclusive Education*, 2 (1), pp. 15–27.

Morley, L. (1999), *Organising Feminisms: The Micropolitics of the Academy*, London: Macmillan.

Morley, L. (2000), 'Lifelong Yearning: Feminist pedagogy in the learning society', in Anderson, P. and Williams, J. (eds), *Identity and Difference in Higher Education: Feminist perspectives*, London: Ashgate.

Morley, L. and Rassool, N. (1999), *School Effectiveness: Fracturing the Discourse*, London: Falmer Press.

National Committee of Inquiry into Higher Education (Dearing Report) (1997), *Higher Education in the Learning Society*, London: HMSO.

Peters, M. (1992), 'Performance and Accountability in Post-industrial Societies: The crisis in British universities', *Studies in Higher Education*, 17 (2), pp. 123–39.

Power, M. (1994), *The Audit Explosion*, London: Demos.

Power, M. (1997), *The Audit Society*, Oxford: Oxford University Press.

Sallis, E. (1996), *Total Quality Management in Education*, London: Kogan Page.

Silver, H. (1993), *External Examiners: Changing roles*, London: CNAA.

Sitkin, S. and Roth, N. (1993), 'Explaining the Limited Effectiveness of Legalistic Remedies for Trust/Distrust', *Organization Science*, 4 (3), pp. 367–92.

Slee, R., Tomlinson, S. and Weiner, G. (eds) (1998), *Effective for Whom? Challenges to the School Effectiveness and School Improvement Movements*, London: Falmer Press.

Strathern, M. (1997), 'Improving Ratings': Audit in the British university system', *European Review*, 5 (3), pp. 305–21.

Trow, M. (1998), 'The Dearing Report: A transatlantic view', *Higher Education Quarterly*, 52 (1), pp. 93–117.

Wagner, L. (1989), 'Access and Standards: An unresolved and unresolvable debate', in Ball, C. and Eggins, H. (eds), *Higher Education Into the 1990s*, Milton Keynes: Open University Press.

Watson, D. and Taylor. R. (1998), *Lifelong Learning and the University*, London: Falmer Press.

Watson, D. and Bowden, R. (1999), 'Why Did They do it? The Conservatives and mass higher education, 1979–97', *Journal of Education Policy*, 14 (3), pp. 243—56.

Yeatman, A. (1990), *Bureaucrats, Technocrats, Femocrats*, Sydney: Allen and Unwin.

5 A Compact for Higher Education: A Case Study of the Thames Gateway

JUDITH WATSON

This chapter seeks to illustrate the concept of a compact for higher education by considering what would be entailed in introducing such a compact to one geographical area of England. The case study area taken is the 'Thames Gateway' – the estuary of the Thames below central London – an area engaged in large scale economic regeneration. It presents the results of analysis of the 1996 Research Assessment Exercise in the Thames Gateway higher education institutions (HEIs) and discusses what this implies for the future of the local learning infrastructure within the local economy and community. It then outlines what a compact for higher education might mean in the Thames Gateway. It argues that further entrenchment of the divide between research and teaching universities is unlikely to serve the needs to regional economic regeneration and that links need to stretch across these sectors and to encompass further education, as well as local economic and community organisations.

Introduction: Regeneration and Learning in the Thames Gateway

The 'Thames Gateway' is a recently-invented term referring to the banks of the Thames from Tower Bridge eastwards towards the sea. It replaces the previously current expression 'East Thames Corridor'. The Regional Planning Guidance (Department for the Environment, 1995) defines it as lying between the A13 road and the river on the north bank and the A2 road and the river on the south bank. From this geographical definition it can be noted that the area:

• is linear;
• is divided by the river;

• and cuts across administrative boundaries.

The Thames Gateway is therefore unlike a city or a town in that it is not organised around a city centre, or town centre. It is a more problematic area for regeneration. The river estuary widens as it leaves London and the crossings become fewer. Beyond Tower Bridge there are only the Rotherhithe Tunnel, the Blackwall Tunnel and the Dartford Crossing for motor traffic, while for rail there are only the old East London tube line and the two newly-opened links of the Docklands Light Railway and the Jubilee Line. The ferry crossings at Woolwich and Tilbury-Gravesend are still important. Cross-river mobility in the Thames Gateway is still very limited, and the farther east one travels the more difficult it becomes. The inhabitants do not see themselves as living in the Thames Gateway, indeed the majority probably have never heard the expression, but consider themselves to be inhabitants of Woolwich or Sheppey, Canning Town or Corringham.

North and south riversides have in common the experience of rapid deindustrialisation in the 1970s and 1980s. This was particularly acute in the London Docklands. Recognition of the problems consequent upon the closure of the London Docks eventually gave rise to the formation of the London Docklands Development Corporation (LDDC) and the redevelopment of the Isle of Dogs and Surrey Docks. The idea of the Thames Gateway is essentially a recognition that the Docklands redevelopment has not resolved all the problems affecting the eastern Thames, and that regeneration is needed further east along the estuary. The LDDC has been wound up without completing the redevelopment of all the former dock sites. In particular, there are still acres of derelict land around the closed Royal Docks in Newham. Further east, both river banks are a mixture of empty former industrial sites, industrial development that survives and in many cases thrives, isolated working-class communities, new housing estates and other new developments.

The term 'gateway' was chosen to express an intention that the estuary should be wrested from its geographical isolation. Until now it has been within affluent South East England but not of it. The intention is to create physical and cultural links not only with the rest of the UK but with the whole of Europe. There are already the ports of Dover, Folkestone and Ramsgate, with road connections through the Thames Gateway into London, container ports at Tilbury and Dartford, and London City Airport in the former London docks. The high speed rail link to the Channel Tunnel will undoubtedly have a massive impact, with new stations at Ebbsfleet near Dartford and at Stratford. Indeed the impact is already being felt, with the last of the great out-of-town shopping centres recently opened at Bluewater and new hotels and other developments at Dartford, located close to the station site as well as to the road bridge and tunnel. The Thames Gateway is also planned to become the site of massive new housing developments, justified on the grounds that much of the land is formerly industrial and classified as 'brownfield' rather than 'greenfield' sites. New housing for the South East can be built there with a clear conscience, away from the protests of residents in Home Counties villages.

Approaches to regeneration in the Thames Gateway are marked by the Docklands experience. It is seen as a chance to complete the Thames-side's renaissance without repeating LDDC's mistakes. Elected local authorities are determined not to be excluded from the Thames Gateway strategies as they were from the centrally-appointed LDDC. Thus 11 local authorities, including ten London boroughs and the Essex district of Thurrock set up the Thames Gateway London Partnership. Dartford and Gravesham in Kent subsequently joined the partnership, although North Kent has also maintained its own development organisations. Crucially, local authorities need to avoid the charge that development is at the expense of local communities and brings employment only to wealthy incomers. They are therefore attracted to strategies relying on 'endogenous growth' as opposed to seeking to attract inward investment. These fashionable theories tend to see economic development as a process of learning, and promote buzzwords such as the 'learning city'. The London Borough of Greenwich, for example, has joined the Learning Cities Network. A high skill economy has a certain logic in the Thames Gateway where wage levels are among the highest in the UK and land prices are also high, but it is not immediately obvious how it can be achieved without further social polarisation.

LDDC did not have a training strategy for the first ten years of its operation (Church 1990), but later began to fund training, mostly in basic skills, through its Skillnet programme. Since that time there has been a shift of central government policy towards a concern for social inclusiveness, in particular with the establishment of the Social Exclusion Unit. Education (education, education) is seen as a privileged mechanism for ensuring social cohesion. This national change of outlook, combined with local experience, means that strategies for educational development in the Thames Gateway are oriented towards widening participation and raising achievement. A group of London boroughs in the Thames Gateway applied for and were awarded a £31 million grant for skills development entitled 'Skills for the Millennium'. However, renewed emphasis upon education and training does not solely or even primarily involve the local HEIs. It was the further education colleges (FECs) in the Thames Gateway that first formed themselves into a local partnership and won a place at the economic development table. However, HE development is now recognised to be a part of the Thames Gateway development strategy. Development agencies are increasingly concerned to foster partnership working between education and training providers, and to ensure that these partnerships work across sectors. The post-1992 HEIs in the Thames Gateway have established strong partnerships with groups of FECs.

In what we might call a 'local learning infrastructure', two dimensions of learning must coexist. Learning as the reproduction of existing knowledge is subject to a series of terms: education, training, skill, knowledge. Learning as the production of new knowledge is subject to a different series of terms: innovation, science, technology transfer. Higher education traditionally is committed to one dimension through its teaching and to the other dimension through its research. A 'research university' might claim to be an organic union of teaching and research. However, the coherence of the whole local learning infrastructure implies coherence:

- within the institutional structure that reproduces existing knowledge, i.e., interaction of the various publicly-funded education and training institutions; and
- between the structure that reproduces existing knowledge and the structure that produces new knowledge, i.e., between educational institutions and innovation within networks of firms.

The need for these two kinds of coherence challenges the claim of the university to be able to satisfy the learning needs of the whole locality within its walls. Therefore HE must make a compact with its communities. As a case study of the relationship of the Thames Gateway HEIs to their communities, the results of the 1996 research assessment exercise (RAE) in the Thames Gateway HEIs will be considered.

The Results of the 1996 RAE in the Thames Gateway

Six institutions provided higher education to the Thames Gateway at the time of the 1996 RAE. Three were former ILEA polytechnics: University of Greenwich, University of East London and London Guildhall University. And each side of the river had a constituent college of the University of London: Goldsmiths College to the south; Queen Mary and Westfield College to the north. The Natural Resources Institute, located at Chatham Maritime, was formerly the research agency of the Overseas Development Administration, and has since merged with University of Greenwich.

These institutions thus had very different research traditions. As polytechnics the three largest institutions had obviously focused upon teaching. However, for some time individual academics and small teams had been building up their confidence as researchers. Many staff welcomed university status as an opportunity to become teacher-researchers of the kind known in the pre-1992 universities. In practice, though, research was often just a source of extra stress. The standard contract of employment in the post-1992 universities still stipulates 18 hours of teaching per week for a senior lecturer, which scarcely permits any time for research. Although seven weeks a year are allocated to 'research and scholarly activity', it is not always possible to produce an assessable output within that time, especially when the surrounding research culture is embryonic. The two University of London colleges continued with a research-teaching mix typical of the pre-1992 universities. Finally, the Natural Resources Institute was more or less entirely devoted to research, mostly very applied in nature, obtaining external funding from contracts with international bodies and developing countries, rather than from the UK research councils.

This was the research capability available within the Thames Gateway in 1996. The aim of the RAE was to assess the quality of research, by looking at the published outputs of researchers and judging them against national and international standards operating within each subject. The 1996 RAE did not seriously attempt to investigate the use of the research within the local or national context. Each subject was assessed in the same manner. However, for the analysis here, we may distinguish four types of HE research by their relevance to local regeneration:

1 increasing knowledge about the processes of economic development;

2 supporting innovation in the industries that the development strategy seeks to promote or attract;

3 supporting business development generally;

4 supporting the community, generally increasing the stock of social knowledge, contributing to other research.

The RAE subject areas may be roughly grouped under these headings. Research in the first two categories will be discussed here. Firstly, looking at the average results across all subjects, it is immediately noticeable that the binary divide persists. There is virtually no overlap nationally between the pre-1992 and post-1992 universities. With only one exception all the old universities are rated higher than all the new. The *Times Higher Education Supplement*'s analysis (*THES*, 1997) shows that Goldsmiths is rated twenty-sixtth of all CVCP member universities. Queen Mary and Westfield College (QMW) is forty-third. Greenwich is sixty-fourth, fourth among the new universities, University of East London (UEL) seventy-eighth and London Guildhall University (LGU) ninety-second. The Natural Resources Institute (NRI, now part of Greenwich) was towards the bottom of the old universities. A major difference between pre- and post-1992 universities was the proportion of academic staff selected for inclusion in the assessment exercise, indicating the different traditions: teaching in the polytechnics compared to teaching-researching in the universities. In the Thames Gateway, proportions ranged from 27 per cent at Greenwich through 36 per cent at UEL and LGU to 81 per cent at Goldsmiths and 83 per cent at QMW.

Table 5.1   RAE grades, all subjects

Grades	**Number of subject areas assessed at each grade**	
	Thames Gateway pre-1992 HEIs	*Thames Gateway post-1992 HEIs*
5*	2	0
5	9	1
4	17	2
3a	4	7
3b	6	8
2	4	18
1	1	9
Total	43	45

Note: NRI excluded.

Table 5.1 shows that the post-1992 HEIs in the Thames Gateway, with 80 per cent of the students, only accounted for just over half the research grades awarded. The top grade, 5*, was awarded only twice (Russian, Slavonic and East European languages at QMW and art and design at Goldsmiths) and not at all to the post-1992 universities. The modal grade for the pre-1992 universities was 4 and for the post-1992 ones, 2. The overlap occurred at grade 3a, which was a very good result in the new universities and a poor one in the old universities.

Research Supporting the Process of Economic Development

There are good arguments for developing the research capacity of local HEIs as part of the process of local economic development. The local HEIs already have knowledge of their local areas, although much of it will be tacit (Polanyi, 1969) – they do not yet know that they know it. As noted already, the Thames Gateway HEIs are developing close links with further education colleges, whose expertise can be pooled in the research. The combined local knowledge of thousands of HE and FE students could be a formidable asset for the development process. By participating in research into economic development, the local HEIs can become more self-aware and more embedded in their local economic communities. Finally, the expertise, capacity and prestige built up in the early stages of the regeneration process should be transferable in the years to come into continuing support for local firms and residents in the form of teaching, R&D, consultancy, and so forth.

However, the process of development may continue without research capacity available in the local HEIs. Development agencies (Training and Enterprise Councils, the new local Learning and Skills Councils, local authorities, development corporations and so on) can commission research from providers anywhere in the UK and even abroad. They may often use market research companies or small consultancies in preference to universities, particularly when they are looking for quick answers rather than deep background. Moreover, they may sometimes be well advised to select specialist or high-prestige institutions, irrespective of location. Furthermore, the process of competitive tendering may preclude them from favouring local suppliers. The HEIs, for their part, may decide not to prioritise research related to local economic development.

Since the Thames Gateway HEIs have no automatic right to carry out research related to Thames Gateway development, the RAE results operate as an indicator for development agencies wishing to commission research. (However, the RAE is separate from the official performance indicators developed by HEFCE.) Table 5.2 shows the results in 16 RAE subject areas that might be thought relevant to the economic development process.

Arguments could be made for the inclusion or exclusion of various areas as relevant and quite a broad definition has been used here. It should be noted that the definitions of these subjects in the RAE are arbitrary anyway, and ignore the many interdisciplinary research programmes running in the local HEIs. There is also a politics of how each HEI categorises staff in order to maximise its RAE ratings. The same individual may have been entered in one research area for the 1992 exercise and another for the 1996 exercise without substantially changing the field of her or his research.

Table 5.2   RAE grades in subjects related to economic development

Subject	Gold.	QMW	Green.	NRI	LGU	UEL
Sociology	5	–	3a	–	2	3a
Communication, cultural and media studies	4	–	–	–	1	5
Statistics and operational research	3b	5	3b	–	–	–
History	4	4	–	–	4	–
Economics and econometrics		4	–	–	3b	3a
Education	4	–	3a	–	–	3b
Politics and international studies	4	–	2	–	3b	–
Psychology	4	–	2	–	2	2
Computer science	2	4	–	–	1	
Geography	4	–	–	–	–	1
Business and management studies	–	–	2	–	1	2
Environmental sciences	–	–	2	2	–	–
Built environment	–	–	2	–	–	1
Social policy and administration	–	–	–	–	2	–
Social work	2	–	–	–	–	–
Town and country planning	–	–	–	–	–	2

We can now see that the institutional divide is also an epistemological one. The more concrete the field, the lower the grade. Most of the subjects relevant to the process of economic development received a grade 4 or 5 somewhere, and many of them also received a reasonable grade in another institution. But there was a group of applied subjects, highly relevant to understanding economic and community development, which received nothing higher than a grade 2 anywhere in the Thames Gateway. In other words, subjects taught and researched mainly in the former polytechnics do not receive high ratings. Pure research is valued more highly than applied research even in closely-related disciplines, so sociology has good grades even in the post-

1992 universities, while social policy and social work are virtually neglected. These Thames Gateway figures reflect the national averages for the various RAE subject categories. Economics and econometrics scored an average of 5.3 nationally, while Town and Country Planning scored only 3.9.

Local research strengths include sociology and communications, cultural and media studies. Education and economics are strong in both old and new universities. However, it cannot be said from these figures that the local research capacity meets the needs of development agencies well. Research in geography should be a major worry for those concerned with regional regeneration. It received a grade 4 at QMW but only a 1 at UEL. Greenwich and LGU both have geography teaching but did not make a submission in the subject for the 1996 RAE.

Research Supporting Key Industrial Sectors

Key industrial sectors for the Thames Gateway have been identified by the Thames Gateway London Partnership. These sectors include 'academic services' and 'technology futures', presumably on the basis that HE and FE are major employers of staff in the area. There is an element of wishful thinking in this. More realistically, the project 'Skills for the Millennium', which was awarded £31 million of public funding from the government's single regeneration budget, identifies four key sectors: construction, manufacturing, leisure and tourism.

To develop these sectors in the Thames Gateway is in a sense to facilitate their institutional learning. Existing firms need to learn how to compete better and expand. New firms attracted to the area have to learn how to operate in a new environment. Learning by firms is usually identified with innovation. It is also recognised that much of the knowledge held by firms is tacit and is not always recognised as knowledge in an academic context. For example, a firm may have adequate scientific expertise available to it (codified knowledge) to operate but fail because of lack of sensitivity to customers (tactic knowledge). Nevertheless, it is generally recognised that access to the latest research findings in HE is a significant asset to firms that wish to innovate. In this section, it will be seen how the 1996 RAE assessed in the Thames Gateway HEIs research areas that are relevant to the four key industrial sectors.

RAE subjects particularly relevant to the construction industry include civil engineering, built environment and town and country planning. These subjects have low research grades in the local HEIs, weaker even than the national averages in these subjects. The highest grade awarded was a 3a for civil engineering at QMW. On the other hand, the local HEIs are very active in running courses relevant to construction. UEL maintains a large construction department, while Greenwich has courses in architecture, surveying and estates management at its Dartford campus, on the doorstep of an area identified for the construction of thousands of new homes over the next few years. The weakness of research in these fields is all the more problematic. The UK construction industry is well known to be slow to innovate, and it seems unlikely that there will be any positive push towards innovation from the local HEIs. The Thames Gateway HEIs are not well known for any particular focus towards the construction industry. Yet it is vitally important that the construction industry operating in the Thames Gateway should be innovative and responsive to change, if the ecological impact of building so many new homes should be minimised.

Cultural industries, by contrast, are well supported by local research capacity with a set of high RAE ratings. Art and design scored a 5* and music a 5 at Goldsmiths. The capacity is further strengthened by the move of Trinity College of Music into part of the former Royal Naval College site. Communication, cultural and media studies scored a 5 at UEL, the only such grade scored in a Thames Gateway post-1992 university in 1996. There were high grades for European languages, including literary studies, at both QMW and Goldsmiths. These grades help to justify the inclusion of cultural industries as a key sector with the development strategy. However, when UEL's success is removed from the equation the strength is somewhat dependent upon Goldsmiths.

Hospitality, leisure and tourism industries do not have any RAE subjects directly relevant to them. History, relevant to museum and heritage work, scored well with 4s at Goldsmiths, LGU and QMW. However, there were no local entries for library and information management, nor for sports-related subjects.

Research related to manufacturing industries varies in the degree of recognition it is accorded. Engineering research is well established at QMW, with 5s for metallurgy and materials, and electrical and electronic engineering, and a 4 for mechanical, aeronautical and manufacturing engineering. Greenwich had 3as for metallurgy and materials, and mechanical, aeronautical and manufacturing engineering, and a 3b for general engineering. Other kinds of manufacturing present in the Thames Gateway do not fare so well. From the RAE subject categories, it can be seen that there is an established tradition of academic research relating to engineering, but no parallel research capacity in support of other manufacturing. For instance, no RAE subject relates directly to the clothing or paper industries. Food science and technology is an RAE subject but is weak in the Thames Gateway as in England as a whole. In the Thames Gateway it only received a 3b grade at NRI. NRI's work has hitherto related mainly to developing countries, but since its incorporation into University of Greenwich, there is an attempt to incorporate the institution as an asset for local development. The institution's capacity is to be disseminated through the 'Medway Regional Technopole', a virtual knowledge centre operated jointly by University of Greenwich, Medway Chamber of Commerce and other partners (Watson and Jones, 1999). The aim was to build up the Medway towns as a centre for biological expertise. At the time of the 1996 RAE, the pharmaceuticals industry in the Thames Gateway was supported by pharmacology research at QMW. However, this industry has been severely hit by the recently-announced closure of the large Glaxo pharmaceuticals plant at Dartford.

The four key industrial sectors vary considerably, therefore, in the support they can expect from the local knowledge capacity. However, a lack of high grades in the local HEIs for sectorally-related research cannot immediately be read off as a problem for economic development in the Thames Gateway. As with research into the process of economic development, R&D for key industries can be sourced outside the region. The variable capacity to carry out research does however put a question mark over the extent to which the Thames Gateway can expect to build an economy upon 'academic services' and 'R&D and technology futures' as key industrial sectors. If sectoral R&D capacity is indeed important to the economic future of the region, three questions should be asked of each sector:

- given the nature of production in the sector, how important will innovation be if the Thames Gateway is to gain and retain competitive advantage?
- with a given need for innovation, how important is a local R&D capacity?
- does the R&D in the sector need to be linked to research in HE?

We are some way from providing good answers to these questions, which would first need a review of existing studies (many from overseas) which show how innovation takes place in different sectors. Some sectors have academic subjects directly linked to them – engineering, pharmaceuticals. Others, like the leisure industries do not have a tradition of linked academic research. These differences are linked to the epistemological hierarchies evident in the RAE, and to overcome them needs an imaginative approach, breaking with the idea of a single scale of 'excellence'. There is no need to break with the idea implicit in the RAE that research should be capable of standing up to international judgement. However, the international community of academic researchers needs to be organically linked to local communities of knowledge and practice. This means involvement of educational institutions that are not primarily involved with research, as well as close links with businesses, especially small firms, local authorities, and community and voluntary organisations. Firms, especially small firms, look for solutions to their problems, and do not necessarily look under headings like 'training' or 'R&D'.

Two examples of research relevant to development in the Thames Gateway, taking place in the local HEIs, show how this kind of research is necessarily interdisciplinary. One is the establishment of the journal of East London studies *Rising East* at UEL. The journal publishes studies across all the social and cultural disciplines, as well as poetry and other items that would not normally be found in an academic journal. The interdisciplinarity arises from a deliberate decision to widen the scope of discussion and make it accessible to non-academics. Recently, and on a smaller scale, University of Greenwich's Regional Regeneration Unit has participated in an OECD study on Cities and Regional Indicators of Learning, using Kent Thames-side as a case study alongside studies of regions in other European countries. This project cut across subject areas, drawing on economic, sociological and educational arguments.

After the 1996 RAE all departments graded at 2 or above received research funding. It is not yet decided which grades in the 2001 exercise will generate funding for universities. The cut-off level may be set higher, at 3b, 3a or even at 4. Any level of cut-off is bound to have an impact on research within the Thames Gateway. Had there been a slightly higher cut-off after the 1996 RAE, at grade 3b, the effect would have been devastating to local research funding. Given that HEIs adjust their research profile to the likely successes in the RAE rounds, six areas of research closely related to the economic development process might well have been wiped out completely, and the embryonic research related to the construction industry virtually eliminated.

The various rounds of RAE, in 1992, 1996 and 2001, have placed the same assessment framework upon all research in HE. This is despite the epistemological differences usually recognised under categories like 'pure research', 'applied research' and Gibbons et al.'s 'Mode 1 and Mode 2' (Gibbons et al., 1994). The result has been that applied subject areas are undervalued in comparison with pure research, and that the divide between research and teaching universities becomes entrenched. However, there is an even more important factor in the exclusion of some types of knowledge. In relation to the local learning infrastructure in the Thames Gateway, FECs are as important as HEIs. James and Clark (1997) make a persuasive case for FE as a strategic partner within economic development. However, FECs cannot join in RAE, nor are they eligible for funding from the research councils, at least not as principal applicants. It has been established that there are various different kinds of research in FE, e.g. market research, research on teaching and learning, commissioned research. In the colleges with substantial amounts of HE work, degrees as well as HNCs and HNDs, there is more research taking place, but none of the FECs in the Thames Gateway have a great deal of HE work. The hierarchy then has three levels: research universities, teaching universities and FECs.

A revised RAE could offer funding for different categories of research, cutting across the type of institution applying for funds, and with different criteria for 'excellence' in each category. These categories might include:

- academic research proper, with peer review;
- capacity to support the local economy, including supporting innovation in SMEs, technology centres and the capacity to undertake projects for development agencies;
- scholarship that supports the quality of teaching, including lecturer updating by reading, placements and other engagement with industrial communities, development of learning materials;
- institutional development, e.g. projects on widening participation.

Conclusion: a Compact for Regeneration

The arguments in favour of a compact between HE and its communities take on a new persuasiveness in an area like the Thames Gateway facing challenges of regeneration. HE takes taxpayers' money (and even people who are called 'non-taxpayers' pay taxes, especially VAT). Yet HE is still selective – the opportunities it offers are not open to all taxpayers. In the Thames Gateway with new housing about to be built the risk is that HE will dedicate itself to the incomers who are already highly skilled and that the current residents will be relegated to lower-level provision in FECs, adult education institutes and private training providers.

A compact is therefore needed to ensure accountability. So far, the need for greater accountability has been approached mainly through performance indicators (PIs). The debate surrounding PIs is currently polarised. One camp argues that they should not exist at all, the other defends their publication. Although PIs are supposed to allow accountability of public money to the general citizenry, the debate about what PIs should include is usually restricted to professionals with knowledge of the field. There are a great number of anomalies in respect of PIs for post-compulsory education and training. Neither RAE nor TQA results count as official performance indicators for HEIs. The HE PIs published by the higher education funding councils in 1999 were surrounded with health warnings and have not yet been used for calculating funding. There are a completely different set of indicators for FECs, yet another set for TECs, while schools results are published in league tables of raw pass rates. Yet how else can the quality of teaching and research to be made known and compared? Both the public and the education and training providers are entitled to better performance indicators than currently exist. PIs have been developed in the context of funding and audit – the assessment of value for money. But in reality it is hard to compare the value for money offered by institutions with different missions. Funding is clearly an important part of social accountability, but it is not the whole story. The concept of a 'compact' for HE takes social accountability to citizens far beyond the limitations of the auditing of performance by targets. The issue is one of information flow need to go beyond PIs and see what information about HEIs needs to go to whom.

What can higher education promise an area under regeneration like the eastern Thames? It was pointed out earlier that the Thames Gateway is linear in shape, with the new housing development promising to create a 'linear city'. Higher education too is spread out along the Thames, but it is not spread evenly. Residents close to London can have ready access to the education institutions based there. Further east, physical access to HEIs becomes much more difficult. UEL has a new campus in Docklands, but the Access to HE courses in Thurrock are linked to Anglia University, with campuses in Colchester and Cambridge, inaccessible by public transport and a long drive by road. The Southend to Fenchurch Street railway line along the northern riverbank is notorious for its unreliability. To the south it is little better, and communities like Sheppey, the Isle of Grain, or Thanet have very difficult access to HEIs. Public transport strategy has concentrated on river crossings, which is helpful for integrating the Thames Gateway from north to south but does not address the east-west dimension. More study is needed of patterns of travel to work and to study, and of the means to improve transport access to educational opportunities.

The development strategies of the largest Thames Gateway HEIs have recently been based on the acquisition of property. At its independence from local authority control, Greenwich found itself on no less than 22 sites. It has now consolidated itself on five main campuses, with the construction of a new student village using the private finance initiative at the Avery Hill Campus. With the NRI, it acquired a campus at Chatham Maritime, into which it moved its schools of engineering and environmental and earth sciences. This was followed by the major investment of the move into the historic buildings of the Royal Naval College in the World Heritage Site of Greenwich. UEL has also made a major investment in physical infrastructure, with a brand new campus at Gallions Reach in the Royal Docks.

Cohen (2000) has written critically of the decision to establish the new campus at the Royal Docks. He questions whether a university with a high proportion of non-white students should locate a campus in an all-white area. It could lead to problems of safety for the students and provide no involvement for the local residents except as low-paid support workers in the university. His case is somewhat overstated. Beckton's new estates, with a high proportion of housing association accommodation and many single parents, are by no means uniformly white, although they still contrast with a student body including many from South Asian backgrounds. Moreover, the new campus is not really 'in Beckton' – it is next to Beckton but separated from it by main roads. At the same time it is not an out-of-town campus either. The success of the campus within the new communities of the Royal Docks depends on what developments follow in the years to come. A significant aspect of Cohen's work is that it shows that researchers in Thames Gateway HEIs can lend a critical approach to local regeneration. This criticality is more valuable in the long term than research that merely supplies 'baseline' data to development agencies.

David Finegold (1999) explores a kind of economic development he understands as the formation of 'high skill ecosystems'. In terms reminiscent of Porter (1990), he stresses the role in economic development of the 'research university'. These arguments are essentially a plea by the high status private universities in the United States to be recognised as contributing to economic development above the publicly-funded universities. They cannot be immediately transferred to non-US contexts; Porter's assertions about the superiority of private above public universities made no sense in the context of his German and Italian case studies, where there is no such divide between private and public higher education. In the Thames Gateway, HE is already polarised between research universities and teaching universities. If this polarisation is allowed to continue it will endanger the contribution made by either sector to Thames Gateway regeneration. Research of the highest calibre needs to continue and to be made available to local communities and their institutions, but it does not need to be concentrated in the institutions that have the weakest local links.

'Widening participation' is the current watchword, but participation does not necessarily lead to achievement. This is particularly true in urban areas where retention and achievement levels are lower. We need to move from 'widening participation' to 'widening progression'. Progression here should be understood in a broad sense. It starts with learners achieving in the education system what they set out to achieve (being enabled to pass exams but also enjoying their learning and benefiting from its social opportunities) and progressing through the education system without encountering unnecessary barriers. Progression also means the ability to move on in life into satisfying work, or non-work activities.

The binary divide in HE remains, but to it is now added a further divide: that between HE and FE. FE is shaking off its image as the 'Cinderella sector' and is seen as capable of allowing access to learning for a widening client group. It is welcomed as a key ally of government in the anti-exclusion struggle. However, the relationship between FE and HE is yet one of equal partnership, but one in which HEIs see FECs are providers of students. This is true even in the Thames Gateway. As young people seek to continue their full-time education for increasing lengths of time, even an institution like Newham Sixth Form College, which is among the English sixth form colleges that have done most to widen their offer and attract a new clientele, is inevitably drawn mainly into becoming a provider of HE candidates.

A new system would be planned as a single post-compulsory system. This would build upon the merger of TECs and FEFC in the Learning and Skills Council. Education and training need a new kind of planning: neither the 'manpower planning' popular in the 1960s nor the non-planning of market forces. Certainly supply and demand are related and there is no point in trying to plan people into things they do not want to do. But purposeful strategic planning is different. It is best based on an information structure that allows one to see what is happening in the labour market and where interventions are best made. Higher education can thrive in such an atmosphere, so long as it does not pretend to provide the entire local learning infrastructure. In its compact with the Thames Gateway communities it must agree to play its part within a whole system orientated towards learning.

References

Church, A. (1990), *Employment in Docklands*, London: Docklands Forum and Birkbeck College.

Cohen, P. (2000), 'The Road to Beckton Pier', in Butler, T. (ed.), *Eastern Promise: Education and Social Renewal in London's Docklands*, London: Lawrence and Wishart.

Department for the Environment (1995), *Thames Gateway Planning Framework* (Regional Planning Guidance 9a).

Finegold, D. (1999), 'Creating Self-sustaining High-skill Ecosystems', *Oxford Review of Economic Policy*, 15 (1), pp. 60–81.

Gibbons, M., Limoges, C., Nowotny, H., Schwartzman, S., Scott, P. and Trow, M. (1994), *The New Production of Knowledge: The dynamics of science and research in contemporary societies*, London: Sage.

James, S. and Clarke, G. (1997), *Investing Partners: Further education, economic development and regional policy*, London: Further Education Development Agency.

National Committee of Inquiry into Higher Education (Dearing Report) (1997), *Higher Education in the Learning Society*, London: HMSO.

Polanyi, M. (1969), *Personal Knowledge: Towards a post-critical philosophy*, London: Routledge.

Porter, M. (1990), *The Competitive Advantage of Nations*, New York: Free Press.

THES (1997), special pages on research assessments, *Times Higher Education Supplement.*

Watson, J. and Jones, L. (1999), 'A Case Study in the Thames Gateway', paper presented to seminar *Further and Higher Education in London Economic Development*, LEPU, South Bank University.

6 Understanding Today and Shaping Tomorrow: The Proper Role of University Research in the Social Sciences, But Under Siege – Towards a Compact for Social Sciences Research

MICHAEL BASSEY

17 November 1999 saw the launching of the Academy of Learned Societies for the Social Sciences:[1] a coming together of 40 learned societies which aims to be an overarching body taking its place alongside the Royal Society, the British Academy, the Academy of the Medical Sciences and the Royal Academy of Engineering.

The Royal Society was launched 339 years earlier: it plays a major role nationally and internationally in the development of the natural sciences and their impact on the world. Why has it taken so much longer for the social sciences in Britain to unite and declare the aim of 'understanding today and shaping tomorrow'? Cynics may say that this is because traditionally the natural scientists have stood on each other's shoulders while the social scientists have stood on each other's faces! Savants respond that the difference is that the natural sciences are able to turn their studies into generalisations or natural laws, while the social sciences can't do this because all of their studies are context bound. Putting it another way, natural scientists are faced with few variables to manipulate, social scientists have a vast number. People are far more complicated than the contents of test-tubes! While the natural sciences can make firm predictions ('Do x in y circumstances and z will happen') the social sciences can only make fuzzy predictions ('Do x in y circumstances and z may happen') or probabilistic ones ('There is a p% chance that ...').

Machiavelli wrote in *The Prince* (c. 1512): 'I believe that it is probably true that fortune is the arbiter of half the things we do, leaving the other half or so to be controlled by ourselves.' Today's social scientists certainly aim to reduce the role of chance. Karl Popper (1945), in *The Open Society and its Enemies*, said: 'We may become the makers of our fate when we have ceased to pose as its prophets.' This is a statement that critical, humane and open enquiry is the proper route of human destiny and not unresearched speculation.

Social science scholars aim for the advancement of knowledge and wisdom about people, individually and en masse. They engage in critical, systematic and creative enquiry within an ethical framework of respect for truth, respect for persons, and respect for democratic values. Social science practitioners use, test and add to that knowledge and wisdom in the same spirit of enquiry and ethics.

The potential agenda of social science is vast, but the current fragmentation of efforts daunts attempts to tackle in a meaningful way the big issues. How do we learn to live together on a small planet; avoid destruction by global warming; practise social justice; provide for the needy while controlling the greedy; prevent genocide, torture, murder; and enable all to lead purposeful lives? If the last 300 years have been powered by the natural sciences perhaps the next 300 will respond to the insights of the social sciences. The tasks set for itself by the new Academy can equally be seen as the proper research agenda for social science faculties in the universities.

How should this feature in a compact between universities, academic researchers, students, and the state – in its various manifestations as government or particular communities or public at large? To answer this question it is worth first analysing the public nature of research. In this account, matters pertinent to such a compact are put in italics.

An Analysis of the Public Nature of Social Science Research

Figure 6.1 relates social science research to public action. It is worth examining this figure in detail, for it can point to some of the issues which must feature in any compact involving university social scientists.

Starting from the top of the figure, researchers in universities may bid for projects which are identified in outline by policy-makers who are empowered to fund them; if successful the researchers design and execute the projects.

Who are policy-makers, how are they empowered, how do they judge researchers' ability to succeed? Are the researchers well trained to conduct research; do they get the resources needed to pursue it effectively? In addition *(and hopefully in equal measure)* the researchers may engage in 'blue skies' research, of theoretical interest but with no immediate pay off, and of their own choosing. At present this depends upon Higher Education Funding Council (HEFC) funds which have been allocated on the basis of Research Assessment Exercises (RAEs). *Will such funding continue to be available? How do different stakeholders (researchers, funders of research, users of research, as well as vice-chancellors and other university administrators, and students) view blue skies work? Will policy- and practice-focused research deteriorate if blue skies work is no longer available to stimulate new thinking?*

When research is completed, or is at an interim stage with some results, reports are written and attempts made to publish them. Traditionally these reports were all written in an academic style, with the perceived audience usually being other researchers, and were submitted to academic journals where they were severely scrutinised by anonymous referees and only published if considered unflawed in argument and worthwhile in claims to knowledge. In response to the need of policy-makers and practitioners to comprehend and apply research findings, 'professional' journals began to appear: these did not necessarily use rigorous referee systems. But there is also the need within researchers themselves to get their findings into the public domain; while many are willing to wait for the slow process of refereeing and journal publication, others have recognised that distributing photocopies of a report or putting it on one's own web pages on the Internet is a quick and effective means of communicating results. Such publication is termed by librarians 'the grey literature'. It has been welcomed by policy-makers as being up-to-the-minute and is often reported in the newspapers. There is, of course, a major problem. *What assurances are available that the grey literature reports are not flawed? The answer is none. The rigorous trustworthiness-testing of the academic community is absent. Falsehoods may abound. This is something that needs to be addressed in any compact involving social science research.*

There are now so many journals, specialist and general, that few researchers, let alone policy-makers or practitioners, can keep abreast of their outpourings. They have to resort to abstract journals, which give summaries of research papers. The publishers of journals are beginning to provide electronic access to publications although a current problem is the cost of such provision. *In compact terms, free access by everybody to a searchable database of social science publication whether in book, learned journal or*

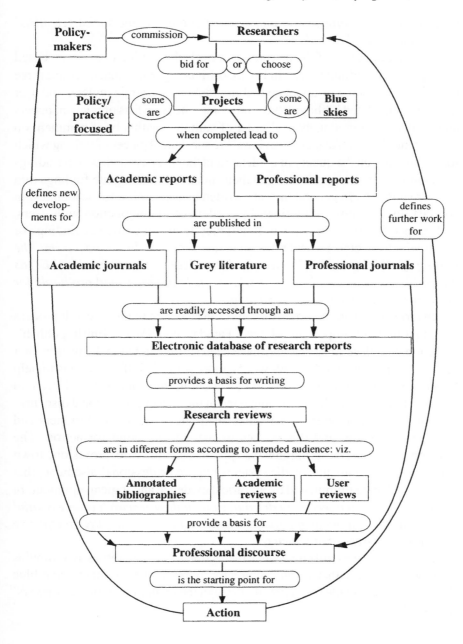

Figure 6.1 From researchers to action: a through-put analysis

*conference proceedings, is an important step towards the social scientists'
aim of 'understanding today'.*

An important part of the research process is the writing of reviews, based
on original articles and books. In Figure 6.1 it is suggested that there are three
main forms of such, viz: annotated bibliographies, academic reviews and user
reviews. 'Annotated bibliographies' are comprehensive lists of relevant papers
and books, often in alphabetical order of author(s) with a brief comment on
the content of each. 'Academic reviews' are substantial pieces of writing which
focus critically on the quality of evidence and the firmness with which findings
are supported by that evidence, and then endeavour to integrate findings into
a coherent theory. In general they are written by academics, for academics. In
contrast, user reviews are written by academics in conjunction with users,
with a specific group of users in mind; they focus on particular findings or
issues which are credible and relevant to that audience. *In compact terms, the
writing of all three kinds of review needs to be seen (for example in RAEs) as
a credible and worthwhile activity which it is both proper and profitable for
academic social scientists to engage in.*

In terms of 'shaping tomorrow', it is the next step in the research process
that is particularly important. Michael Faraday said, 'Work, finish, publish':
in the nineteenth century that may have been sufficient, but in the twenty-first
century, in a world flooded with words, more is needed. If research is to help
'shape tomorrow' it is necessary to talk about it, think about it, and strive to
act on it. In Figure 6.1 this is encompassed in the idea of professional discourse
– the interaction between social scientists, policy-makers, practitioners and
the public at large; and this is seen as the starting point for action. The
development of schools, highways, prisons, health care provision, town
planning, entertainments, media systems require professional discourse, that
is ongoing debate illuminated by empirical evidence and logical argument. *In
compact terms, engagement in discourse about their research is an essential
part of the work of academic social scientists if they are to play an effective
role in the progress of our society.*

Figure 6.1 comes full circle when the 'action' of society serves as a stimulus
for new research, either taken up directly by researchers (if they have blue
skies funding available) or indirectly through the mediation of policy-makers'
sponsorship.

Relationship between Government and Social Science Researchers

It is too facile to talk of 'the attitude of government towards social science research' as though 'government' embraces a seamless fabric of policy-makers and civil servants working with a common set of aims, methods and assumptions. Even to refer to the attitude of an individual government department is simplistic, for anyone who has had research dealings with but one of these is likely to have found that within the department there are factions and groups, some institutional, others based on personal friendships or animosities, such that to the outsider it seems that a variety of agendas are being addressed. And, inevitably, the parliamentary policy-makers often arrive in post fairly ignorant of the key issues surrounding their responsibilities and so are on a steep learning curve. Having reached a plateau of understanding they often seek quick answers to major issues because they know that they will be in office for a relatively short period of time, and political advancement depends upon evidence of decisive action.

Nevertheless government is often an important source of funding for the academic community and so researchers try to keep good working relationships with government departments. But the pursuit of truth (by researchers) and the pursuit of power (by politicians) can lead to clashes and it is not unknown for researchers to consider that government utterances have distorted their research findings or indeed suppressed them and prevented publication. On the other hand politicians can consider that researchers are unhelpful if criticisms of policy developments are forthcoming and there is then the perceived threat of no funding for future projects. The problem, of course, is that in the pursuit of truth, criticism should be perceived as a welcome friend, whereas in the pursuit of power, criticism is perceived as an unwelcome enemy. In part the problem is that the media will always turn a minor criticism into a major setback, and the public is ill-equipped to recognise this.

Thus while our compact needs to ensure that researchers are free to publish their findings, in the name of truth, they should find ways of so doing that respect the task of government to govern.

Relationship between Particular Communities and Academic Social Science Researchers

The community of school teachers has traditionally denied the value of educational research, often claiming that it is written in unintelligible language, or if intelligible tells nothing new. Other communities of professionals (psychologists, town planners, social workers for example) have a similar perception although less markedly than amongst teachers.

Our compact needs to recognise this problem and indeed ideas like the user-reviews, mentioned in the analysis of research above, may slowly change this perception. Again, if the professional communities can contribute to the agenda of researchers, this might help allay suspicion that academics are playing trivial pursuits in their ivory towers!

Under this heading it is worth considering the role of research agencies that lie outside the universities. For many years there have been agencies which sample public opinion and now, increasingly agencies are developing which will conduct any social enquiry for a fee – and are being used by government. There is a concern that while university researchers usually belong to a learned society with a code of research ethics, the new agencies may be less concerned about issues such as the peer validation of research conclusions.

A compact needs to embrace the idea of all social science researchers subscribing to an ethical code based on respect for truth, respect for persons, and respect for democratic values.

Relationship between the Media, the Public and Social Science Researchers

Some researchers shy away from the press, fearing – with some justification – that their work may be trivialised and savaged by reporters looking for a newsworthy story. But those who are committed to the idea of 'understanding today and shaping tomorrow' recognise the importance of trying to communicate to the public at large. Indeed the larger learned societies in the social sciences employ press officers in order to help their members disseminate their findings to the lay public and some provide training on writing press releases and advice on giving media interviews ('Don't wear dark glasses on television – it makes you look like a criminal').

Social research is essential for democracy. Government of the people, for the people, by the people, needs research about the people: research into people's needs, problems and aspirations; research giving knowledge in the forms of theoretical understandings, policy implications and practical applications; research making knowledge available to all to ponder over, criticise, reflect on, argue about and build on. Democracy means that the adult members of society try to share responsibility for managing the affairs of society and deciding how it shall develop. It follows that the members of society need deep insights into how society functions and intelligent ideas on where it might go. In other words democracy needs research.

It follows that social science researchers have a responsibility to research into significant issues and to disseminate their findings not only to their academic peers but, as far as possible, to the general public.

In particular there is a need to create a public climate that recognises and values rational argument, empirical evidence, critical debate and creative insight. When a politician stands on a platform and says, 'When elected, my party will adle and botack', instead of half the public saying 'hurray' and the other half 'rubbish', we need a climate in which everyone asks, 'What is the evidence or argument that adle and botack will work?'

Thus our compact stretches from academia into the world at large and needs to recognise that universities are not only educating their students but have a major role in educating everyone!

Towards a Compact for Social Science Research

From this discussion ideas can be listed that could contribute to a compact between the social science research community and the rest of the world. These are in Figure 6.2. Advance humanity!

Note

1   The arena for this article is the United Kingdom

References

Machiavelli, N. (1979), *The Prince*, Manchester: Manchester University Press.
Popper, K. (1945), *The Open Society and Its Enemies*, London: Routeledge and Kegan Paul.

a) Social science research needs to be recognised as attempts 'to understand today and shape tomorrow'.

b) Ultimately the social science research agenda should help humanity focus on questions like: How do we learn to live together on a small planet; avoid destruction by global warming; practice social justice; provide for the needy while controlling the greedy; prevent genocide, torture, murder; and enable all to lead purposeful lives?

c) All researchers need effective training in research.

d) All researchers need to work within the expectations of a code of research ethics based on respect for truth, respect for persons and respect for democratic values.

e) Those who commission research are entitled to dedication and competence from researchers, and in turn should respect the integrity of findings and the right of the researchers to publish.

f) Academic researchers need adequate funding for both policy/practice research and for 'blue skies' research.

g) All research publication needs some independent guarantee of trustworthiness.

h) A freely searchable electronic database of all social science research publication is needed.

i) Academic researchers need to accept responsibility for trying to communicate their findings not only to each other but also to the public at large.

j) Universities need to work with the media in accepting the challenge to educate the world to value rational argument, empirical evidence, critical debate and creative insight.

Figure 6.2   Towards a compact for social science research

7   The Virtual University

IAN JOHNSTON

Relevance to the Compact

Communications and information technology (CIT) and the development of web based virtual universities have the potential to revolutionise both the delivery and the pedagogy of higher education. In doing so they also have the potential to fundamentally alter the nature of the compact between Universities and various stakeholders.

For example, in relation to the student or learner CIT enables the customising of learning to the individual student's specific needs and interests, including prior knowledge, pace, style of learning, as well as time and place and the injection of the student's own content.

In relation to the state it will make it possible to offer a national curriculum in key vocational subjects anywhere in the United Kingdom or indeed world wide; to realise the still elusive potential to hugely reduce the unit cost of education; to access obscure subjects for widely distributed minorities; to provide an instrument to force collaboration between institutions; to become a big export earner; to allow ways of widening participation in education at all levels by attracting learners via entertainment into education, i.e. 'edutainment'; and, finally, slightly similarly to form a vehicle for enticing the whole population to practise the skills to operate effectively in the e-economy.

In relation to employers it should dramatically widen access for their employees to higher education, and by introducing new pedagogies allow higher proportions of their employees to achieve higher level skills.

For unions the benefits for union members are similar to those for employers – e.g. wider access in many senses, leading to higher skills and potentially to more satisfying careers and greater job security, through improved personal and company competitiveness.

For academics, CIT and virtual learning offers the prospect of enriching on-campus delivery and accessing off-campus learners. It should therefore contribute to important aspects of the compact, for example, to both raising and maintaining quality and to widening participation. However, for academics and others who work in conventional universities it presents the challenge of very significant and rapid changes in role from controlling and delivering information towards managing and counselling students, who will access information and learning materials direct. New forms of learning and assessment will be needed, and students can be expected to become more demanding. Experience of CIT-assisted services in other walks of life suggests expectations of 24 hour, 365 days per year service-on-demand, at service levels and quality matched by broadcast quality entertainment, computer games, and e-banking.

The Third Revolution

Outside the cloistered higher education sector there is a wider appreciation that CIT constitutes nothing less than a revolution in the concept of work and society, on a par with the agricultural and industrial revolutions. The full implications are impossible to predict. However it is clear that this new revolution will add 'new capacities to human intelligence and how we work together' (Bangeman, 1994).

It is widely accepted that there is an accelerating and widening diffusion of CIT, combined with other new technologies, producing historically high and rapid change in both production and services. A global 'information economy' is emerging.

As a result there are significant and rapid changes in the skill profiles of jobs and in the organisation of work in this modern economy. But the initial education and qualifications system has been arguably slow to respond. Companies, sectors, regions, countries and economic trading blocks that identify the best approaches to human resource development will be the most prosperous and competitive. Universities which adapt quickly *may* survive. But it is entirely possible that universities as institutions that we currently recognise will disappear.

The pace of change can be illustrated in several ways (Johnston, 1999) by the exponential growth in computer networks over the last decade from near zero to approaching 20 million; by the exponential reduction in processing costs over three decades; by the approaching near universal use of mobile phones with the recent addition of web access; and by the development of e-commerce and e-entertainment, in particular in the UK via digital interactive television.

The lowering of capital cost of networks means it is perfectly possible for developing countries to enter and compete in software development markets. For example, India is now a serious global provider of software.

In European Union and member state policy terms there have been several macro shifts in education *policy* in response to this third revolution, including the concept of transition to a 'learning society':

- encouraging lifelong learning;
- longer schooling/more higher education;
- more emphasis on generic skills for employability;
- efforts to minimise social exclusion; and
- increasing realisation of the potential of new technology itself to assist the learning and assessment process.

The Paradigm Shift

Many observers (Harrison, 1998; Guile and Fonda, 1998) consider that we are only seeing the beginning of the paradigm shift both enabled and in some senses required by the information explosion. The shift arises as a result of the 'liberation' offered by information technology in terms of real time instantaneous access to data and to intelligent systems. These are able – much more rapidly than humans – to offer authoritative interpretation of rules or carry out systematic diagnosis or routine operations on known facts.

As a Royal Society of Arts Study (1995) put it:

> The information society can be defined as one where stocks and flows of information are the dominant feature, determining social structures, economics, ethics etc. Information itself has no inherent determining force. The information society is value-free and purpose-less; it is the purposes to which people decide to put information that determines society ... Using information creatively leads to a creative economy ... across all sectors – the arts and business – if we are to make links between them and have a truly creative economy.
>
> In the creative economy the creation and trade of intangible intellectual goods is important – led by human creativity. Today's scarce resource is not land, labour or money, but human attention: the ability to give it and to attract it.

This emphasis on creativity, lateral thinking, making connections presents a further challenge to traditional pedagogies.

In this paradigm shift, hierarchies and specialised monofunctional departments tend to give way to small autonomous multi-disciplinary teams looking after the total needs of specific groups of internal or external customers. The skills required broaden out from low level repetitive specific skills to holistic management of the process of meeting the customers' needs from product design and specification through to aftercare service. Staff are no longer 'following instructions' set by senior management. They have to act independently, planning, executing and controlling their work. Competitive advantage comes from going beyond this to encouraging creative solutions, and identifying strategic niches as Michael Porter (1991) advocates.

The primary task is to:-

> ensure that core business processes add value by developing more innovative work practices. In the process-based organisation (of the future), employees at all levels carry responsibility for their own performance. Managerial control is replaced by self-discipline within a framework that encourages creativity, organisational learning and development of core capabilities (Harrison, 1998).

This has implications for universities both in terms of how they themselves organise internally and in terms of the skills they need to impart to their students as they enter the labour market.

Most of the skills currently demonstrated in such modern organisations have been developed informally by experience by the organisations and individuals rather than by formal development in higher education. Such organisations have a culture of continuous improvement; emphasise communication; encourage experimentation; focus on outcomes and practical results; and give time to reflect on experience either as an individual or in the team, with or without the assistance of a mentor – in other words in 'learning organisations'.

According to Harrison (1998), and Guile and Fonda (1998), a new learning paradigm 'needs to accompany the changing nature of work. Whereas most companies invest more in management development than in training front-line staff, in the process-based organisation all staff take responsibility for added value and front-line employees share responsibilities for, for example, managing change and innovation – activities previously seen as managerial prerogatives. Their learning is as critical as anyone else's in the process'.

In the learning paradigm, individuals need to develop the behavioural characteristics to be able to take responsibility for their own performance. Guile and Fonda (1998) identify 20 of these behaviours. They include maintaining clarity about the scope and boundaries of your work, and judging your work and that of others by its contribution to business objectives.

Part of any compact between universities and students or employees has to concern the relevance of what is learnt. The above analysis suggests that the development of virtual universities should be accompanied by a new curriculum, new learning objectives, and new learning methods which are developed to match those that the student will experience in a modern CIT-based learning company.

Service sector growth is being accelerated by CIT (OECD, 1996). History suggests that 'when technological progress accelerates so do growth, living standards and employment' (OECD, 1994). The reverse would be true 'only in a world of saturated wants or perpetual restriction of demand – conditions that have not occurred in the past and seem unlikely in the foreseeable future'. In the very long term, concerns about environmental sustainability could alter this equation. But for now it seems likely that new technology equals new products which by 'supply push' create new demand which creates new jobs – the mobile phone being perhaps the most stunning example.

Transition from old to new technologies is a demanding process that can create skill mismatches. Some workers losing their jobs are – or perceive themselves to be – incapable of learning the new skills. Hence the risk of social tensions and divisions.

In education and training terms a compact for higher education leads to: (1) the policy of lifelong learning for all; and (2) the need to develop new vocational subjects much more quickly, e.g. e-commerce.

In organisational terms too, the high performance workplaces for the future will be those which adapt and apply CIT the quickest. In general these will be organisations that emphasise:

- self-managed teams;
- flexible job design;
- multi-disciplinary, multi-skilled teams/individuals;
- continuous improvement/quality circles/business excellence quality;
- approaches;
- being a learning organisation;
- just in time learning/team learning/virtual teams;
- other forms of flexibility including self-employment and portfolio or part-time working.

Implications for Education Policy and Practice

Many of the stakeholders in the compact, particularly the state employers and unions, have been directly experiencing this paradigm shift in their own sector of employment, and for some time policy makers have been attempting to think through the consequences for education policy and strategy (e.g. European Commission, 1997).

This has centred on creating a 'learning society' directly matching the 'information society' in which:

• encouraging lifelong learning;
• longer schooling/more higher education;
• more emphasis on generic skills for employability;
• efforts to minimise social exclusion; and
• increasing realisation of the potential of new technology itself to assist the learning and assessment process

are all key strands of policy. In general this has served to increase state propensity to fund increasing numbers of initial entrants to further and higher education and to encourage mature entrants and continuing professional development all of which have led to a rapid doubling of numbers of students in higher education in Britain.

The impact of CIT and globalisation is also apparent in research. While 'big science' capital requirements have long required international collaboration, CIT has enabled rapid cheap global communication between research groups in most areas of academic activity including humanities and social sciences (e.g. Newby, 1999). This collaboration has been encouraged by the successive European Union 'Framework' programmes and by the early universal linking of universities by e mail via the joint academic network (JANET).

Emergence of Virtual Universities

Before the development of CIT, Britain established a world lead in distance higher education with the Open University which has traditionally used the postal service to distribute printed and audiovisual learning materials, combined with a physical network of tutors and physical attendance at assessment centres and 'summer schools'. This has been very successful and the Open University launched in the 1980s now has over 150,000 students at any one time, including many in Europe and with potential to expand in the USA and indeed any English speaking market.

To date the Open University has not been in any sense virtual. Access to materials is not instant, the learning programmes tend to be linear, i.e. sequential, and physical attendance is required. However, it is now experimenting with on-line delivery and on-line access to tutors, particularly for courses in information technology itself.

In Europe the Catalonian Open University, which started operating in 1995, was the first to use the Internet for a high proportion of course material delivery and some forms of assessment, though the course materials are not extensively developed for the potential of an interactive pedagogy.

In the USA, the University of Phoenix is a private company producing high quality web-based materials supplemented by a nationwide network of local study centres giving access to learning support from 'course assistants'. Possibly much more significant, as Newby has pointed out, is the number of major American research-led universities such as Berkeley, Michigan and Columbia which have linked up with private sector knowledge and entertainment providers such as Time Warner, Disney, Microsoft and Cisco to develop and exploit their expertise in CIT and entertainment for education applications distributed on the Internet. This is potentially an ideal win–win partnership between on the one hand the private sector expertise and access to the capital to fund the very high developments costs of genuinely interactive materials, and on the other hand the intellectual understanding of subjects and pedagogy, quality control, assessment, accreditation, and global status of these US universities. In the long run some observers believe three or four such partnerships might dominate the global English speaking higher education market.

Newby (1999) raised concerns about the long term capacity of the British higher education sector, lacking access to large corporations with comparable resources, and fragmented at institutional level, to compete for this market.

In Britain the Labour Government in 1997 adopted a concept termed 'the University for Industry' or UfI: Learndirect. As the first Chief Executive of the UfI Anne Wright explained in late 1999, UfI will not be a 'provider' of learning in the traditional or conventional sense, but will provide learning opportunities both directly to learners, *on-line*, and through a national network of selected partner providers operating an array of CIT equipment from local learning centres with in situ physical tutorial support. The high quality on-line learning it will pioneer will offer enormous scope for extending learning opportunities to people whose access to learning is presently limited by its largely traditional institutional setting. The UfI will cover all skills levels from basic through intermediate to higher level.

UfI: Learndirect is expected to create access to learning opportunities which are:

- accessible on a 'roll-on-roll-off' basis to suit the needs and requirements of learners themselves;
- in 'bite-sized' chunks of learning;
- based on the most up-to-date on-line learning information, provision and tutorial support;
- supported by integrated self-test formative assessment;
- susceptible to collective study by virtual teams or networks of students; and
- described by an on-line prospectus which incorporates interactive advice and a web site with tasters.

The UfI individualised electronic learning log will provide the state and employer/union partnerships with valuable anonymous data for measuring the extent of learning virtual nationally and the characteristics of learners.

UfI intends to pioneer the development of high quality on-line learning courseware utilising the latest techniques and standards. It is doing this by commissioning new materials from a list of suppliers selected through a rigorous competitive bidding process which includes universities and other education and training providers.

In Britain, therefore, the state is funding a vehicle which in principle should allow universities to collaborate in: (1) the developing courses; (2) providing local learning centres; and (3) in providing virtual 24 hour tutorial services.

In terms of the compact, UfI is already (2000) working closely with employers and unions, often through National (sectoral) Training Organisations and trade associations as well as directly with companies in developing the UfI corporate and individual membership schemes. Employers sit on UfI sectoral advisory panels which advise UfI on the commissioning and development of suitable learning courseware.

In March 2000 the Higher Education Funding Council announced funding for a further experimental project, the e-university. Unlike UfI, which is mainly aimed at the domestic market, the e-university will be specifically designed to market British higher education to the world.

Economies of Scale

There are enormous capital costs in developing truly interactive virtual higher education learning programmes that fully use the Internet's multimedia capacity and maximise, within the programme, intelligent interactivity replacing tutorial support, while allowing the learner to build on their personal knowledge and experience and input their own content.

In very broad terms an investment of around £1 million (US$1.6 million) would be required for a relatively straightforward humanities degree. But all the market research by UfI: Learndirect suggests that the learning materials can represent only about 15 per cent of the cost per learner and that the learning materials will have a usable shelf life of about three years, with the remaining delivery costs being variable. This translates to needing about 1,500 learners per year at current British levels of state subsidy or 3,000 in the private market to break even, (assuming that tutorial support can be spread over several programmes and an income of £1,500 per public programme per annum per student with six year completion and half that income from private students). Since universities deliver over 500 programmes it would require an indicative 1.5 million new private students in Britain (or in round terms a doubling of the existing higher education student population) to break even if the portfolio of programmes was to be comprehensive

Calculations of this sort, *however approximate*, indicate clearly that success as an interactive high quality virtual university will only come for providers who can reach out to a mass market, *probably global* given language restrictions, though US providers probably alone have a sufficiently large domestic market.

Since the state is most unlikely to subsidise a growth in learners on this scale, inevitably the virtual learners will tend to be full cost private individuals or employers on behalf of their employees. This is one driver in the growth of corporate universities. It also explains why the partially virtual universities that have emerged so far have concentrated on that part of the market where private students are most active, i.e. professional qualifications, MBAs, and continuing professional development together with newly emerging skills of use to professionals such as information technology and the legal and commercial implications of e commerce.

All of these cost implications of virtual universities put aspects of the grand compact under strain. Since the state probably cannot deliver, leaving provision increasingly to private global providers for the benefit of privately funded students, the state will be failing to deliver universal wider participation, with all the subsequent problems of social inclusion that that will bring. From the provider's perspective the high costs of development will produce incentives to minimise these costs by:

- cutting quality and interactivity;
- restricting choice *within* programmes;
- restricting the choice *of* programmes to those most in demand in the private market.

This means providers will be failing on both the quality and choice aspects of the compact.

The Costs of Networked Learning

While for many people the concept of virtual universities is thought of in the context of virtual access from afar, at least as important an aspect is provision of networked learning to on-campus students even though possibly in different locations.

Bacsich et al. (1999) define networked learning as 'using a networked computer for the purposes of learning, blurring the boundaries between on-campus, distance and flexible learning'

In an extensive literature review Bacsich et al. (1999) highlight significant costs:

a) to institutions e.g.:
- installing and equipping institutional infrastructure, computer laboratories possibly equivalent to five years of a lecturer's salary (Arizona Learning Systems, 1998);
- technician support;
- computer rooms (estates);
- computer software licences and Internet access charges;
- learning material development (though much lower than for interactive materials);

b) to academic staff e.g.:

- overtime on materials development;
- increased tutorial assistance possible up to four hours per student per

week more than with conventional methods (Arizona Learning Systems);
- on-line tutorial support;
- self purchase of home computers to students, e.g. charges for accessing university computing facilities;
- costs of purchasing their own pc or laptop;
- costs of maintaining and insuring these.

All of these threaten aspects of the compact. If access to quality modern learning materials forms part of the compact, extending students' previous use of CIT at work or at school, then these costs certainly erect a barrier to wider use of CIT and networked learning, and make it less likely that the 5:1 ratio implied by the Dearing Report (1997) of students per pc will be achieved quickly.

Of course the benefits of networked learning are also significant especially for students in avoiding travel, and freeing up time to do other things, including earning. From the perspective of an employer whose employees embark on a learning programme, the advantages of networked or virtual learning are enormous in permitting much learning to be done out of working hours at no wage cost to the employer, and with no disruption to production or services arising from absence while learning.

Implications of a Compact for Higher Education

The implications for universities of both the development of global virtual universities and the wider use of networked learning are extensive and can be categorised as:

- profound, altering the meaning, mission and place of universities in society;
- instrumental, altering learning outcomes;
- altering delivery;
- altering organisation and skills.

Profound

Universities began as developers and keepers of knowledge that they disseminated to an elite. The CIT revolution (combined with the emergence of multinational company investment in R&D) means that universities are minor players in the creation of knowledge which is held in cyberspace and available to all. If access to cyberspace is uncontrolled, academic freedom is arguably automatic.

No student anywhere can get to the leading edge of anything but an increasingly narrow specialism at initial taught degree level. This has profound implications way beyond the scope of this chapter, encouraging the fragmentation of subject; the development of multi-disciplinary studies; the introduction of taught Masters and Doctorates to reach the leading edge of knowledge; the reduction in the need for institutional autonomy; and indeed questioning the need for institutions at all. There is an extensive literature that has been conveniently reviewed (Association of Commonwealth Universities (ACU), 1998).

Instrumental

If knowledge and even commercial and industrial processes are changing so fast that it is impossible for education providers to keep up, the unavoidable conclusion is that there will be a shift to just-in-time virtual training and education which inevitably will be mainly for employees already working in the processes concerned, and mainly on-the-job.

For learning outcomes, instead of leading edge knowledge and techniques, initial higher education should increasingly focus on equipping students with the flexible generic skills that will enable them to react quickly to change, leaving specific process and vocational skills largely to their future employers to develop. This is partly behind the government's proposals in England for two year degrees.

The Dearing Report's (1997) emphasis on breadth versus depth and on key skills (communication; numeracy; IT; and learning how to learn) took the thinking further.

However this approach could be taken a lot further still. The full range of skill outcomes to be developed and accredited might include:

- team working, project/process approaches;
- interpretation of data;
- continuous improvement;
- quality awareness;
- self management;
- team leadership.

'Creativity' could be encouraged by undertaking projects focused on processes, working in teams, and being provocatively inspired to engage in lateral thinking to identify new ways or routes to achieving the same outcomes. Or better still outcomes that better meet the customer needs. Creativity is then seen as a skill that can be developed, not just an intuitive or inherited talent.

Such an approach is likely to put the compact under further strain. It will be welcomed by the state unions and employers. It may not be understood by students or parents. It may be resisted by academics who see the importance of 'their' subject eroded, 'deep learning' lost, and shorter learning programmes predominating.

Delivery

Tomorrow's learner will not sit at a desk in a classroom, but will be able to interact anywhere with the world wide wireless web. This may lead to the development of education space envelopes specifically designed for group social interaction, and for only those bits of laboratory work which cannot be simulated.

In the short-term a huge contrast will develop between vibrant, colourful, multiple choice, interesting, interactive, fast, funny, virtual learning, and conventional classroom delivery. As an interim step, lecture theatres will be increasingly linked to cyberspace and networked learning will become the campus norm. Apart from making classes more attractive and more relevant, the new technology will enable the lecturer to monitor instantly the progress both of individuals and the whole class, transforming formative assessment and requiring a whole new responsive pedagogy.

The presumed advantages of CIT are well known (EC, 1997) and include:

- individually routed learning paths;
- suiting pace, place, time, past experience;
- encouraging networking across frontiers;
- broadening and enriching the curriculum;
- accessing world class expertise;
- simulation of practical applications;
- automated instantaneous assessment.

Much further work still needs to be done to maximise the interactiveness of learning materials; to allow students and lecturers to introduce their own content; to develop virtual ways of student-student interaction; and to eliminate fraudulent misrepresentations and plagiarism in assessment.

It is unclear for how long most students will continue to prefer to have a human tutor and a collective learning experience, which is perhaps more of a social than a pedagogic necessity. Early market research by the UfI: Learndirect confirmed that when virtual learning opportunities were described to potential learners, they immediately imagined and preferred going to a learning centre supplemented by a friendly human tutor. UfI: Learndirect compromised by planning to provide both virtual online information and internal support *and* learning centres with social facilities such as coffee bars and child care.

Organisation and Skills

Significant changes in the delivery of teaching and learning will inevitably lead to changes in the organisation of higher education and in the skills required. Moreover CIT can and should be applied much more effectively to all academic and administrative processes in higher education.

On-campus multi-disciplinary teams of academics and administrators managing cohorts of students through their learning experiences, with the same team and contact point dealing with everything from enrolment, registration and Assessment of Prior Learning (APL); through learning delivery and resources, credit accumulation, assessment, and graduation and on to alumni contact and selling and guidance on further learning opportunities.

Some academics will focus on curriculum development, on the pedagogies of interactive computer based learning materials, and on automated assessment techniques.

Some academics may have a role more akin to that of facilitator in organising both real and virtual socialisation events. There will be a move along a spectrum away from being the deliverers of knowledge towards managing the individual's learning process.

For administrators it would mean becoming adept at managing the whole process. Expert CIT systems are on hand to give correct information and solutions to complex and highly varying circumstances of individual students.

Many administrators will find great satisfaction in the customer orientation that such CIT-backed arrangements will provide, and of course there will still be a need for policy reviewers to keep university-wide policy embodied in the expert systems up-to-date and effective.

The need to achieve economies of scale will emphasise the desirability for merger and collaboration in the delivery of networked learning. However, relatively few British universities are likely to have the will, ability or opportunity to engage with the private sector to form consortia strong and large enough to become truly global virtual providers. Moreover, the pace of collaboration will have to quicken significantly if as a country or Europe as a whole we are not to be left completely behind by the exponentially changing knowledge revolution.

In practical terms there are four likely scenarios:

* academics swallow their pride and buy in the software from global distributors, thus changing the role of the lecturer fundamentally towards managing and guiding the learning process. As the learning software becomes more and more effective the need for the academic in learner support mode to be a real expert in the subject is removed;
* academics provide the global online tutor support in their subject specialism – not just for their university's students;
* those academics who are real global leaders in their subject or in the pedagogy of virtual learning are hired by the global distributors to become curriculum and learning material developers;
* existing universities compete by both improving the conventional on-campus experience – much better holistic student guidance covering academic and pastoral issues – *and*, by maximising their links with real local employers so that there is a seamless progression for students in at least initial higher education from study into employment, with the probably shortening of initial higher education courses supplemented by continuing virtual part-time study from work.

In these radical scenarios the compact would have to be redrawn. Higher education would be less compartmentalised into early career years, and less specialised. In virtual reality the distinctions between leisure, study, and work will be blurred. Access to all three will be instantly available. Social contact may be replaced by virtual contact, with global not local outreach. The immediate gains for the learner stakeholder are very significant and include access to world class expertise and learning methodologies, and assessment techniques that through automation are very largely free from discrimination on grounds of gender, class, race or religion. Choice in some ways would be bewilderingly large once forced into virtual mode. Choice of conventional learning opportunities may be more restrictive.

If teaching, curriculum development, and learning design are really removed from the duties of the vast majority of academic staff, huge rationalisation of research and subject specialisation might be possible into just a handful of globally distributed centres, or experts might simply occupy cyberspace. The mainstream research academic might tend to gravitate towards private sector research centres.

Conclusion

Where virtuality is more cost effective or more quality effective or more discrimination neutral in assessment, it will inevitably seep into more traditional institutional practices. Both national and international competitive pressures and consumer expectations will force such changes. There will also be supply-push as digital television brings both interactivity and virtual education into the home.

The only safe conclusion is that the future for higher education is changing unpredictably fast. While the public funding arrangements and degree awarding licences in most countries give existing institutions a kind of monopoly, learners as customers will increasingly realise the convenience and advantages of virtual learning. Branding, e.g. the Disney or Microsoft university, will eventually be more desired/respected by employers and students alike. This will produce an unstable situation in which politicians eventually remove the conventional monopoly, probably in the face of both employer and consumer demand.

For staff in higher education the challenge will be to adapt.

In a nice twist, the problem is in itself the solution. Adopting lifelong learning for their own staff offers institutions a way to adaptability. Virtual learning offers flexible delivery. Virtual team working and virtual team learning enhance that flexibility. The special dynamics of 24-hour global team working are only now being properly explored. However they offer many things which universities have traditionally held dear, in particular the possibility of widespread international collaboration and partnership in both research and teaching.

All these changes will put pressures on the compact itself to change. The learner may no longer relate to a particular institution or a particular group of academics, instead constructing their own learning programmes from a globally available selection. So both the stakeholders and the objectives of the compact could be fundamentally altered, perhaps to put less emphasis on institution or accreditation and quality, and more emphasis on enjoyment and the immediate application of knowledge to the task in hand.

References

Arizona Learning Systems (1998), *Preliminary Cost Methodology for Distance Learning*, State Board of Directors for Community Colleges of Arizona.

Association of Commonwealth Universities (1998), 'University Visions', *Bulletin of Current Information,* No. 132, p. 34.

Bacsich, A. and Boniwell, K. (1999), *The Costs of Networked Learning*, Sheffied: Sheffield Hallam University.

Bangeman, M. (1994), *Europe and the Global Information Society*, Brussels: European Commission.

Business Strategies Ltd (1997), *Occupations in the Future*, London: Business Strategies Ltd.

Consulting on the National Endowment for Science Technology and the Arts (1997), *RSA Journal*, CXLV.

European Commission (1997), *Accomplishing Europe through Education and Training.*

Guile, D. and Fonda, N. (1998), *Performance Management Through Capability*, Brussels: IPD.

Harrison, R. (1998), 'Move with the Goal Posts', *People Management*, Vol. 4, No. 2, 22 January, p. 33.

Johnston, I. (1999), Virtual Chalk: The future of work in higher education', *Perspectives*, Vol. 3, No. 1, pp. 28–33.

National Committee of Inquiry into Higher Education (Dearing Report) (1997), *Higher Education in the Learning Society*, London: HMSO.

Newby, H. (1999), 'Higher Education in the Twenty-first Century – Some Possible Futures', *Perspectives*, 3 (4), pp. 106–13.

OECD (1994), *Jobs Study*, Parts 2a and 2c, Paris.

OECD (1996), *Lifelong Learning for All*, Paris.

Porter, M. (1991), *The Competitive Advantage of Nations*, New York: Free Press.

PART III
TOWARDS A COMPACT FOR INCLUSIVITY

8   What Kind Of Place Is This? Cultures of Learning, Student Identities, and the Process of Disqualification in British Higher Education[1]

PHIL COHEN

Rights of Passage?

Every year tens of thousands of people young and old get offered a place at university and tens of thousands more graduate. Freshers' weeks and graduation ceremonies mark the rites of passage of studenthood. But what kind of a place and what kind of a passage is it? In order to answer that question we have as always to 'think global and act local'. Firstly, because students who come from or have their roots in many parts of the world outside Britain attend our universities; in some cases, as at the University of East London (UEL), they comprise a majority of the student body. Secondly, we need to locate the issues of equal opportunity which are emerging within higher education in a wider sense of what is happening not only in this country, but in the rest of Europe and, indeed, across what is sometimes known as the Western world.

The insularities that have traditionally informed university cultures in Britain are no longer (if they ever were) useful. Consequently, the main argument of this chapter is that multicultural societies require multicultural universities. This is the nature of a new compact which present circumstances demand. It is as simple and as complicated as that. Simple because it embodies a clear statement of principle: the university should draw its students and staff from every section of society and ensure that this diversity is actively articulated by its procedures of recruitment and assessment, by its pedagogies and curricula, and in its general intellectual and social life. The question is complicated because there is no consensus, few guidelines, and a lot of quite heated argument, about what might be entailed in turning this new compact into workable policy and practice. All too often we get much rhetoric in the form of university mission statement, but precious little reality.

The issue of a new compact is fraught not just because of the usual institutional inertias and resistances, but because it means putting in question the historical role which the Western university has played since the Renaissance in the development of European culture and thought. It is one thing to recognise the implication of universities in the colonial mission which set out to civilise and conquer the non-European world, quite another to admit that as an inevitable part of the process of decolonisation, the very model of the Western university is being challenged by the counterflow of populations and ideas from South to North and East to West.

Before we consider how the university might best respond to this challenge it might be worth taking a moment to consider what exactly is being challenged. Is there anything in the traditional form of the Western university worth defending or even extending?

In the space and time available to me I can only provide the briefest of sketches, starting, but not ending with Oxbridge. Any guided tour of the ancient universities will reveal an archaeology of Western reason, in its successive transformations, from the medieval community of scholars, and the institutions of Renaissance humanism, through to the eighteenth century Enlightenment, the so-called Age of Reason, followed by the Victorian Age of belief in science, progress and modernity and thence on to the twentieth century megastructures modelled on corporate capitalism. It would be wrong to see this as a simple story of linear progression, one institutional form giving way to another, as knowledge is disseminated to ever-wider sections of society. That is the Whig interpretation of intellectual history and it is only believed in nowadays by Whig intellectuals, most of whom are to be found in the Tory party.

Rather, each of these instances – liberal humanism, enlightenment rationality, techno-modernism and corporatism-provides a paradigm of how the business of teaching and learning in a university might proceed. Each of them is reproduced in a variety of weak and strong combinations in contemporary forms of higher education. We are not talking here so much about the content of education as its underlying form, the hidden curriculum and invisible pedagogies that inform the transmission and validation of knowledge. Different university cultures and different academic disciplines adopt different elements from these various models and shape them into unique regimes of truth. So, for example, certain ritual occasions of university life (like degree ceremonies) might still conform to medieval protocols, marking off a kind of sacred space and time in contrast with the decidedly profane priorities, which govern the institution for the rest of the time. Lecture styles might run the gamut from charismatic displays of erudition designed to evoke the ghost of some eminent Victorian, or Renaissance polymath, to the impersonal transmission of soundbite sized packets of information in so called active learning programmes. Seminars might equally be a cross between scholastic disputation and encounter group! There certainly continue to be great tensions between the traditional ideal of the liberal university as a seat for the pursuit of learning and critical enquiry by and for an intellectual elite and its new function as a mass provider of vocational qualification and training for the post school population.

There are continuities as well as contradictions between these different types of university. The aspect I want to look at is inscribed in the name itself – namely the claim that these institutions dispense universalistic forms of knowledge. The claim can be dated from the rise of medieval scholasticism and the development of Latin as a kind of *lingua franqua* amongst the educated elites in the Christian West. This common culture linking feudal state and Catholic Church was centred in the university and did two things at once – it drew a rigid dividing line between those who had access to higher forms of understanding or reason and the vernacular or common knowledge available to the mass of the people. This distinction concealed its own intellectual foundations in the work of Islamic scholastics such as Averroes and Ibn Khaldun who had accomplished much of exegesis of the classical texts upon which Thomas Aquinas and others drew so heavily and without acknowledgement.

In general, then, the claim to universal knowledge, whether based on classical or Biblical foundations, or both, turned out to be the assertion of a particular kind of cultural hegemony exercised within each nation by its hereditary elite, and was also deployed to construct a superior civilisation of the Christian West over and against the non-Christian East.

It seems to me that this strategy, whereby a line is drawn that marks off Europe's internal and external Others from forms of high culture guaranteed by the university, is repeated in the other decisive moments of its history, but with different disciplines at the cutting edge of the distinction. With Renaissance humanism it was the language and texts of Ancient Greece that provided the privileged sites of knowledge and power. Thus began the long slow construction of an imaginary geography, history, and philology of Classical Antiquity which stressed its uniquely Aryan or European origins and increasingly overlooked its Afro-Asiatic roots. Classics, that unholy alliance of Profane Power exemplified in the Roman Imperium, and Sacred Knowledge – The Ideal Proportions of the Greek Body and Mind – became the centre piece of the Humanities curriculum in the Western university in the nineteenth century. In Britain especially, it became the core curriculum of the Victorian public school system, providing a moral education for those who were to prosecute the civilising mission to the domestic working class and native populations in the colonies overseas.

As the West shifted its economic and cultural axis from the Christian Mediterranean to the capitalist Atlantic, the challenge to classical humanism and the core curriculum of the ancient universities came from disciplines associated with the scientific enlightenment and the technologies of modernity: biology, physics, medicine, psychology and most recently, the social sciences. A dividing line was drawn between these new universalisms of Western reason, and the particularistic, vernacular cultures of the primitive and the poor, which could now be transformed into objects of scientific study and social management.

The anti-industrial, anti-modern spirit which continued to dominate English (but less so Scottish) universities until well after the second world war, meant that this scientific enlightenment culture had a very weak implantation within them. The cultural insularity and conservatism of the English intelligentsia can be traced to the peculiar conjuncture of Classics and Empire in the late Victorian period when so many of the institutions which we still think of as characteristically modern took shape. English Literature, even as it supplanted the Classics as the key humanistic discipline in the inter war period, nevertheless drew on many of its procedures of reading and textual exegesis, not least in its obsession with establishing the Great Tradition.

The Thatcherite revolution in higher education was a characteristically contradictory enterprise. It aimed to preserve so called traditional values at a symbolic level while in practice it ensured their destruction and replacement by much more utilitarian structures of learning. It was not a question of returning to the Classics (unless that meant Adam Smith!), but of promoting Business Studies and Civil Engineering as an alternative to Sociology and Social Engineering as the basis of a new core curriculum.

Even if this shift was intended to make higher education less elitist, more open to students from non traditional backgrounds, in practice the simple redescription of polytechnics as universities, without any redistribution of resources, did little to disturb the two tier structure of higher education. Students from professional and elite backgrounds continued to dominate the intake to the old universities. Young people from working class and ethnic minority backgrounds, if they go to university at all, are concentrated overwhelmingly in the former polytechnic sector.

This two tier system is underwritten by an unequal distribution of social and cultural capital between the two sets of institutions. Every time I travel from the UEL campus at Barking to give a lecture or seminar at an 'old' university I am made all too aware of that! (see Ainley's (1994) comparison of UEL with the University of Kent). And sadly, but predictably, this structural inequality is actively reproduced by student choices, especially as these are influenced by sixth form teachers' recommendations and parental ambitions. For example, unless some special, extra academic factors intervene, the brightest and best young East Enders do not make UEL their university of first choice. Even if they have not yet set their sights on Oxbridge, they would prefer to go to a higher status, red brick, university such as Manchester, or Leeds, or Liverpool.

To understand – and challenge – the continued power of the 'old university' over the popular imagination of higher education we need to look a little more deeply at what is in play.

Ancient and Modern

The ancient or premodern university was essentially a finishing school for a largely hereditary political and social elite; the cultivation of taste and superior sensibility through gentlemanly pursuits – of which learning was only one and the least important amongst many – was what counted. Some of this is still retained in Oxbridge culture, where extracurricular activities continue to lay the social foundations for subsequent careers. The old boys' network has not so much disappeared as been transformed, we might say reinvigorated, by widening its scope, both in terms of recruitment and influence. In the era of globalisation, Alumni associations constitute powerful sources of patronage and preferment which extend throughout civil society and around the world. More locally, the settlement of academic staff and students in and around the campus creates an extended residential community that lays claim to privileged amenity and resource. Linking the global and the local, the foundation myths of the institution and its culture of collegiality support the fiction that this is a hothouse community of scholars engaged in the disinterested pursuit of truth, while at the same time, supposedly equipping graduates to go out and become captains of industry, international civil servants, and the like.

The hidden curriculum of the 'old' university is still underwritten by the notion that the student is being initiated into an inherited body of knowledge, strongly identified in an academic discipline which in turn translates itself into professional credentials and career. The whole enterprise is premised on a model of learning and teaching which privileges the individual pursuit of excellence, over and against any more collective, peer-oriented process. As such it is based on the internalisation and defence of disciplinary boundaries. Curriculum development thus consists in extending the range and scope of a particular discipline, making raids into neighbouring territories of knowledge – colonising other fields, building academic empires, and yet more ivory towers.

The modernisation of this process in the last twenty years has produced a new kind of university in which the model of the independent minded scholar has given way to that of '*homo academicus*' – the academic whose value is measured in terms of volume of specialist research output, the teacher whose success is assessed by numbers of students who stay and pass the course, the administrator whose professionalism is recognised in terms of purely managerialist criteria. The 'modern' university is a place where specialised knowledge is accredited, examined and turned into academic qualification. Extra curricular activities, however important they may seem, and however much they may actually shape the student culture, simply do not count in this version of HE.

This shift from an aristocracy of learning to a meritocratic culture of achievement is supposed to ensure that the criteria which regulate access to and advancement within the good academic life are substantively, and not just formally, universalistic. Academic success is no longer supposed to take account of any particularisms of origin or position. Whether your parents live on a council estate or millionaires row, and whether you study at Barking or Balliol, the education you get is supposed to represent the same degree of opportunity for self-advancement. Graduate qualifications are supposed to enable students to go places, to transcend the specific gravity of local histories and geographies, shed the burden of birth, become citizens of the global economy, travellers at home everywhere in the new space of information flows. That at least is the official version of reality. In practice, the modernisation of the traditional university has served to reproduce the hidden curriculum and invisible pedagogies associated with the transmission of cultural capital within the governing elite, whilst only slightly widening access to non-traditional students.

The question of a new compact then becomes – is it possible for a university to develop a different kind of relationship to its environing communities, whilst still retaining its place at the cutting edge of intellectual innovation and change?

From the 'Third Way' to The 'Polyversity'

The new universities are in a sense caught between two stools. They do not want to be poor relations to the ancient universities with whom they cannot possibly compete in terms of prestige or resources but nor do they want to embrace a form of modernity which condemns them and their students to second-class citizenship.

One of the difficulties in finding a 'third way' is the ambivalent position which the university occupies as a symbol or instance of Western modernity. A modularised curriculum with a strongly vocational emphasis, while it may speak powerfully to the individualistic aspirations of non-traditional students also discriminates against those whose cultures operate on a different basis. Many of UEL's students have come from countries or cultures which have been excluded from or made the object of the kinds of modernist knowledge associated with the global success of Western capitalism. Now, as active subjects, they want to get their hands on this precious cultural capital and the social status which they associate with higher education. At the same time, many of them want to have the grand narratives that secure their own sense of cultural heritage affirmed rather than questioned. They may be especially sensitised to processes within these newer universities which mirror forms of discrimination in the wider society. So, although the new universities may open up a space for the reassertion of marginalised identities, they also undermine the traditional paradigms of knowledge production and transmission on which these identities depend.

One response to this situation has been the emergence of new kinds of student culture, centred around the militant assertion of Afrocentric or Islamist agendas. Although this development is usually seen as a threat to traditional liberal values of academic freedom, it must be understood in part as a reaction against the deconstruction, or degradation of these same values. Many of the attacks on the university culture for being 'Eurocentric' are in fact tilting at windmills, because the imagined object of the critique – the traditional humanistic/scientist curriculum of the Western university – no longer exists. The real, but disavowed object of critique is precisely the absence of an alternative, equally coherent set of intellectual foundations, and the lack of a common culture or purpose that ensues. It is this vacuum or gap that is filled with new orthodoxies of belief, new fundamentalisms, and new forms of student identity politics.

To respond seriously to these new challenges we have to begin to articulate a third way, another type of university which conforms neither to the traditionalist nor modernist models, but which starts precisely from a nuanced critique of their complimentary elitisms. Such a critique would certainly embrace a multicultural approach to higher education, which would conserve what is best in European traditions of scholarship while drawing on what is most relevant in non-European traditions of science, philosophy and the arts as well.

This would result in a pluralistic learning environment, where a wide range of informal cultures of student learning enter into dialogue (and sometimes confrontation) with hybrid cultures of academic teaching and research.

In fact, the epistemic foundations for this shift have already been created by the recent emergence of theoretical languages and methodologies which are transdisciplinary in form and produce new patterns of intellectual convergence, viz. catastrophe theory, chaos theory. At the cutting edge of advanced research, semiologists, mathematicians, historians and geneticists may find they are using very similar grammars, to elicit, represent or analyse their various objects of study.

These new regimes of truth provide provisional homes from home for a wide range of disciplines, from architects, engineers, mathematicians, to historians, writers, artists and social scientists where they can become conversant with the convergent grammars of each other's respective trades. Whether in the study of fractal geometry, or tectonic plate geology, or the use of rhizomes, and butterfly attractors to model processes of social/cultural change, or the emergent arts of the Internet, there is a common enterprise which has, as its prime referent, topics of investigation which give priority to the *linkage* between local and global phenomena, rather than their separate or oppositional frames.

The so-called post-modern turn in the politics of knowledge, which some people have attributed to 'foreign influences from across the channel' has certainly contributed to ending the hermetic insulation of the Anglo-Saxon intellectual world. Whether it has contributed to the final decolonisation of the western mindset is a much more moot point. At any rate the turn is also present in the way the HE curriculum has developed.

But here its downside also becomes apparent. As the traditional fields of disciplinary research have fragmented into ever more diverse specialisms, so the grand narratives that previously gave them some overriding coherence or sense of wider social purpose have given way to much more localised forms of special pleading. The current vogue for inter-disciplinarity attempts to paper over the cracks in the edifice of knowledge, but it does not address the fundamental epistemic crisis of cultural relativism that is so easily exploited by student identity politics.

The problem is also reflected at the level of the curriculum. Modularisation of degree courses dissolves academic disciplines into more flexible and fragmentary units of knowledge which can be mixed and matched in all kinds of permutations to allow for easier consumption. This is supposed to enable the student to produce an individualised portfolio of so-called transferable skills attractive to their prospective employers. The evidence unfortunately is that it does no such thing. Most graduate employers prefer students from 'traditionally modern' universities with a good degree in a non-vocational subject. Advertising agencies can train history graduates to write good marketing copy because they are already adept at parsing texts. Media studies graduates might have all kinds of hands-on experience, but are much less likely to have grasped the generative grammars of textualisation.

So the question remains as to whether giving a post-modern twist to the vocationalist agenda in fact offers a realistic framework of aspiration for the average student. In order to answer this question, we have to take a step back both in time and place and look at what has happened in British schools over the last decade.

Schooling for the Dole?

What schools were experiencing a decade ago universities are experiencing now – namely, the advent of a highly motivated politically self conscious and self confident generation of black and Asian students who see good academic performance as the key not only to personal success, but to the collective advancement of their communities, and who are critical of many aspects of the educational environment which they see as standing in their way.

The identity politics which inform much of this critique tend to be essentialist, and to advocate monologic regimes to truth. I have already suggested that these movements are threatened by the hybridised, transversal forms of knowledge that are emerging at the cutting edge of the human and natural sciences. However we also have to understand the development of student cultures in their sociological context.

Education is about qualifying some students and institutions as academic success stories and disqualifying the rest as failures. Part and parcel of this process is the making and breaking of identities. Teachers approve and reward the performance of certain kinds of student identity and disapprove and punish others. These identities are both highly gendered – in terms of certain educationally normative versions of masculinity and femininity and also highly racialised. In many cases teachers actively construct and impose these identities on young people in schools and they always come out as specific educational identities. So and so is an academic star, so and so is a trouble maker. Academic sheep have to be sorted from non-academic goats. These identities may be internalised, or acted up to by young people, or they may be challenged in the name of an alternative identity set provided by families, communities or the school counter culture. In general, the wider and more divergent the range of identities the educational institution can accommodate, the more open and inclusive its academic opportunity structure. The problem is that schools – and increasingly universities – are under pressure to restrict the range of approved student identities to an ever more narrow and convergent set, and to marginalise or exclude those whose faces do not fit. It is in reaction to this process that student identity politics have been formed. And like all reaction formations, they tend to mirror the very thing they are opposing.

Yet there may be a way of reconfiguring student identity work in a way that does better justice to the social aspirations they embody. This can be done by relating student identity work more closely and clearly to the cultures of learning they bring with them into the university.

Cultures of Learning

It is worth reminding ourselves that learning activities don't take place in isolation, inside an individual's head. They always take place within specific communities of practice. Some of these communities may be formal, institutionalised and face-to-face, viz. a first year undergraduate class; others may be informal, or virtual, as with a group of skateboarders, or an Internet users group. But in every case a similar process takes place. People start as beginners from a peripheral position where they are encouraged to watch what other, more skilful and experienced exponents are doing, and then, if properly supported, they move step by step to emulate their betters, until they reach a point where gaining in confidence and authority they are able to improvise and innovate and hence graduate to a more powerful and central role in the community of practice, where finally a few may become teachers of beginners in their turn. This process is not about role modelling or mentoring as commonly conceived, since this tends to fix people at the first passive imitative stage; it refers to a more subtle and ambivalent kind of learning process, in which rivalry and challenge are integral to the process of identification and mastery. A properly educational process is one which facilitates the transition from simple unreflective mimetic observation to a more complex and conjectural kind of endeavour, one that does not merely repeat the real, but questions it.

Now the point is that if you can't learn to do the appropriate kind of identity work, if you can't imagine yourself as a part of a particular community of practice, or if you are denied access to it, if once you are in you can't tolerate the initial peripheral beginner's position and react by elaborating a culture of defiant outsiderdom, or by dropping out, if you aren't encouraged to move on from that to a position of creative emulation, then you won't learn how to learn and you will never graduate to a position of authoritative innovation.

What stalls so much educational ambition is the absence of coherent and credible strategies of envisagement, of taking the next step. If you can't imagine yourself playing in a rock band or working in a laboratory you are not likely to get your head and hands round a guitar or a Bunsen burner. But equally until you do you cannot fully put yourself in the picture you have created for yourself of your own future.

There are two aspects of this model which are germane to the task of devising better student access routes into higher education as part of the new compact between the university and society. Firstly, if the community of academic practice does not offer an identity which makes sense as an extension of existing informal cultures of learning then it will not be properly taken up. It is a mistake to think that this identity is necessarily or primarily vocational. In the first instance what people learn, or fail to learn is how to be students – and they learn how to be students from other students who have been at it longer and know the ropes. Academics think this is all about study skills. But actually it is about studenting skills. This for many people who do not come from a background where going to college is the norm is the hardest lesson of all to learn.

Secondly – unless there are informal mentors already in place to help newcomers acquire these studenting skills, they are unlikely to master them and this in turn will affect their academic performance. Mentors in this context are people who exemplify appropriate forms of student identity work. And here we come up against a curious paradox. We know what a black or Asian student identity is about, partly because mentoring schemes have been put in place to help these students assert their specific cultural identities, partly because there are strong ethnically based student organisations and partly because they come from communities where identity politics are already highly developed and narratives of aspirations are correspondingly strong. But we do not know what a white working class student identity looks like, indeed it strikes us as a kind of oxymoron – students may be from the working class, but their move into higher education seems to involve them in surrendering that identity; and if they are white their terms of placement are not recognised as an equal opportunity issue, and they are simply subsumed within a cross class category. Or to put it in another slightly more theorised way, the racial body count renders their contradictory class location invisible. The establishment of a mentoring scheme for white working-class students would thus seem to be an essential provision for the new universities .

Thirdly, the trajectory of studenthood will not necessarily follow the continuous upwards line of a 'career'; the learning curve may describe a series of random broken and irregular turning points, but in every case it creates a frame within which a new student identity is formed. We need to find a model of cultural apprenticeship that makes sense to people who customarily regard formal education as being beyond their scope or beyond the reach of the stories they tell themselves about how their lives should unfold.

This approach also challenges many of the criteria for educational success and failure stories. From this vantage point, good teaching is no longer just about 'filling the gaps' in the students' knowledge, through the administration of a set curriculum, or motivating them to achieve through maximising individual competitiveness. A more fundamental task of higher education in a new compact with society is to help students perform the identity work needed to envisage 'taking the next step' in constructing their own aspirational pathways.

To sum up, polyversities occupy a highly contradictory front line position in the contemporary politics of knowledge. Potentially they are at the cutting edge of intellectual change, in so far as the research agendas mandated by their situation challenge existing academic divisions of labour and point towards new transdisciplinary paradigms. At the same time because their vocationalist emphasis leads to the structured neglect of the internal research culture, they are not likely to realise this potential in terms of creating new cultural capital. The most innovative and productive scholars are likely to continue to migrate to the older universities. This same narrow focus also leads polyversities to ignore the informal processes of learning and identity work that shape the extra-curricular aspects of student and staff culture, because their relevance to academic performance is not grasped. So we arrive at the familiar scenario of having the worst of all possible worlds. And yet with a little bit of vision, and a little bit of courage, the story could still have a very different ending in a new compact between higher education and society. (See appendix for an illustration of some strategies towards a new compact for a multicultural university).

Notes

1   This chapter draws on a Keynote Address at Homerton College, Cambridge, in May 1998.

References

Ainley, P. (1994), *Degrees of Difference: Higher education in the 1990s*, London: Lawrence and Wishart.
Amin, S. (1989), 'Eurocentrism', trans. R. Moore, New York: Monthly Review Press.
Anderson, P. (1968), 'Components of the National Culture', *New Left Review*, 50, pp. 3–57.
Arthur, J. (1995), *Campus Wars: Multiculturalism and the Politics of difference*, New York: Westview Press.
Bernal, M. (1987), *Black Athena: The Afroasiatic roots of classical civilisation*, New Brunswick, NJ: Rutgers University Press.
Bloom, L. (1994), *The Western Canon*, London: Macmillan.
Blum, L (1995), *Multiculturalism, Racial Justice and the Community*, New York.
Cohen, P. (1992), *For a Multicultural University,* London, UEL.
Donald, J. and Rattansi, A. (1992), *Race, Culture, Difference*, London: Sage Publications.
Doyle, B. (1989), *English and Englishness*, London: Routledge.
Dunant, S. (1994), *The War of Words*, London: Routledge.
Fuss, D. (1993), *Essentially Speaking*: London: Routledge.
Gates, H.L. (1993), *Loose Canons*, New York: Routledge.
Kerr, C. (1995), *The Uses of the University*, 4th edn, Cambridge, Mass.: Harvard University Press.
Lyotard, J. (1993), *Education and the Post Modern Condition*, Manchester: Manchester University Press.
Taylor, C. (1992), *Multiculturalism and the Politics of Recognition*, Princeton, NJ: Princeton University Press.
Williams, J. (1995), *Classrooms in Conflict*, New York: State University New York Press.

Appendix: The Multicultural University – Towards a New Compact

Reactive Strategies

1)   Piecemeal and Opportunistic

Involves: initiatives taken in particular subject areas to change curriculum content and styles of teaching/evaluation.
Aim: to respond to student interests in especially sensitive subject areas.
Likely outcomes: may buy off student discontent, and develop a partial multiculturalism, but leaves the hidden curriculum and its knowledge/power structure intact.

2)   Ethnicist

Involves: setting up of special provision for minority student groups viz black studies programmes, African or Asian world studies programmes etc.
Aim: to institutionalise the recognition of collective difference.
Likely outcomes: may create limited power base for minority ethnic staff and students, by endorsing essentialist forms of identity politics but does not involve majority in curriculum change and is open to ghettoisation.

Proactive Strategies

1)   Core Curriculum
Involves: setting up a multicultural pathway or foundation course taken by all students in each department.
Aim: to induct student into a common multicultural framework of learning.
Likely outcomes: may focus culture wars around rival claims to relative legimacy but does introduce students to hybridised forms of knowledge.

2)   Permeation Model
Involves: setting up an institutional body to link race equality policies (viz. staff recruitment and training) to curriculum reviews by Subject Area Coordinators and student representative.
Aim: to identify problems and develop new courses across the whole university.
Likely outcomes: risk of focusing staff/student conflicts and frustrations; if done with sensivity may help generate a framework of negotiation around convergent definitions of racial (in)equality.

9 Equality, Inclusion and Higher Education (HE) for Students with Disabilities

VIV PARKER

Introduction

Disability has only recently found a place in the discourse on equal opportunity. It has taken 18 attempts over 13 years to achieve disability discrimination legislation in the UK and the resulting Disability Discrimination Act (DDA, 1995) should help remove many of the barriers that confront disabled people. However many disabled people see it as 'a sham' (Gooding, 1996, p. 1) because of the exclusion from the Act of crucial aspects of services such as education and transport. If the Act can be construed as a major part of a compact between the Government and disabled people it is a compact with too many 'let out' clauses. It is still lawful to discriminate against disabled students in higher education (HE) although the strong lobby against this exemption has achieved some success and the Education Secretary, David Blunkett, is initiating consultation on a bill on disability rights in education with the aim of securing early legislation in the current parliament (Skill, 2000). In terms of a social compact between the state, the higher education institutions (HEIs) and their students, disabled people are in many ways still a very marginal and marginalised group.

Disabled people experience marginalisation and oppression comparable to that experienced by women and ethnic minorities but have further to go in their campaign to have this recognised and redressed. The explanations given for this oppression are typically rooted in the alleged personal deficiencies or impairments of functioning attributed to disabled people. The disabled people's movement has campaigned vigorously against this and one of its major successes has been the deconstruction of the medical model of disability and the:

development and articulation of the social model of disability which, by focusing on disabling environments rather than individual impairments, freed up disabled people's hearts and minds by offering an alternative conceptualisation of the problem (Campbell and Oliver, 1996, p. 20).

Once disability is seen as the social oppression of people with impairments rather than focusing wholly on impairments the imperative for action shifts from changing the individual to changing society. The disabled people's movement has developed this understanding and conceptualisation of disability through political struggle and now has the responsibility for prompting the HE sector into deconstructing and reconstructing disability in the same way.

There are many ways in which society, and higher education as part of that society, must change if disability equality is to become a reality beyond the rhetoric of policies on social inclusion, equal opportunities, widening access and accommodating diversity. The justification for these changes is primarily a matter of social justice and fairness. Disabled people should have the same opportunities to engage in all the activities that constitute social life as their non-impaired peers.

The present government has committed itself to a form of compact focused on tackling social exclusion and, in a report by DEMOS (Christie, 1999, p. 18), has defined this as 'exposure to long-term problems which cut people off from 'mainstream' opportunities for work, learning, a decent quality of life and participation in civic life'. Opening a consultative conference on this report Margaret Hodge, Minister for Disabled People, emphasised that 'social inclusion and equality are central to the agenda of New Labour' (Hodge, 1999). She acknowledged the difficulties of turning rhetoric into reality but emphasised the need for government to put resources into appropriate areas to tackle entrenched prejudices in society and seek other levers to achieve cultural change. She also affirmed the fundamental commitment of New Labour to 'work for those who can and security for those who can't'. The implicit assumption in this is that where access to work is dependent upon study in HE that too will be provided.

What does this sort of compact imply for the state and students with disabilities and how does the HE sector contribute to this process? As a basis for exploring these issues it is necessary to review the current experience of people with disabilities and how limited access to, and participation within HE, significantly limit, directly and indirectly, their participation in other aspects of life. HEIs have to recognise that although one important aspect of the compact involves them in encouraging and enabling the admission of students with disabilities there are many responsibilities consequent to this that they have yet to meet.

Disabled People and Social Inclusion

The experience of disabled people ranges from marginalisation and neglect to a form of 'design apartheid' which Imrie identifies as where:

> building form and design are inscribed with the values of a society which seeks to project and prioritise the dominant values of the 'able-bodied'. From the shattered paving stones along the high street, to the absence of induction loops in a civic building, people with disabilities face the daily hurdles of negotiating their way through hostile environments which the majority of us take for granted (Imrie, 1996, p. viii).

These physical barriers also characterise university campuses. The one most frequently identified at my own university campus for example is the proliferation of very heavy fire doors which means that students have to be accompanied just to get through them. It is ironic that where the predominant ethos of HE emphasises independence and autonomy for most students many with disabilities experience enforced dependence on others through the built environment and the failure of many teaching learning strategies to accommodate their requirements.

In the lobby against including HE in the DDA during 1995 one significant factor was the claimed high cost of making the campus accessible. The brief report on David Blunkett's announcement about legislation for disability access to education emphasises the high cost of making colleges accessible and quotes an estimate of £150 million for colleges and a similar sum for universities (THES, 1999, p. 2). This is, however, an effective strategy for ensuring that any legislation is limited in scope and extended in timescale for implementation. In fact the costs of physical access may not be high; The Higher Education Statistics Agency (HESA) suggests only 2 per cent of disabled students have a mobility impairment or use wheelchairs (Chard and Couch, 1998, p. 603). A recent survey of 1,500 service providers about disability provision found that cost was not raised as a major issue either by those making, or those failing to make, access improvements (Meager et al., 1998). Research based on 40 case studies of employers found that '44 per cent of adjustments to help disabled employees function effectively at work cost between nil and £49' and only 5 per cent cost over £5,000 (Christie, 1999, p. 43).

Free access to the environment and personal mobility are prime conditions for participation in work, leisure, education and social life. Negative attitudes and ignorance can limit access as much as poor design through inefficient policies and management of the built environment. Well designed toilets, libraries and restaurants can be made inaccessible by badly placed rubbish bins, chairs, tables and the failure to systematically unlock both sections of double doors; parking bays for disabled users may be unusable because they are blocked by service vehicles, rubbish skips and the lack of dropped kerbs (Parker, 1999b).

These physical barriers are significant for many people who experience difficulties because of limitations in stamina or strength and not just for the estimated 5 per cent of disabled people using wheelchairs. Christie suggests at least 12 million disabled people and their carers are affected directly by 'disability-related exclusion (1999, p. 25). He also notes the increasing incidence of disability with age. This suggests that most of us are likely to experience disability directly or through close friends and relatives, as we grow older.

Disabled people frequently experience discrimination and oppression in their social and economic lives (Imrie, 1996, p. 3). They are 'more likely than the non-disabled to be unemployed, long-term unemployed, in low paid and low skilled jobs' (Christie, 1999, p. 31). Higher education correlates positively with employment and offers greater access to a wider range of employment opportunities with better pay and conditions. Disabled people have a right to these opportunities and, through them, will be enabled to participate more fully in leisure, social and civic life. The government has legislated, as promised, through the DDA to remove disability discrimination in employment. One important contribution that HE can make to put a compact into practice is to enable more disabled people to join the professions. This should eventually impact on the design and delivery of the structures and services that currently exclude them. If disabled people are enabled to participate more widely in HE they can contribute to the generation of new knowledge and research to contest 'normative ideologies and values of what constitutes disability (and "ablebodiment")' (Imrie, 1996, p. 9).

Improved access to HE for disabled people will also benefit society, which needs to draw on all its resources and not continue to ignore or limit the talents of those with impairments.

Although estimates of the number of disabled people in the community vary, depending upon how statistics are collected, they indicate that disabled people do not constitute a small minority. A recent report by DEMOS for the National Disability Council quotes estimates from the Department for Education and Employment (DfEE) 'that there are 8.7 million people in the UK of all ages with a current disability' and from the 1998 Disability Follow-up Survey which suggests 'there are 8.6 million disabled adults'. DEMOS emphasises that, whatever definition is used, 'the total disabled population is very large – we are not discussing a small minority group' (Imrie, 1996, p. 17). In the age of lifelong learning there are many potential learners with disability. They are a significant part of the market for HE and this has implications for how HE must market and restructure itself.

HE and Students with Disability

Until quite recently disabled students were largely invisible and little was known of their presence or experience in the sector, 'statistics for disability in higher education are not readily available' (Higher Education Funding Council for England (HEFCE), 1995, p. 17). A review of Further and Higher Education (FE) noted that, although 97 per cent of institutions had a written equal opportunities policy and often referred to access and participation, 'specific references to students with learning difficulties and disabilities are extremely rare ' (Department for Education, March, 1995, p. 7 para. 3.13). More recent figures indicate that 3.4 per cent of students enrolled on higher education courses in Britain report that they have a disability (HESA, 1997, cited in Chard and Couch, 1998, p. 603). 'People with disabilities have been under-represented within HE for some time' (Quality Assurance Agency for Higher Education (QAAHE), 1999, p. 3).

The main source of funding for HEIs is from the Department for Education and Employment (DfEE) through separate Higher Education Funding Councils for England (includes Northern Ireland), Wales and Scotland. These councils allocate annual block grant to each HEI based on overall student numbers and certain historical features of each institution. The strong tradition of academic autonomy in higher education inhibits the funding councils from designating block funding for any specified purpose. Once the block is allocated the institution has autonomy to spend it as it wishes. No money is systematically allocated for disabled students, consequently institutional provision for disabled students across the UK is very variable. Some institutions have a national reputation for excellence for their disability provision, for example the University of Central Lancashire first appointed advisory staff to support students with disabilities in 1987. Such institutions typically 'top slice' their budgets to fund this provision. More usually many HEIs have had little or no provision or policy and were first prompted to designate a person with responsibility for disability and to audit their provision in 1997 by the requirement to produce a disability statement (Parker, 1997, p. 96).

The main means of funding support for students with disabilities in higher education is via the DfEE Disabled Student Allowances (DSA) which are grants paid directly to these students by their Local Education Authorities (LEAs) as part of the student maintenance awards. They have been increased annually and currently stand at £4,055 per course for equipment, £10,250 annually for non-medical personal support and an annual allowance of £1,350. The introduction of the DSAs, in 1990/91, has been quite a pivotal factor in enabling institutions of HE to develop policies and services for students with disabilities and most important in enabling these students to enter higher education and study successfully on a full time basis. The total number of awards made in the first three years they were introduced almost trebled, from 1,497 in 1991/92 to 4,050 in 1993/94 (DfEE, 1995, p. 11).

The DSA are an excellent resource but not sufficient to ensure access to HE and successful study for all disabled students as some students are ineligible for it, e.g. those not in receipt of an LEA maintenance award. If what a student requires cannot be formulated in what an LEA sees as clearly justifiable financial terms it cannot be funded. Students with mental health difficulties often need university-based provision which cannot be funded via the DSA. Spending and managing the DSA and securing and managing the support it funds can also impose a considerable extra burden on disabled students for whom HE study is in itself already very challenging (Parker, 1999a). Many students require support of an institutional kind that the DSA cannot, and the HEI does not, fund; for example assistance in finding, managing and paying for interpreters or scribes; the provision of lecture handouts or the use of a PC in examinations for students; interpreters for deaf applicants. In FE funding is provided by the Further Education Funding Council for England (FEFCE) directly to the institution for support for students with disabilities/learning difficulties and this enables the FE colleges to provide institutional support. However, students in FE do not receive the DSA. This difference in systems between FE and HE in itself can result in difficulties at the point of entry to HE. Every year some students, who have been supported in FE by college staff arrive at the HEI in September expecting to find similar support staff in place and are not then able to find appropriately qualified support through their DSA at such short notice.

The other main means of funding provision for students with disabilities has been a series of special initiatives from the Funding Councils. In the period 1993-1999 the funding council for HE in England and Wales invited institutions to bid for two tranches of £3 million for special initiatives to widen participation for students with special needs and two of £6 million for projects to improve provision for disabled students. A wide variety of projects, 168 altogether, across a large number of institutions and a coordinating/dissemination team were funded (HEFCE, 1999). The first two HEFCE funding rounds were directed to HEIs demonstrating good practice and commitment to disabled students. This did not address the problem of how to develop services in those institutions which seemed less committed so the more recent funding has been offered to institutions lacking base-level provision and for collaborative projects to promote and share good practice. The Scottish Council adopted a different strategy and provided funding for some basic provision across all Scottish HEIs.

Funding for these initiatives was offered to HEIs on the condition that the HEI would subsequently 'embed' and continue the project activity within its own provision. As manager of three funded initiatives I know from my experience and that of colleagues managing projects in other universities (through the regular networking meetings) that this was one of the less successful outcomes of these initiatives. Recurring resource cuts and increasing demands on the HEIs over recent years meant that there was great pressure for them to seek the special funding but there were disincentives to continuing to fund the initiatives. The projects made very apparent the extra costs that an institution must meet if it is to enable disabled students to study effectively and the funding councils are actively reviewing strategies, including the possibility of a weighted funding, for meeting some of these institutional costs. One difficulty with this strategy is the traditional freedom of universities to spend allocated funding as they wish. If funding was allocated to the HEIs on the basis of the number of students with disabilities that they have there is currently no means of ensuring that it is spent on them.

The special initiatives referred to above, have had immense impact in raising awareness across the sector, in promoting policy and practice, disseminating good practice and identifying key issues to address further. One such issue is the need to ensure that, once within the university, disabled students have full access to the whole HE experience. Inclusive education is still 'in its infancy in colleges and universities' (Hayes, 1997, p. 258). Disabled students do not yet have a full and free choice of where, what and how to study. Universities are effectively free to refuse to provide any facilities for students with disabilities and are not required to take any steps to develop services. Many offer no support to students during the pre-entry stage, for example deaf students may have to provide or pay for their own interpreter at interviews and blind students may have to provide their own scribes for an entry test. This limits choice for disabled students even at the pre-entry stage.

When students with disabilities are enabled to study in higher education, their participation may be on a more limited basis than that of other students. One study of students using personal assistants (Parker, 1999a, p. 496) found that none of them used facilities that might be described as 'extra curricular' such as sports, student union, social activities or clubs. The main reason seemed to be difficulties in securing funding of the personal assistants and transport for the extra hours that would be involved.

The effects of this have not been well researched in the UK but studies in the USA indicate that limited access to student life may limit academic attainment and the chances of course completion. Aune (1998, p. 199) describes a 'climate of exclusion from campus life' as one of the main barriers identified by students with disabilities. She cites one study that reported that disabled students experienced social isolation, ostracism and scorn from their instructors and fellow students either because of their disabilities or because of the accommodations they requested as disabled students. Opportunities for students with disabilities to develop leadership skills and engage in international exchanges are also limited at a time when this is becoming increasingly significant. Students with disabilities often miss out on:

> important peer group interaction. Non-disabled students continue to experience little interaction with disabled students and thus perpetuate existing stereotypes on campus and also in the workplace (Aune, 1998, p. 199).

In the longer term this also means that disabled students will continue to be under-represented amongst professionals and policy makers who are recruited via the higher education system, thus perpetuating an excluding system.

Effectively many disabled students are experiencing what could almost be described as a form of social apartheid in HE. This must be explicitly addressed in any compact between the institution and the student as it would be quite unacceptable to admit students and make it an explicit condition that they would not engage in any social or extra curricular activity.

The barriers to study in HE faced by disabled students are many and varied. They may be at institutional level, for example the absence or inadequacy of policies on assessment, admissions or student support; course level, for example a requirement to complete a placement abroad or work experience; or tutor level, for example a failure or refusal to provide handout material or allow tape recording of lectures They may come from outside the institution through professional bodies which impose conditions on their training courses such as teacher training. The study commissioned by the HEFCE and Higher Education Funding Council for Wales (HEFCW) to offer guidance to institutions on 'the base-level provision they should all aim to make for students with disabilities' (Segal Quince Wickstead, 1999, foreword) found disability discrimination in HE in many forms. These included physical access issues, indifference and complacency, and ignorance about the capacities of disabled students. The study indicated that ' there is a great deal to be done to inform attitudes within the sector so that the diversity of students' experiences, perspectives and abilities is respected and valued' (ibid., p. 6).

HE and the Policy Agenda

A leading disability activist and academic, Professor Mike Oliver, points out that Giddens, the leading sociologist of his generation, 'produced one of the most popular introductory sociology texts (1989) and in it, there is not a single mention of disability; close examination of many other introductory texts will yield similar results' (Oliver, 1996, p. 18). Academic engagement with issues of disability has developed since then, largely through the work of disability activists such as Oliver, but there is still considerable truth in the claim that 'academic and policy communities continue to pay scarce attention to disability and the experiences of disabled people' (Imrie, 1996, p. 3). A recent text on negotiating access to HE indexes only one reference to disability and this is a comment about policy initiatives launched to recruit from groups under-represented in HE which emphasises that 'there seems to be a growing assumption in the policy discourse that expansion has taken care of most of these groups with the exception of people with disabilities' (Williams, 1997, p. 12).

Several under-represented groups were mentioned in the terms of reference of the National Committee of Enquiry into Higher Education chaired by Dearing in 1996, but people with disabilities were not. When the report of the committee was published it did include a supplementary report on widening participation about disabled students which indicated that 'higher education does not have a particularly well-focused understanding of disability' (Dearing

Report, 1997, p. 4.17) and that understanding of disability in schools and colleges was well in advance of HE. It emphasised that disability was seen as a problem by hard-pressed academics, resource-strapped administrators and senior managers. The report itself then proceeded to demonstrate some oddities and limitations in its own conception of disability and the actions it recommends (Hurst, 1999, p. 78). However one positive recommendation it made was for a strategic review of sectorial provision to identify longer term proposals possibly using the model of the Further Education Funding Council (FEFC) review which resulted in the report 'Inclusive Learning' (FEFCE, 1996).

Inclusive Learning

Inclusive learning is an important concept in Further Education and arose from the work of the Tomlinson committee which was set up in 1995 to examine post school provision for those with learning difficulties and / or disabilities. One of its main recommendations was that in providing for 'inclusive education' the aim must be to move away from:

> offering courses of education and training and then giving students who have learning difficulties some additional human or physical aids to gain access to these courses

and move towards:

> redesigning the very processes of learning, assessment and organisation so as to fit the objectives and learning styles of the students ... only the second philosophy can claim to be inclusive, to have as its central purpose the opening of opportunity to those whose disability means they learn differently from others (FEFCE, 1996, p. 4).

This process is an attempt to apply the social model of disability to learning and promote access for all students. It proposes that access should be integral to the system rather than a series of special 'add-on' initiatives for special groups like those that have characterised HE to date. How viable is this for the HE sector? One concept, which offers a useful tool for reviewing access to HE, is that of *universal instructional design* (UID), a term introduced by Silver, Bourke and Strehorn (1998), in the USA. It developed from the concept of universal design as used by architects to describe comprehensive plans to meet the requirements of *all* individuals using space. Applied to educational environments it 'places accessibility issues as an integral component of all instructional planning' (Silver et al., 1998, p. 47). It means that tutors will design into their curriculum, course delivery and learning environments many of the modifications that students with disabilities would typically request. This removes the need for students to identify themselves as disabled and ask for special adjustments to be made. It is also likely to benefit all students not just students with disabilities as it is often said that effective teaching for students with disabilities is likely to represent good practice for all students.

The study by Silver et al. (1998) of how teaching staff might define, implement and identify barriers to the implementation of UID in a university setting produced some interesting findings. The strategies listed as definitive of UID for students with disabilities largely amounted to a list of current best practices for promoting active learning with strategies such as cooperative learning, using a team approach and contextual learning. The main barriers noted were the time required to introduce and implement such approaches, staff 'attitudes as barriers' and the fact that most staff are not trained to teach and are not aware of diverse learning needs in HE and, lastly, their sense of academic freedom to choose how to teach. One conclusion of the study was the need for a transformation of the culture of the university to enable the implementation of UID and the fact that its development seems most possible in those sectors of the university with a commitment to 'innovative teaching approaches and self renewal' (Silver et al., 1998, p. 50).

Transformation of the Culture of the University

One major factor which could help bring about this transformation of the HE sector is the extension of the DDA to include HE as the Disability Rights Task Force has recommended (Skill, 1999). If it becomes illegal to discriminate against disabled people by denying them access or failing to provide them with the same service once they are within the university this must provide a new urgency and incentive to the sector to review and improve provision. All HEIs are required to revise and update their disability statements by August 2000 and, in the context of disability discrimination legislation, this should provide an opportunity for a more formal and explicit compact between the student and the university.

In Australia and the USA it is unlawful for tertiary institutions to discriminate against a person on grounds of disability and this requires institutions to be considerably more explicit and comprehensive in the service they provide. In Australia public universities are required to report annually on progress made towards 'increased participation and improved educational outcomes for students with disabilities' (O'Connor et al., 1998, p. 3). Statistical reporting on this progress is a statutory requirement linked to public funding. In the UK there are moves in this direction as discussions continue on the use of the new benchmarks 'to drive funding' (Major, 1999, p. 1H). HEIs do need to be made more accountable to demonstrate that the large amount of public funding they absorb is used for the benefit of the whole community.

However, there is a need to develop performance indicators and accountability systems for the HEIs that more appropriately reflect success in wider access policies. The 1999 publication of league tables in the press were used to praise HEIs for their success in wider access policies while publicly castigating, in several instances, the same HEIs for high student drop out rates (Major, ibid.). The presumption of the calculation of drop-out was that any student not completing within three years of enrolment has dropped out. Students recruited from under-represented groups, and this includes disabled students, frequently cannot complete their studies in the 'normal' three year period for reasons directly related to their under-representation in HE.

Two other initiatives which have potentially wide implications for improving the quality of provision for disabled students across the sector as a whole are the work of the Institute for Learning and Teaching (ILT) and the Quality Assurance Agency (QAA). The QAA is in the process of issuing a Code of Practice, which will inform the procedures for Institutional Audit. The third section was issued in October 1999, and is entitled 'Students with Disabilities' (QAAHE, 1999). HEIs have a year in which to prepare themselves before QAA visits can explore the extent to which institutions are implementing the Code of Practice. This Code identifies a series of precepts and examples of good practice covering the whole range of provision within an institution with the object of assisting institutions to ensure that 'students with disabilities have access to a learning experience comparable to that of their peers' (QAAHE, 1999, foreword).

To date, provision for students with disabilities and learning difficulties has been subject to QAAHE audit but usually in only one of the six audit categories, that for student support and guidance. This conceptualisation of provision for disabled students as a matter of support and guidance has reflected the limited focus of many institutions and the new code should encourage significant improvement and ensure greater accountability as HEIs will be required to review and develop provision for disabled students across the whole HE experience. A compact between students and institutions must involve reconstruction of the issues. An inclusive university is one which focuses on providing a whole-institutional service to enable the learning of all its students and not one that identifies the students with problems and offers special learning support.

In a university one of the main meanings of access must be 'access to the curriculum' (Borland and James, 1998, p. 85). Recognition is growing, amongst those providing disability services, of the need to review teaching strategies and learning environments if students with disabilities are to gain equality of access to the HE curriculum. A Scottish Council for Research in Education report on disabled students in HE (Hall and Tinklin, 1998, p. 89), identified the importance for HEIs of raising awareness of barriers created by inappropriate methods, promoting staff development in disability issues and promoting good practice in teaching all students. The ILT has been recently set up as a membership organisation for all those engaged in teaching and learning support in HE. It aims to enhance the status of teaching, improve the experience of learning and support innovation in HE. If it is successful in its aims, this should significantly improve curricular access for all students.

Avoiding New Barriers

As universities seek to restructure themselves it is important to ensure that innovations in teaching and learning and responses to current and anticipated changes in the learning environment enable the learning of students with disabilities and do not present new barriers.

The serious problems of access for visually disabled users posed by graphical user interfaces (Petrie and Gill, 1993, p. 153) have been recognised for some time by those working with visually impaired students and need to be widely recognised as Communication and Information Technology (CIT) becomes increasingly important in HE learning environments. DISinHE, a project offering advice on disability and computer and information technology, emphasises how easy it is for websites to present barriers to disabled students. In spring 1998, over 70 websites aimed at disabled people were analysed and rated against recognised standards of good programming practice. The study found that only 12 scored highly on general accessibility, 44 were found to have considerable accessibility problems and 12 were totally inaccessible (Clarke, 1998, p. 8). These were websites targeted at people with disabilities, so it seems probable that other websites will be less satisfactory in terms of access (see Cast Bobby).

Networked or resource-based computers for group and independent study are a very useful teaching and learning aid but they can be disabling in how they are used, the software, the hardware, or the environments in which they are located. The desks, chairs and input devices may be difficult for students with mobility and manual dexterity impairments; the screen may be unsuitable, queuing systems may make short periods of use, with regular breaks for students who need them because of pain or discomfort, impossible. All these difficulties can be rectified providing tutors are aware of them and offer appropriate support or alternative access routes.

The new information and communication technologies may enable greater access and empowerment in many ways but also carry the risk of 'over-emphasising IT and under-emphasising real social contact in promoting inclusion, leaving disabled people in an "electronic ghetto"' (Christie, 1999, p. 20). For many years disabled students have had access to HE via the Open University which has been a major provider for large numbers of disabled students; it provides funding and equipment for disabled students from its own resources as those choosing to study with it do not receive LEA/DSA support. It has long provided materials in alternative formats, it enables great flexibility in the place and timing of study, provides good staff development for its staff and has an excellent track record in supportive policies and practices. As HEIs move towards distance, dispersed and networked learning, it is important to recognise the importance of social contact, group- and campus-based learning as a significant part of the attraction of campus universities for many disabled students.

New Directions

How, then, do all the above contribute to a compact for Higher Education? It is useful to focus on the recommendations of the SQW base-level study which found that disability was still a barrier to higher education and 'that there is still discrimination to be tackled' (SQW, 1999, p. 7). It identified the following 12 constituents of base-level provision that all universities should aim to make for students with disabilities (ibid., p. 1):

A Comprehensive Disability Statement

- An admission policy, and procedures, that specifically address the needs of disabled students.

- Well-publicised arrangements for the assessment of individual needs, with target times for completion.
- Provision of services to meet assessed needs.
- Clear internal communication and referral policies.
- Monitoring of the provision of support services that have been agreed.
- Access to networks of suitable trained support workers.
- An institution-wide policy and procedure to cover exams and assessments.
- Staff development programmes on information about students with disabilities and the support available.
- Dedicated staff including a permanently employed disability coordinator and administrative support appropriate to number of disabled students.
- An estates strategy to cover physical access.
- Monitoring procedures for procedures, policies and their impact.

Although these are described as constituting the *minimum* level of support that each HEI should provide, but not best practice, they are not widely in evidence across the sector. The report emphasised that implementation of these recommendations will require institutional funding and commitment from the funding councils and the HEIs. These recommendations provide the minimum core ingredients for a compact between the state, the institution, and the students if the barriers to HE that have excluded disabled people to date are to be removed. The justification for this claim is nowhere better expressed than in the words of the SQW study (ibid., p. 8) which emphasised that:

> In a civilised and liberal society, affirmative action to enable disabled people to benefit from, and contribute to, HE should need little justification. There is a strong economic argument, since people will be better equipped to make a productive contribution to society. There is an equal opportunities argument, since no individual or group should suffer disadvantage or discrimination on the basis of disability. There is an academic argument, since enabling people with disability to access higher education more easily will result in a bigger pool of students and talent. We are also committed to a more cohesive society which values diversity, and which encourages individuals to play a full and active part within it.

In the context of lifelong leaning and the learning society universities are finding that they must compete with other providers in the learning market in higher education. 'Participation in UK higher education is becoming ... part of the welfare bargain that individuals expect to reach with the state'

(Robertson, 1997, p. 75). Disabled people rightly expect to share in this bargain. According to Robertson the challenge for universities will be to 'define the characteristics of a 'new' bargain which would be acceptable to themselves as well as the other parties to the contract' (ibid.). He emphasises the heavy cost to the whole community of universities and that to survive they must be seen to meet the needs of all their stakeholders by offering flexibility and choice and delivery of a 'customised' rather than 'mass' product. If universities are able to change in these ways it should greatly enhance the opportunities for participation by disabled students.

What are the components of a compact between the state, the HE sector and disabled people? The government's declared aim of social inclusion entails a commitment to ensure that disabled people have a full share in the benefits and responsibilities that society offers; this must include access to education at all levels. However, for some years this commitment has remained largely a matter of policy rather than practice. The financial autonomy of HEIs coupled with the established tradition of academic freedom has, with few notable exceptions, rarely been used to promote disability access and more typically has contributed to the barriers that have limited the participation of disabled people in HE. In the early 1990s government and HE sector awareness of these barriers, and strategies necessary to remove or reduce them, were very limited. However, between 1993–99 several rounds of special project funding were offered across the sector to promote access to HE for disabled people. The outcomes were well documented and publicised such that now neither the HE sector nor the government can claim to be unaware of the strategies required to promote access for disabled people. A compact requires that action is taken to enable or require the sector to become fully inclusive. There are currently several initiatives that should significantly move the sector and individual institutions in this direction. The first, and arguably the most important, is legislation.

The Disability Rights Task Force was set up in 1997 to advise the government on the action necessary to promote comprehensive and enforceable civil rights for disabled people. The report of the Task Force, published in December 1999, proposes that future civil rights legislation should include a separate section on further and higher education with rights that are, ultimately, enforceable through the courts (CVCP, 2000). The legislation will also strengthen the current law covering employment and transport and give disabled people who do acquire skills and qualifications through HE more comprehensive access to the labour market and higher earning potential. This will benefit them and wider society.

This legislative framework should provide the incentive to institutions to review their policy and practice and identify clearly what access they can currently offer to disabled students and an action plan to develop and improve this. The HEFCE funded institutions are required to review and republish their disability statements by summer 2000. Previously the statements merely indicated what was and was not provided, and institutions could legally indicate that they provided no access to disabled students. The new legislation should make this unacceptable and the disability statement will be, in itself, a written compact between the institution and its students, identifying the rights and responsibilities of all parties. Applicants and students will have a responsibility to make their disabilities and study requirements known to the institution as early as possible to enable them to help provide for these needs.

To make full participation a reality each institution will need to review its current practice, promote staff awareness of the requirements of students with disabilities and provide the means to enable staff to meet these needs. This will be encouraged and prompted by the recently issued QAA Code of Practice on Disability. The strength of this code is that it places responsibility for meeting the needs of disabled students firmly on the agenda of the whole institution rather than allowing it to rest with a few specialist staff running the disability services. The institution will need to identify a resource to meet the needs identified and this is difficult in the current climate of competing demand and limited resources. However HEFCE has announced that from autumn 2000 it will provide premium weighted funding towards the institutional costs of provision for disabled students through the formula funding system (Skill, 2000). The institution's responsibility will be to ensure that this funding is spent on disability provision but there is currently no system or precedent for HEFCE to require this. This is one area in which financial autonomy and academic freedom may conflict with a commitment to promote the inclusive university. In such circumstances the compact between the government and the community should override this autonomy and ultimately the civil rights legislation should make this unnecessary.

References

Aune, B. (1998), 'Higher Education and Disability in the United States of America: The context, a comprehensive model, and current issues', in Hurst, A. (ed.), *Higher Education and Disabilities: International Approaches*, Aldershot: Ashgate.

Borland, J. and James, S. (1999), 'The Learning Experiences of Students with Disabilities in Higher Education. A case study of a UK university', *Disability and Society*, Vol. 14, No. 1, p. 89.

Campbell, J. and Oliver, M. (1996), *Disability Politics: Understanding our past, changing our future*, London: Routledge.

Cast Bobby can be found at: http://www.cast.org/bobby and will provide an accessibility check on any website.

Chard, G. and Couch, R. (1998), 'Access to Higher Education for the Disabled Student: A building survey at the University of Liverpool', *Disability and Society*, Vol. 13 (2), pp. 603–23.

Christie, I. (1999), *An Inclusive Future? Disability, social change and opportunities for greater inclusion by 2010*, London: Demos.

Clarke, A. (1998), 'Research Highlights Major Accessibility Problems', *Ability*, 24, Spring.

CVCP (2000), Information for Members, 1/00/19, Disability Issues.

Department for Education (1995), *Further and Higher Education Review Programme; Disability Discrimination Bill*, London.

Department for Education (1993), *Disabled Students' Allowances*, ACL 10/93, 23 September, para. 2, p. 1.

Department for Education and Employment (1995), *Mandatory Awards and the Administration of Disabled Student Allowances, Final Report, Further and Higher Education Review Programme, Disability Discrimination Act 1995*, London.

Disability Now (, 2000), 'Schools to Come Under the DDA'.

DISinHE, *Teaching Everyone. Disability and New Technology a Guide for lecturers*, University of Dundee, SEARCH-ED Project: http://www.disinhe.ac.uk.

Gooding, C. (1996), *Blackstone's Guide to the Disability Discrimination Act*, London: Blackstone.

Further Education Funding Council (FEFC) (1996), *Inclusive Learning. Report of the Learning Difficulties and/or Disabilities Subcommittee* (the Tomlinson Report), London: HMSO.

Hall, J. and Tinklin, T. (1998), *Students First. The Experiences of Disabled Students in Higher Education*, Edinburgh: The Scottish Council for Research in Education.

Hayes, J. (1997), 'Access to Higher Education: An exploration of realities and possibilities', *International Journal of Inclusive Education*, Vol.1 (3), 257–65.

Higher Education Funding Council of England (1995), *Access to Higher Education: Students with Special Needs. An HEFCE Report on the 1993–94 Special Initiative to Encourage Widening Participation for Students with Special Needs*, HEFCE.

Hodge, M. (1999), opening address to *An Inclusive Future*, conference on the Demos Report, Imperial College, 3 February.

Hurst, A. (1999), 'The Dearing Report and Students with Disabilities and Learning Difficulties', *Disability and Society*, Vol.14 (1), pp. 65–83.

HEFCE (1999), *Special funding programmes to improve provision for, and widen participation of, students with learning difficulties and disabilities*, http://www.hefce.ac.uk.Initiat/SLDD/siall.htm.

HESA (1997), 'HESA Data Report: students in Higher Education Institutions Cheltenham, Higher Education Statistics Agency', in Chard and Couch, op. cit.

Imrie, R. (1996), *Disability and the City. International Perspectives*, London: Paul Chapman.

Major, L.E. (1999), 'Improve or Else', *Guardian Higher Education Supplement*, 7 December.

Meager, N., Evans, C. et al. (1998), *Baseline Survey of the Measures in Part III of the DDA*, London: DfEE.

National Committee of Inquiry into Higher Education (Dearing Report) (1997), *Higher Education in the Learning Society*, London: HMSO.

O'Connor, B., Watson, R., Power, D. and Hartley, J. (1998), *Students with Disabilities: Code of Practice for Australian Tertiary Institutions*, Brisbane: Queensland University of Technology Publications (online at http://www.qut.edu.au/pubs/disabilities/national_ code/ code.html).

Oliver, M. (1996), 'A Sociology of Disability or a Disablist Sociology?', in Barton, L. (ed.), *Disability and Society: Emerging issues and insights*, Harlow: Addison Wesley.

Parker V. (1997), 'The Disability Discrimination Act 1995,Disability Statements and the Effect on Higher Education for Students with Special Needs in England', *Research in Post-Compulsory Education*, Vol. 2 (1), pp. 89–103.

Parker, V. (1999a), 'Personal Assistance for Students with Disabilities in HE: the experience of the University of East London', *Disability and Society*, Vol. 14 (4), pp. 483–504.

Parker, V. (1999b), unpublished report of meeting on access at Docklands Campus, 9 December.

Petrie H. and Gill, J. (1993), 'Current Research on Access to Graphical User Interfaces for Visually Disabled Computer Users', *European Journal of Special Needs Education*, Vol. 8 (2), June, pp. 153–57.

Quality Assurance Agency for Higher Education (1999), *Code of Practice for the Assurance of Academic Quality and Standards in Higher Education. Section 3: Students with Disabilities*, October, Gloucester: QAAHE.

Robertson, D. (1997), 'Social Justice in a Learning Market', in Coffield, F. and Williamson, B. (eds), *Repositioning Higher Education*, Buckingham: SRHE.

Segal Quince Wickstead (SQW) (1999), 'Guidance on Base-level Provision for Disabled Students in Higher Education Institutions', report to HEFCE and HEFCW, Cambridge.

Silver, P., Bourke, A. and Strehorn, K. (1998), 'Universal Instructional Design in Higher Education: An Approach for Inclusion', *Equity and Excellence in Education*, Vol. 31 (2), pp. 47–51.

Skill (HE Working Party) (1999), *Newsletter*, Issue 40, September, London: Skill: The National Bureau for Students with Disabilities, p. 1.

Skill (2000), verbal briefing by official of DFEE, 8 February.

THES (1999), 'Disabled Access Law will Cost Unis Millions', *Times Higher Education Supplement*, 17 December, p. 2.

Williams, J. (ed.) (1997), *Negotiating Access to Higher Education. The Discourse of Selectivity and Equity*, Buckingham: SRHE.

10 Still on the Margins: Towards a Compact between Higher Education and the Lower Socioeconomic Constituencies in Britain

CORNEL DaCOSTA

For the past five decades or more, the sociological evidence has been clear – that those in the lower socioeconomic groups have obtained far less higher education than those from the higher socioeconomic groups in society. Moreover, this situation has remained relatively consistent despite increased opportunities for higher education over the years. Indeed, there is a risk that this has been taken so much for granted in theory and practice that nothing can or will be done about it.

Nevertheless, we need to recognise that in the late 1980s and early 1990s, increased and widening participation in higher education did take place, especially among women, mature students and ethnic minorities, and by those in the Registrar General's socioeconomic groups III to V. However, when compared to the participants from socioeconomic groups I and II (professional and managerial groups) the share of the lower socioeconomic groups for higher education has been proportionately less than would be expected from members of the economically active population. Thus, access to social justice in relation to higher education and its related benefits has been less accessible to such groups (Halsey, 1993).

Historically, evidence from Glass (1961) to Reid (1999, p. 161), focused on social class as a significant variable relating to educational disadvantage by using a variety of scales including the Registrar General's scale or the Registrar General's socioeconomic group scale (RG SEG). However, there is a clear need to widen the remit of those disadvantaged to include social class, ethnic minorities and those in poverty. Indeed, despite recent government social initiatives such as the implementation of Education Action Zones, the New Deal programmes and a concern about social exclusion and marginalisation in society, the problem of greater inclusivity at all levels and particularly in relation to access to higher education for lower socioeconomic groups remains deep rooted and this chapter provides a proposal for a way out of this continuing dilemma and problem.

Various reasons have been provided in the literature as to why the lower socioeconomic groups do not engage in higher education as much as could be expected in a self-professed meritocratic society. Goddard (2000), drawing upon an earlier report to the Committee of Vice-Chancellors and Principals in Higher Education, reported that lack of money and an aversion to debt for higher education were the main obstacles to poor students who might otherwise enter higher education. Additionally, Goddard (2000, p. 8) referred to other barriers:

> Ignorance, exacerbated by marketing strategies that focus on the middle classes ... Lack of aspirations and confidence: parents, schools and advisers convince young people that higher education is not for them ... Lack of traditional entry qualifications, exacerbated by universities not considering non-traditional qualifications.

Further, the Higher Education Funding Council's (for England) (HEFCEs) published data on the link between university intakes and postcodes has demonstrated that those from richer neighbourhoods tend to go to the older, higher status universities and that those from poorer neighbourhoods attend the lower status new universities. The evidence is indeed stark. In reporting on the findings of the Sutton Trust which focused on access to the top UK universities, by tracking equally achieving pupils at entry to secondary school, and then following their progress through different school avenues, *The Times*, in an editorial (2000, p. 17), stated that:

> ... the top five universities admit 50 per cent more privately educated students than would be expected, and 40 per cent fewer than expected from lower social classes. When the study widened its focus to the top 13 universities, it found that the probability of winning a place was some 25 times greater for those educated privately than from those from a low social class or a poor area. These discrepancies cannot be explained away by differential ability ... It is time that universities took more seriously their obligation to offer the best education in the country to the best pupils in the country.

The association between social origins, academic opportunity and success has remained fairly constant over the past half century (Turner, 1960; Morgan, 1990) and there is little evidence that the picture is likely to alter unless a concerted effort is made to bring about a change in such a situation. Indeed unless some action is taken, our universities will wittingly or unwittingly perpetuate the class system which has been endemic in Britain in which 'applicants progress from privileged pasts to privileged futures or from less privileged pasts to less secure and lower status futures' (Dearing, 1997, p. 106). The scenario also has significant implications for the liberal view that higher education is worthwhile in its own right and also for the market view that higher education contributes significantly to individual wellbeing and to the economic welfare of a nation. And, as no persuasive case has yet been made that participation in higher education can be detrimental to one's wellbeing, we, as educators, surely need to seek ways and means to make access to higher education from among the lower socioeconomic groups a tangible reality and thus reposition the place of such groups in relation to higher education through a necessary compact between the two and the wider community and society. But this is unlikely to happen unless we can persuade the policy makers to take a determined view to bring about a necessary transformation.

Chapter 1 of the Dearing Report (1997), specifically focuses on the need for such a compact when Dearing draws our attention to the necessary linkage between higher education and the different constituencies in Britain. In proposing a new compact, Dearing (1997, p. 11) states that:

> At the heart of our vision of higher education is the freestanding institution, which offers teaching at the highest level in an environment of scholarship and independent enquiry. But collectively, and individually, these institutions are becoming ever more central to the economic wellbeing of the nation, localities and individuals. There is a growing bond of interdependence, in which each is looking for much from the other. That interdependence needs to be more clearly recognised by all participants.

In then going on to emphasise the notion of a compact, Dearing (1997, p. 12) says that:

> We think in terms of a compact between higher education and society which reflects their strong bond of mutual interdependence: a compact which in certain respects could with advantage be made explicit. A compact which is based on an interpretation of the needs of both sides at national, regional and local level

requires continuing dialogue and a framework within which it takes place. It needs to be informed by disinterested advice. It should not be another 35 years before a group like ours looks again systematically at the issues.

Indeed, it would be a shame if yet another report, in a few years, were needed to confirm, yet again, that the lower socioeconomic constituencies in society were still not gaining access to higher education in equitable numbers in a modern democratic state (Levitas, 1998). Moreover, in the light of the continuing discourse about the role of human capital, globalization and international competitiveness (Ashton and Green, 1996; Currie and Newson, 1998), increased participation in higher education is a desirable and necessary objective in Britain for the near and long term future. Further, the objective of reducing the differences in participation rates in higher education so as to meet the large potential and aspirations of currently non-participating groups is clearly of prime concern today.

There are in place today government-initiated strategies which encourage wider participation rates from among the less privileged in society. These include the availability of additional funds to those institutions accepting non-traditional entrants into higher education. However, as indicated above, the poorer students tend to gain places in our less prestigious institutions for a variety of reasons. Clearly, what is needed now is a more robust strategy which works and is applicable at national, regional and local levels. A framework is needed in which higher education institutions are made accountable to demonstrate a commitment to widening participation, a workable participation strategy, clear monitoring of progress made and an on-going review of policy and practice in this endeavour.

There are in place too a number of schemes in different universities to recruit from a wider band of entrants into higher education but they do not as yet appear to be making a significant dent into the intended project and there is a risk that some universities may give up on their initiatives for lack of faster progress. A workable compact is therefore needed by which each university and institute/college of higher education initially works locally to 'adopt' or twin with local educational institutions from primary, secondary and further education within their local purview to generate the seamless robe within which education should be provided for the widest participation rates possible. Thus from primary school, pupils need to see a progression route which takes them through to secondary schooling, further education and to higher education in the first instance, and to lifelong learning as a continuing opportunity.

Despite the recent expansion of higher education, it is still those mainly in the higher socioeconomic groups who conceptualise a progression from school to higher education and into the professions. In turn, those in the lower socioeconomic groups do not generally have a similar educational vision as their counterparts in the higher socioeconomic groups. Indeed, a progression into further and higher education is often an alien concept for those in the lower socioeconomic groups in society. Higher education is simply not central to their consciousness and significant numbers know little about the existence of universities and what they stand for. This is not particularly surprising as higher education has been highly elitist and a secret garden for generations for those who have been able to use the facility to gain in status, power and privilege. Historically, the lower socioeconomic groups have not been encouraged to taste the fruits of higher education, and undoubtedly, higher education has been shielded away from them for so long that it is a hard task to bring about a reasonably swift transformation in such a situation. Further, it can be argued that much theoretical work on widening participation for low socioeconomic groups has been largely presented as an act of faith, when clearly, what is needed is more in the nature of praxis. Consequently, what is now proposed is a practical facilitating process which largely eliminates the psychological, physical and symbolic boundaries between higher education and schools so as to encourage those who do not normally enter higher education to do so. Further, the proposal is testable in practice.

We need academic and other higher education personnel, who genuinely believe in widening participation, to participate closely in a continuing personal dialogue with teaching colleagues in schools and further education, and especially with parents of pupils/students who can in turn play a significant part, once persuaded, that their offspring can benefit from seeking and obtaining higher education. In such a situation, it should be normal for school pupils to get to know individual university academics as friends of the school and also as mentors. Further, they should have relatively open access to their local universities, albeit with some initial adult supervision. They should be encouraged to attend appropriate university teaching sessions, to ask questions and to feel the ambience of higher education including an awareness of the learning and teaching resources and the 'public' university utilities like cafeterias and sports facilities. In short, knowledge of, and the higher education physical experience, should be an integral part of their learning experience while still at school so that higher education ceases to be an alien concept to them.

Further, in terms of working within an operational framework, academic staff in higher education should also play a more central part in participating as school/college governors, and in particular in engaging in the curricula of the educational sector outside the university. At present, there is unfortunately very little interaction between the two parties and this is often confined or limited to the university/school liaison officer. In general, university academics are gatekeepers and by and large only receive and make judgements on university entry applications. In this situation, the schools are effectively very junior partners of the universities, except where good on-going links have been developed between schools as in parts of the private sector and the more prestigious universities. But the time has come when university presence in varying capacities has to prevail in schools and vice versa. This will not only help importantly to promote in children thoughts about entry to higher education, it will also make their teachers much more knowledgeable about on-going higher education and even encourage them into becoming continuing students themselves. In turn, university academics would get a good opportunity for continuing professional development.

In trying to create greater cooperation between higher education and schools/colleges, the more senior of the higher education personnel also need to play their part in local school affairs. Unfortunately, too often, deans, pro-Vice-Chancellors and Vice-Chancellors are extremely remote from local matters such as local schools and a change in this practice would seem to be long overdue to offset the ivory tower image of the university which has prevailed for so long in our institutions and in the media and thus played a part in limiting wider student participation in higher education.

The closer links suggested above between higher education institutions and their local schools, in particular, become increasingly important as reduced funding for students will deter them from going too far away from home because of the costs involved. This will unfortunately reduce the opportunity for student personal autonomy, personal development and maturity as well as the opportunity to meet with people away from other localities. But if this will, on the other hand, help towards wider participation into higher education at the local level it is perhaps a price worth paying.

Apart from closer involvement with schools, it becomes necessary for higher education personnel to work closely with other agencies, which are local, national and international. This must include key stakeholders such as the professional bodies, training agencies, unions and employers.

All the above suggestions for promoting and widening participation into higher education from among those who traditionally have not gained from higher education do however need financial support as it is clear that funding is increasingly a major problem for those contemplating higher education.

The government has a responsibility to provide financial allowances which are needed to help with costs of widening participation. This can be at a number of levels. Access students need more support than they are getting now, mature students with mortgages and families to support have additional needs. Bursaries as opposed to loans to poorer students may indeed be a critical consideration. Further, higher education institutions needing to provide additional support for those disadvantaged through disability or special learning needs should be 'compensated' to help meet their obligations arising from widening the student intake.

To conclude, it would appear to be self-evident that widening participation so as to make higher education much more inclusive (Daniels and Garner, 1999) than it is at present is a goal which can and should be achieved. However, for such an aspiration to be fulfilled, there needs to be a compact operating to a schedule, between government, higher education and the wider community. The compact has to have a clear accountability remit and a direct bearing especially on schools in poorer neighbourhoods so that higher education is decreasingly privileged for the few but becomes more available for the many in an inclusive society.[1]

Note

1   At the time of going to press, the Education Secretary, David Blunkett, made a keynote address reported as 'Reaching out to make society just' (*THES*, 12 May 2000, p. 14) in which he unveiled a seven point plan to bring more people from all backgrounds into higher education.

   It echoed some of the points considered in the above chapter, thereby drawing the marginalization of lower socioeconomic groups into the mainstream debate.

References

Ashton, D. and Green, F. (1996), *Education, Training and the Global Economy*, Cheltenham: Edward Elgar Publications

Currie, J. and Newson, J. (1998), *Universities and Globalization*, London: Sage Publications.

Daniels, H. and Garner, P. (eds) (1999), *Inclusive Education*, London: Kogan Page.

Goddard, A. (2000), *Unequal Opportunities, a University Challenge*, London: *THES*.

Glass, D. (1961), 'Education and Social Change in Modern Britain', in Halsey, A., Floud, J. and Anderson, C. (eds), *Education, Economy and Society*, New York: The Free Press of Glencoe.

Halsey, A. (1993), 'Trends in Access and Equity in HE: Britain in International Perspective, *Oxford Review of Education*, Vol. 19, No. 2, pp. 129–40.

Levitas, R. (1998), *The Inclusive Society? Social Exclusion and New Labour*, London: Macmillan Press.

Morgan, H. (1990), 'Sponsored and Contest Mobility Re-visited: An Examination of Britain and USA Today', *Oxford Review of Education*, Vol. 16, No. 1, pp. 39–54.

National Committee of Inquiry into Higher Education (Dearing Report) (1997), *Higher Education in the Learning Society*, London: HMSO.

Reid, I. (1998), *Class in Britain*, Cambridge: Polity Press.

The Times (2000), Editorial, 'Dreams of Aspirers', 10 April, p. 17.

Turner, R. (1960), 'Sponsored and Contest Mobility and the School System', *American Sociological Review*, No. 25, pp. 855–67.

PART IV
CONTRIBUTIONS TOWARDS
A COMPACT: PERSPECTIVES
FROM THE CONSUMERS

PART IV

11 Prospects for a Compact with the Learning and Skills Council

PATRICK AINLEY

Introduction

This chapter begins with a brief history of university expansion to date. A second section then relates the new system of higher education funded through its own funding council to the new unified system of further education and training that will be introduced under the Learning and Skills Council on 1 April 2001. A third and final section looks briefly at the two separately funded systems (though both are nominally under the Department for Education and Employment's Lifelong Learning Directorate) to ask how they could be related – and related also to their students and other partners in their regions and localities – through a new compact. Other than a radical and democratic reconstruction, the chapter questions whether any such compact can be viable and suggests that the relations likely to obtain between higher education and its various consumers in the future are those of contract.

Brief History

The recent expansion of higher education was justified by a vocational imperative. Yet originally, all higher education was vocational, developing on the European university self-governing model from the monastic disciplines for training the priesthood and only later embracing the other original professions of law and medicine. Later, with Oxbridge dominated by the classics, the development of technical training required for industry was undertaken by the Victorian redbrick foundations in the commercial and industrial centres of London and the North of England. In one of the earlier of several attempts to emulate foreign industrial competitors, the German university model was influential in the establishment of single science disciplines based upon research. The same process of 'academic drift', as Pratt and Burgess (1974, p. 23) first called it, that repeats itself throughout English educational history, saw the steady depreciation of vocational training at the expense of the Victorian cult of Classics-based gentlemanly amateurism.

On the eve of the Second World War, the elite system of medieval Oxbridge Colleges and Victorian redbrick universities were attended by about 50,000 students, mainly young men, that is only 3 per cent of the 18–21 age range, growing to 6.2 per cent by 1962/3. Under pressure from service-class professionals in the growing post-war welfare bureaucracies, a rapid growth was recommended in the 1963 Robbins Report. The Robbins principle that 'courses of higher education should be available for all' was qualified by the proviso that it applied only to those whom academics considered 'able to benefit'. Nevertheless, the acceptance of the Robbins Report led to a pattern of transition for growing numbers of middle-class youth, female as well as male, moving from school to work and from home to living away, via three or four years of residential higher education. This 'finishing school' model of higher education was firmly established in what were largely liberal arts institutions patterned upon the Oxbridge original. Informally-structured arts courses tended to dominate these new foundations and enjoyed higher status within them than the more rigidly patterned, technically-applied and vocationally-related, lab-based, science courses.

Instead of bringing all higher education under the university umbrella, the 1964 Labour government instituted a 'binary line' between the polytechnics and the rest. This decision institutionally polarised higher educational values and goals. It generated and sustained – in this sector of education as elsewhere – a simplified opposition between academicism and vocationalism, education and training, cultural knowledge and occupational competence. Despite this, the binary policy saw an expansion of Further Education (FE) colleges and polytechnics under the control of local education authorities. Together with the Open University (established in 1969), the foundation and subsequent growth of the polytechnics brought the percentage of full and part-time higher education (HE) students to 12.7 per cent of the age group by the end of the 1970s when a short period of cutbacks followed consequent upon the ending of the long economic boom in the 1973 oil crisis. When government policy changed again at the end of the 1980s towards the introduction of a market-driven expansion of higher education, the elitist option of, as Fulton (1991, pp. 589–605) says, 'raising the grades they required for entry rather than squeezing in all those who meet previously acceptable standards', was no longer available to most universities. In addition, their reliance upon state funding meant the loss of their much cherished but largely illusory independence (see Fraser 1983). Despite 'the concept of autonomy' being, as Tapper and Salter (1992, p. 228) put it, 'central to ... the traditional idea of the university, only the most perverse re-reading of history could claim that British universities remained autonomous institutions by the final days of the Universities Grants Council'. Instead, the university authorities accepted expansion on a reduced unit of resource to include one third of the age range in some sort of higher education by the end of the millennium (half of the 17–20 population in Scotland).

The increase in total numbers was achieved despite an increase in fees (then still recoverable by the universities and colleges from public funds) and the introduction of loans to pay for student grants. Flat-rate fees were differentiated by subject area in an unsuccessful effort by the Conservative government to go against the operation of the free market it favoured and to direct more students into science and technology and away from the cheaper but more popular arts and social sciences. This made some subjects more expensive to study than others and invited institutions to charge 'top-up' fees for their popular courses. Indeed, this development is widely regarded as inevitable. In addition, the contradictory recommendation of Dearing's Report on higher education to recommence expansion by charging fees further undermined the Robbins' principle of state support for all qualifying students and predictably discouraged would-be students from applying. This was seen in the immediate fall in applications from mature students in 1998 and a later fall in under-21 year olds (confirmed by the *THES*, 3 July 1998). The removal of grants, which the New Labour government unexpectedly added to Dearing's expected recommendation to introduce fees, now saddles students with total debts/ loans estimated by the Campaign for Free Education to vary by course and institution from between £10,000 and £20,000.

The introduction of the market in higher education provided a model for the type of differentiated market that Conservative governments intended to replicate in independently competing schools and colleges of further education. Only minor changes were necessary to produce such a result in the HE sector as an elaborate hierarchy of universities already existed in which independent, self-governing institutions competed with their various specialised course offerings in an academic market place for state-subsidised students. The removal of the binary divide between universities and polytechnics in 1992 completed this differentiated hierarchy at the same time as it removed the last vestiges of local accountability and democratic control over higher education.

By taking the former polytechnics and colleges, together with FE and sixth-form colleges, away from administration by the local state and funding them per head through funding agencies, the hierarchy of Higher Education Institutions (HEIs) competing in the academic market place also provided an example of the new organisation of quangos in what has been called 'the Contracting State' (Harden, 1992) run on the franchise or contract principle. This semi-privatised state sector complements the state-subsidisation of the private sector in a new mixed economy (Ainley, 1999).

With research increasingly concentrated in specialist centres, as government clearly signalled even before Dearing by hiving off responsibility for the research councils to the Department of Trade and Industry's Office of Science and Technology (via a staging-post in the Cabinet Office), it is predictable there will be a new binary divide as the new (and some not so new) universities at the bottom of the pile become teaching-only institutions. This can only be confirmed by Dearing's recommendation for research to be concentrated in 'centres of excellence' – predictably in the elite, Ivy League. For, as Scott (1997) writes, 'Since the onset of "consolidation" many universities have concentrated ... on improving their research performance [and] the [Dearing] committee has perhaps not been sufficiently bold in recognising that renewed expansion may have to lead to a clearer division between research-oriented and access-oriented universities.'

In the latter, recruiting and teaching universities, 'skills' courses related to employment will be concentrated, along with two-and-a-bit year Foundation Degrees delivered in their associated FE colleges. It is unlikely however that such Americanised arrangements of 'state universities' with their associated 'community colleges' can meet the ambitious expansion targets that government have set for half of the age range to be in HE in England and Wales by 2002. Indeed, expansion has already peaked as consolidation takes its place (Ainley, 1998). Meanwhile, at the other pole of the widening spectrum, in selecting and researching 'Ivy League' universities, courses unrelated to any specific employment but serving as a cultural apprenticeship to core management positions in business and finance also pander to the academic consumerism of overseas students and those who can afford to take courses for their intrinsic interest. Fees raised to full cost for such prestigious courses can be anticipated as the old universities privatise themselves out of the state system, raising their entry requirements to preserve their elite status rather than admit more students who meet their old standards. As it is, the more culturally prestigious the institution and the course, the more white, male and middle-class the students are. Older universities also have younger students. In other words, expansion thus far has resulted in the worst of both worlds – a mass system for the many combined with an elite system for the few.

Enter the Learning and Skills Council (LSC)

Democratically accountable Local Education Authorities (LEAs) have seen their influence much reduced in the move from the national system of education they formerly locally administered. Now we are moving towards a national system of education nationally administered through 'quangos big and small', as Lord Nolan, Chairman of the Committee on Standards in Public Life, described the elements of the new state (Radio 4, 16 May 1996).

LEAs lost all vestiges of control over the polytechnics and other colleges of higher education of which they were often so proud when these were incorporated in 1988. The FE colleges followed the polytechnics into the semi-privatised 'quasi-market' in 1993. LEAs still retain responsibility for their schools but local management means that funds for them are delegated from the DfEE on a formula per head so that former control is lost. The same is proposed for the surviving remnants of local authority Adult and Community Education under the latest proposals for implementing the 1999 'Learning to Succeed' White Paper. LEA youth services are also to be merged with the various careers companies through the 'Connexions' strategy into the Youth Support Service, following the 'Bridging the Gap' suggestions of the Social Exclusion Unit. Together with training management agencies, they will be administered by a Learning and Skills Council from April 2001, bringing together the Further Education Funding Council and the Training and Enterprise Councils National Council into one super-quango funding all post-compulsory non-higher education and training from 2001. Local LSCs will also 'steer the distribution of funds for school sixth form provision' that LEAs will hand on accordingly. LSCs could logically and eventually take over responsibility for funding all the schools in their localities from the LEAs, as predicted by Peter Kingston in *The Guardian* on the 29 February 2000. After all, as Stephen Byers warned the first North of England Conference under New Labour government, 'LEAs have no God-given right to run schools'. Democratically elected local councils are, after all, associated as much by New Labour as by the previous Conservative governments with the old corruption of Old Labour.

Employers' nominees are to hold a 40 per cent representation on the LSCs local and national, as well as on college corporations and elsewhere via the

Lifelong Learning Partnerships that have been set up by employers and others with colleges and through the already existing Education and Business Partnerships with schools. With its 47 local arms (reminiscent of the 50 Manpower Services Commission Area Manpower Boards and based on existing TEC offices), each employing between 55 and 150 staff under the direction of executives paid from £50,000–80,000 to spend budgets typically over £100 million to fund on average more than 100,000 learners, the LSC is a quasi-autonomous non-governmental organisation contracted to the Department for Education and Employment. In an untidy compromise, the DfEE is bringing in its notorious Office for Standards in Education to divide responsibility for inspection of LSC institutions with the Adult Learning Inspectorate (the old TEC national inspectorate) which retains responsibility for those over 19. Higher Education – with the exception of the mistrusted Schools of Education inspected through the Teacher Training Agency – (as yet) sorts out its own inspection arrangements through the Quality Assurance Agency. The Adult Learning Inspectorate will however liaise in a manner yet to be imagined with the Training Standards Council. The TSC is to be phased out as a separate entity alongside the formerly target-setting National Advisory Council for Education and Training Targets – national targets now being set by the LSC. Local LSCs meanwhile will set local targets/ plans, possibly with different funding tariffs for different localities.

Only plainly partial opposition spokespersons could describe the new system as a 'confused spaghetti' (Teresa May, quoted in the *Times Educational Supplement* (*TES*) on the 21 January 2000). Although the latest (at the time of writing) Eighth Report of the Select Committee on Education and Employment records its 'concern' that:

> the different geographical coverage of, for example, the Careers Service, RDAs, the proposed LSCs, the UfI, the proposed Youth Support Service and the New Deal Delivery Units ... are likely to create new obstacles to the delivery of a seamless service, both vertically, across different age groups, and horizontally, within specific age groups, across a range of policy challenges (para. 72 and in conclusion).

The Committee therefore advised that 'careful attention' (para. 68) will have to be paid if the 'duplication, confusion and bureaucracy' that the 1999 White Paper 'Learning to Succeed' noted resulted in 'an absence of effective co-ordination or strategic planning' (as quoted in para. 57 of the Report) was to result in the 'seamless web' that the White Paper aspired to.

Distinct regional patterns of clearly structured routes or pathways are already emerging both within and between institutions in the new system to which social groups defined by class background, gender, ethnicity and ability are relegated or promoted (Ainley et al., 2000). This is but one instance of the 'new regionalism' emerging in response to re-regulation of the economy through globalisation, leading to what is referred to as 'glocalisation'. These divisions both between and within regions have not yet become so entrenched that they are plainly apparent to all who are involved or to outside observers, though they are becoming marked in the national regions of Wales and Scotland, especially the latter which was always differently administered anyway. Moreover, they are obfuscated by opportunities for transfer between routes and by extension beyond previously sharp cut-off points into 'Lifelong Learning' with recurrent returns to learning and new combinations of learning with (often part-time) employment. The new system thus appears fluid and changing with successive new initiatives for particular groups and individuals at different times and in different places. It is also, like the new contracting state of which it is a part, inherently unstable and internally competitive despite the New Labour emphasis upon 'partnership'.

In a significant continuity with the old arrangements whereby the universities were separately funded from the Treasury via the University Grants Council (UGC), the implicit privileging of the academic progression route to higher education via sixth forms echoes the way that HE was altogether omitted from the Learning and Skills Review of non-advanced FE that preceded the White Paper. Beyond the Education and Employment arena, interdepartmental conflicts and rivalries dispute the boundaries of social security (already closely collaborating with Employment Services foreshadowing a possible merger, as in New Zealand. Merger of the ES and DSS would explain the divorce remarked by the Select Committee of New Deal from the broader learning system). As noted above, the Department of Trade and Industry (DTI) has claimed research and enterprise support from the DfEE (i.e. knowledge production as opposed to its reproduction by education and training). Meanwhile, both the DTI and DfEE's relations with the new 'super-Ministry' of Environment, Transport and the Regions are unclear. It is the DETR's Regional Development Agencies with which the local and national LSCs will somehow coordinate their funding activities on a regional basis, especially for the distribution of European funds. While amalgamations into such super-ministries as the DETR and the DfEE itself (see Aldrich et al., forthcoming) – appears to be the order of the day, there is also the overarching question of the contractual relations of the various government departments to the Treasury, which becomes ever more powerful in this new contracting state.

Competition, inherited from the Conservatives who set up the new system, is built into it and intended to drive up standards. The aim is for provision of education and training, as of other services, to be responsive both to the changing demands of the economy and to individual demand dependent upon reading the market signals of 'employability'. Individuals may be 'empowered' by a basic voucher entitlement through Individual Learning Accounts administered by the Learning and Skills Council and not the University for Industry as was originally intended. The UfI has now been renamed and relegated to a phone-line brokerage service called 'Learning Direct', although still aspiring as 'a driver of virtual learning' – as it describes itself – to franchise to thousands of 'learning centres' in FE colleges, employers' premises, libraries, community centres, supermarkets and pubs). ILAs may optimistically be topped-up with financial investment or loans and could be tied in with ISAs and even pensions in a totally voucherised welfare system.

Individual Learning and Savings Accounts would ensure that responsiveness to consumer demand replaced the rigidities of universal provision as an entitlement of citizenship. For universal principles are dismissed by the new government, as by postmodernists, as 'totalising' and therefore totalitarian. In their place, New Labour proposes to 'modernise' such classic welfare state measures into the individually and locally customised services of a 'postmodern' society. Significantly, the government proposes to begin in education by changing the national and uniform terms and conditions of school teachers – a feature of the bids accepted for Educational Action Zones (EAZs), which, in this respect as in others, differ profoundly from the Educational Priority Areas and Community Development Programmes of the Wilson era (see Hatcher, Nixon, Ranson and Rikowski, forthcoming). As in FE, where a prolonged dispute saw the eventual deregulation of the former 'Silver Book' agreement in favour of local negotiation of pay and hours by individual college corporations, staffing is the most expensive area of expenditure where the most savings can be made. The removal of security of tenure for academics in HE had the same deregulating effect (Ainley, 1994).

There have it is true been some concessions to national and regional feelings through devolution and promised regional assemblies – the London mayor, for instance. The changes to and prunings of the local state made by Mrs Thatcher remain firmly in place, however. Arguably they will be taken further under the 'new regionalism', which echoes the 'new federalism' of Reagan and Bush and shadows that of the EU and existing government offices. For the surviving democratically elected councils have already had their role recast by central government from being responsible to their local electorates towards becoming boards of managing directors under directly elected mayoral Chief Executives seeking tenders, issuing contracts and monitoring the performance of separate subcontractors (see Cochrane, 1993). Such so-called 'enabling' local authorities, endorsed by all three main electoral parties, mirror the 'contracting' or 'franchising' that has occurred in the central state, again with a parallel loss of accountability and democratic control.

The new form of public administration reconstructs the state along the lines of a holding company producing an inherently unstable system. Holding companies suffer particular organisational dysfunctions, managing at arm's length a complex range of diverse organisations to which self-management has been devolved. Subcontracting can be a way of reducing the price of a product or service by squeezing the contract, but it typically involves loss of detailed control, although financial control is increased. The relationship between contractor and subcontractor is one of mutual dependency, yet another effect is fragmentation, for it is difficult to maintain and enforce national standards or public goods without considerable interference in the activities of the subcontractor.

The 'new public management' of this semi-privatised state sector is potentiated by new technology ('management by e-mail'). This uses indirect quality indicators as performance targets of outputs ('management by objectives'). A contracting core of management no longer in direct contact with the work being undertaken comes to rely on such indirect indicators of performance. This leads to the well-known 'All Pigs Flying' scenario (Ainley, 1997). As well as new divisions between core management and a periphery of contract workers, this makes it difficult to determine which are real indicators and which are virtual ones. As well as being 'The Audit Society' described by Power (1997) with its 'Rituals of Verification' run by accountants, the contracting, post-welfare or workfare state may therefore also become the virtual state.

So Where Do We Go From Here?

What sort of a compact is possible for the competing and semi-privatised institutions of higher education in a contracting state? And with whom are they to make such a compact? Or is it contract, as Lord Meghnad Desai predicts in this volume, which is to govern the financial transactions of individuals and institutions? In my opinion, the marketisation of the state and society that has been allowed to happen in recent years must be reversed to return public services to democratic control, extending that control so as to really serve the people. Thus a democratic compact is the only alternative to a commercial contract.

In particular, if educational institutions at all levels were returned to the democratic control of their communities and regions, this could serve to generalise science and stimulate imagination of the radical transformations required to avoid ecological catastrophe through a genuine modernisation of the economy and society. It appears that, due to the government's difficulties with the Scottish Parliament, Welsh Assembly and London mayor, New Labour's regional agenda is being vigorously back-pedalled. The DETR's Regional Development Agencies as presently proposed do not formally represent the regions to which they were once intended to be democratically accountable through regional assemblies. Even without such a mandate, it is also doubtful that the RDAs will possess sufficient financial muscle to attract education and training institutions that will now be directly funded by their local LSCs. In particular, HEIs funded separately through their own funding councils will need very substantial incentives to enter into regional compacts with their RDAs. This applies especially to those universities that see themselves selecting home students from the better state and private sixth forms nationally and from which their students graduate to national if not international labour markets. The concentration of research into national 'centres of excellence' that may also be internationally renowned also directs these selecting and researching institutions away rather than towards their regions. It is the recruiting and teaching universities across the new binary divide that will perforce seek to relate to their regions and to the FEIs that represent for them a source of local students.

Yet amongst especially these students and despite – or perhaps because of – the relentless vocational pressures for conformity to which education at all levels now subjects students, alternative cultures generally oppose the whole work ethic, or what Aronowitz and DiFazio (1994) called 'the Dogma of Work', which derives identity from occupation. It is commonplace to remark that as employment loses its centrality in social life, consumer and leisure identities become more important. There is a contradiction, however, in that conventional consumer and leisure identities are harder to sustain without regular income and this has been widely held to partly account for the proliferation of counter-cultures amongst the young. Many in the new mass of students working their way through schools into further, higher and continuing education and training are beginning to shape such a challenge in the ways in which they struggle to make lives for themselves in the new circumstances in which they find themselves. Teachers and trainers at all levels of learning can help them to do this at the same time as they help them to achieve their learning goals even though these too often promise only an illusory connection with worthwhile employment.

For this is the question most deeply rooted in the consciousness of all learners – what is the purpose of my learning? And it is at this point that thinking about a new compact should begin because the contradiction between endless academic selection and employment that cannot be guaranteed at the end of the course is today more clearly apparent to more students and their teachers than ever before. Before literacy and numeracy hours in primary and (from September 2000) in secondary schools, 'democracy hours' should be introduced in all schools and colleges to debate and decide what is worth learning and researching at all levels of learning. Having so many full- and part-time students in some sort of education at least provides opportunities for such a 'Rethinking [of] Education and Democracy' (Hillcole, 1997).

The purposes of learning are ultimately related to the nature of work (White, 1997) and at present the prime purpose of institutionalised learning is selection to the employment hierarchy. Yet nobody should be relegated by 'failure' in often irrelevant tests and examinations that deny them the basic right to contribute creatively to society and in exchange for such work to receive a living wage. The imbalance between the work rich but time poor and the work poor but time rich needs to be redressed (Gershuny, 2000). Guaranteed employment need no longer, however, be the same as the full-time, male, lifelong earning, eight hours a day five days a week, that was lost in this country with the collapse of heavy industry. It should be a matter of celebration that the long hours of work of yesteryear are no longer necessary as a rule. Leisure can increase, as it would if work were genuinely shared. Thus the individual right to work must involve work-sharing to reduce hours worked, not only to ensure that all have work to sustain themselves but also to give those in work a chance to participate in increased learning at work, as well as in cultural consumption out of work.

Learning at all levels will be integral to such a real cultural revolution but will not be limited to formal education. It will include recreation, sport and many other cultural and self-directed activities, including the ecological and community activity urgently required in so many parts of society. This could happen possibly through a Ministry of the Arts, Sports, Science, Education and Culture rather than the separation of all these activities and the subordination of education to employment. For once education is no longer primarily about selection for the employment hierarchy, we will be free to learn from work but never just in order to work.

References

Ainley, P. (1994), *Degrees of Difference: Higher education in the 1990s*, London: Lawrence and Wishart.

Ainley, P. (1997), '"All Pigs Flying" – A Consequence of Indirect Management by Outputs in Further Education, unpublished paper for 1997 Vocational Education and Training Conference, Huddersfield University.

Ainley, P. (1998), 'The End of Expansion and the Consolidation of Differentiation in English Higher Education', *Teaching in Higher Education*, Vol. 3, No. 2, pp. 143–56.

Ainley, P. (1999), *Learning Policy: Towards the certified society*, London: Macmillan.

Ainley, P. and Bailey, B. (1997), *The Business of Learning, Staff and Student Experiences of Further Education in the 1990s*, London: Cassell.

Ainley, P. and Corney, M. (1990), *Training for the Future, the rise and fall of the Manpower Services Commission*, London: Cassell.

Ainley, P., Smith, D., Watson, J. and Yeomans, D. (2000), report to the ESRC on research into 'Progression and Pathways in 16–25 Education and Training'.

Aldrich, R., Crook, D. and Watson, D. (2000), *Education and Employment: the DfEE and its place in history*, London: London University Institute of Education.

Aronowitz, S. and DiFazio, W. (1994), *The Jobless Future, Sci-Tech and the Dogma of Work*, Minnesota: University of Minnesota Press.

Cochrane, A. (1993), *Whatever Happened to Local Government*, Buckingham: Open University Press.

DfEE (1999), *Learning to Succeed: A new framework for post-16 learning*, London: HMSO.

DfEE, Select Committee on Education and Employment (2000) *Eighth Report*, London: DfEE.

Fraser, J. (1983), *The Decline of Autonomy of British Universities in the Robbins Era 1963–83*, unpublished MEd, Deptartment of Education, Stirling University.

Fulton, O. (1991), 'Slouching Towards a Mass System: Society, government and Institutions in the United Kingdom', *Higher Education*, 26, 3, pp. 589–605.

Gershuny, J. (2000), address to the British Sociological Association annual conference 'Making Time, Marking Time' , York University.

Harden, I. (1992), *The Contracting State*, Buckingham: Open University Press.

Hatcher, R., Nixon, J., Ranson, S. and Rikowski, G. (forthcoming), *Report on Education Action Zones*, Universities of Birmingham and Central England.

The Hillcole Group (1997), *Rethinking Education and Democracy, A socialist alternative for the twenty first century*, London: Tufnell Press.

Pratt, J.and Burgess, T. (1974), *Polytechnics: A Report*, London: Pitman Publishing.

Power, M. (1997), *The Audit Society: The Rituals of Verification*, Oxford: Oxford University Press.

Scott, P. (1997), 'The Dearing Report' , *Parliamentary Monitor*, August, p. 3.

Tapper, T. and Salter, B. (1992), *Oxford, Cambridge and the Changing Idea of the University*, Buckingham: Open University Press.

White, J. (1997), *Education and the End of Work: A New Philosophy of Work and Learning*, London: Cassell.

12 Students Learn to Adapt

ANDREW PAKES AND MARTIN O'DONOVAN

Students have moved on. Life in the twenty-first century differs unimaginably from the 1960s, or even the 1980s. A third of school leavers enter higher education, rather than one in 10. Over half of students work part-time to supplement their income. Most students are computer literate. More students than ever are careers-focused. Most students pay fees. Whether we like it or not, students often see themselves as *consumers* of higher education.

Likewise, the NUS (National Union of Students) in the twenty-first century is different from the NUS in the 1960s because the mood and culture of the country has changed, and education has changed with it. Many part-time students do not consider themselves to be 'students'. There have been fundamental changes to what exactly constitutes an 'average' student. Mass expansion, the huge growth in part-time study, debt, the end of the binary divide. The 'average' student is an illusion.

There have been major changes in the student support system and the quality of the student experience has been adversely affected. Many students face serious debt and hardship, funding per student has collapsed and lecturers do not earn what they deserve. This should not deflect us from the precious outcome of increased participation, greater opportunity and, albeit on a limited scale, widened access. We firmly believe that expanded tertiary education in the new century is better for students and better for society than that of the largely elitist 1960s. The increased debt may not be better, but this is outweighed by the participation revolution.

The contribution of students and their representatives in higher education towards the notion of a compact for higher education needs to be properly addressed. In recent years there have been two independent inquiries set up to examine, among other things, student support – one chaired by Lord Dearing, the other by Andrew Cubie. Their independence is beyond question, if for no other reason than their findings have caused such monumental political headaches for the administrations to which they reported. Both reached similar conclusions, through different mechanisms: students from the lowest socioeconomic groups should receive support to help them through university, and graduates should make a contribution to their education on graduation. These principles are reflected by current NUS policy, and by 80 per cent of the people in Scotland, according to an opinion poll taken by *The Herald* in January 2000, shortly after the publication of the Cubie Report.

If it is widely accepted that students must make a contribution, the question moves on to how much should be contributed, and how this contribution should be met. These questions are examined fully later in this chapter, but before examining the detail of policy, it is instructive to pull together trends and developments in higher education.

Students in the Learning Age

The government has set out a vision, albeit without a clear indication on funding for 'the learning age'. Many jobs now require training on a regular basis – a trend likely to continue; and educational structures are likely to become more fluid than the conventional nursery–primary–secondary–further–higher–postgraduate model that has existed throughout much of the twentieth century. This may involve rethinking the GCSE–A level–GNVQ–Degree–Masters qualification model, or a least a 'pop in, pop out' mechanism for people wishing to gain new qualifications. Recognition of short courses will also need to be improved if lifelong learning is to offer best value to learners.

It is important that we examine the mission of lifelong learning. Who is the target student? What is the focus of the learning age? Is it leisure learning ('my granny learns Spanish in the upstairs room of our local pub') or skills-based learning (renewal of job-relevant skills)? If it is – at least to start with – the latter, is the focus on the socially excluded and the poorly paid or is lifelong learning to be made available for all? We clearly need to prioritise within the questions and suggest mechanisms to deliver this learning within a new compact.

The first target must be to tackle social exclusion. Basic skills come first. Funds as are available should then focus on re-skilling, leaving leisure learners down the priority list (my granny may have to pay for that course in Spanish). The interesting aspect in lifelong learning is the development of a mechanism for proper contributions from business – the Individual Learning Account (ILA). As this system develops, it is important that businesses are not allowed to pick and choose. If businesses will pay for a subsidised course for retraining some skilled employees, there must be a financial commitment to the basic skills agenda. Otherwise, the ILA could be manipulated as a perk for businesses, which is clearly not the policy intention.

Internet Learning

The new compact in tertiary education will evolve as lifelong and distance learning takes hold. Contributions from stakeholders will alter, and employers may contribute more through individual learning accounts – particularly on the costs of retraining.

Students are one of the groups within the population that has been the quickest to adapt to new communications and information technology (CIT/ICT). This trend will continue. Students are CIT-friendly, and they will need to be. New technology is dictating much of the jobs' agenda. While concrete predictions on the future of technology are likely to become hostages to fortune (the world of technology is progressing at a breathtaking pace), what is clear in 2000 is that today's student is tomorrow's CIT-friendly employee, employer, tomorrow's Internet consumer and tomorrow's Internet learner.

Internet learning should not be seen merely as a useful mechanism for delivering extra learning for graduates. Internet learning offers an extra option to those wanting to learn whom classroom-based learning in the past may have disenfranchised. As schools hook up to the national grid for learning, the Internet user will move on from late twentieth century notions of being the 'nerd' or the 'swot'. All young people will have used the Internet, and the educational opportunities that arise, particularly as regards 'second chance' learners, should not be overlooked.

ICT-based learning is not only inevitable, but is also desirable for students. Some in education may feel threatened by this but the opportunities offered by the Worldwide Web are extraordinary. This agenda of ICT-based learning poses particular challenges to lecturing staff. However, the suggestion that face-to-face learning will somehow be replaced by the Internet is misguided. The challenge to students and lecturers is to ensure that the changes ahead enhance quality and add to the student experience, rather than developing into a cost-cutting agenda.

ICT has the potential to improve the student experience for all learners. This learning will take place in colleges and schools – which may increasingly become a hub of community learning programmes. For example, as after-school clubs and homework clubs develop, parents may be encouraged to undertake courses within the school environment.

Trends Towards Part-time Study

The government is keen to fund an expansion in further and higher education. That expansion is likely to focus largely on part-time provision. The shift towards part-time study may impact on the sector quite dramatically.

In a sense, the first wave of this revolution has already happened, and universities and lecturers have adapted extraordinarily well. If the next wave of expansion takes us to 50 per cent participation, the squeeze on timetables and space will become tighter. One area of concern for students' representatives is that the traditional Wednesday for sport will be eroded, as will the opportunity for student development activities, community work, and even the opportunity to be active in a students' union. While these activities are traditionally the preserve of full-time students, a greater focus on part-time learning will put these activities at risk. And a weak students' union is detrimental to all students – full- and part-time.

The impact on lecturers may also be dramatic: a further increase in teaching hours, and no guarantees that the Bett agenda is poised for full implementation. A higher education system of 50 per cent participation will need extra government funding and perhaps a new stream of funding. This is something addressed later in the chapter.

The Future Role of FE – Social Inclusion

The further education sector is now the focus of the Government's policy on tertiary education. Most of the new funds allocated to tertiary education in the 1998 Comprehensive Spending Review were channelled into further education. Whereas the higher education sector has seen the abolition of the grant (partially reintroduced from September 2000) and the introduction of a means-tested tuition fee, the further education sector has seen the piloting of an Education Maintenance Allowance and new funds to enhance quality and improve access. The key to this development is the government's drive against social exclusion. Further education is seen as the sector where social exclusion is tackled; the development onto higher education is seen as desirable, but the higher education sector is seen as having a less significant role in the inclusion agenda.

The Future Role of HE – Raising Horizons

Higher education will therefore need to reinvent itself if it is to thrive and survive in the future. There will always be the traditional pillars of research and excellence that are UK higher education's great international strengths, but higher education is losing out on the social agenda to further education. The government's emphasis on lifelong learning focuses almost entirely on the further education sector. This presents the higher education sector with a dilemma: how can higher education tap into a government agenda of tackling social exclusion? The answer may be to encourage a more natural development for students from further to higher education – a seamless sector. If a student from a very poor background goes on to higher education, then society gains enormously, alongside the individual. The move towards a bursary for students from the lowest socioeconomic groups moves us closer towards this in terms of funding. On a structural level students will benefit through the continued development of learner-focused partnership agreements between further and higher education institutions, encouraging the idea that they belong in higher education.

Representation at the Study Place: the Future of Students' Unions

Lifelong learning, part-time learning and distance learning are all set to impact on education at the start of the twenty-first century. How will these developments affect student representation? How can students' unions represent part-time students? Can students' unions address the needs of distance learners, or do most part-time learners simply not consider themselves to be 'students'? On the other hand, an ICT-friendly membership may welcome a representative body that communicates through new technology: web democracy, representation and advice is certain to increase.

The Future of NUS

The National Union of Students should survive well into the new century, providing a national voice for students. NUS will only survive, however, if it adapts to the modern era.

Representation at the Work Place

Students' unions and the National Union of Students can provide representation at the study place. However, over half of today's six million students (further and higher education, full- and part-time) work while studying. Worryingly, few appear to understand their rights at work and fewer still are represented by trade unions. As the trend towards part-time learning continues, so will the need for the NUS to develop relations with trade unions to ensure that students are represented in the workplace, the NUS is developing a strong working relationship with the Trades Union Congress (TUC), and this will be vital if students are to be informed of their rights at work and the role of trade unions in society.

What is the situation facing working students? The NUS' students at work survey, 1999, reached the following conclusions on students who work part-time to supplement their income:

- students are forced to work to meet their basic living costs;
- their jobs are not relevant to their chosen careers;
- they are being poorly paid. Half earn under £3.80 per hour;
- they are working around 20 hours per week;
- their jobs are non-unionised;
- they are poorly treated by their employer;
- their work is having a detrimental impact on their studies;
- there are health and safety problems at work;
- they suffer poor health due to their job, but leaving is not an option.

NUS and TUC research indicates that students are not 'anti-trade union'; rather, they do not understand the support a trade union can offer. Furthermore, students do not understand the difference between the dozens of trade unions that exist. A natural progression would be if the NUS and the TUC provided a joint card, which could offer students a gateway to trade unionism – trade unions would gain members and students would gain a voice in the workplace, where currently they have none.

Expansion: in Defence of Luton

Damian Green MP, when Conservative higher education spokesman, described suggestions of a reverse away from expansion as 'entirely facile'. The expansion vs elitism debate is a nonstarter. Expansion is welcome. Employers want more graduates, all the political parties want more graduates, and students are increasingly graduating as IT-friendly people with good transferable skills. These are the skills employers want.

If a student studying media studies at, say, Luton, gets a degree, goes on to have a career enhanced by their period of study, where is the harm – or the bad investment – in that? On a more concrete level, why is it better for a student to read seventeenth century French texts at King's College in London for two years, before being forced to go to Paris for a year with no support from their institution when a student at the Wolverhampton University studies French culture, history, literature, politics *and* language before being offered institutional support and EU funding to live in, say, Toulouse?

Most distressing in the debate on expansion is the 'ladder up' mentality of people who have benefited from higher education. Expansion has led to many people gaining opportunities their parents could never have dreamed of. How do we respond as a society? Sadly, we are too happy to leave unchallenged the proposition that exams are easier, students are more stupid and standards are slipping. This assertion, never more tangible than after August's publication of A level results, is insulting to students, teachers and everyone in education. Quality and access can and do go hand in hand. The fact that our concept of quality no longer revolves around caps, gowns and Latin is a cause for celebration.

Funding the Future

The government sees higher and particularly further education as vital in developing a highly skilled workforce. Fifty per cent of people are to undertake higher education, and lifelong learning is set to become a reality. The implications for the funding of all stakeholders in tertiary education, including student funding, are immense. This increase in numbers is likely to take place largely among part-time students.

How should students and their representatives adapt to these revolutionary changes? For students to yearn for the elitism of the 1960s and conclude that all students should receive a grant is not helpful. The sums simply do not add up. Pie-in-the-sky politics that fail to address the economic reality of expansion present an open goal to elitists ('charge more') and conservatives ('admit less').

As learning patterns change students will increasingly have to be treated like others in society. When students fall below the poverty line, they should receive benefits. If students work, they should receive a national minimum wage and representation from a trade union. Where a student is socially excluded, they should receive a bursary, or an education maintenance allowance, as proposed by the government's social exclusion unit. Students with childcare responsibilities should receive a childcare allowance, to enable them to fulfil their potential. A new age of learning cannot be funded by the methods of the past. Given the post-Cubie agenda in Scotland and the reintroduction of a bursary for English and Welsh students from the lowest socioeconomic groups, this is an argument that progressives are winning. Students and their representatives must embrace change and move on.

The key political questions are 'what contribution should students make?' and 'how should they make it?' To state glibly that everyone should get a 1979-level grant and no one should pay fees is economically incoherent. It is clear to us that such funds as are available should be targeted on those who need it most. We believe, as did Cubie and Dearing, that it is also necessary and fair that full-time students make a contribution to their higher education upon graduation.

The make up of this contribution is key. There are two key developments in the debate on post-fees, education funding. Many in education believe that the government's post-Dearing settlement, arrived at in August 1997, looks increasingly like a stopgap measure. 'Dearing II', due to be commissioned in 2001, will need to move the debate on.

Cubie vs Campbell

Two ideas prevail at the start of the new century. While changes in learning patterns may eventually move us further away from 'one size fits all' funding systems, the two proposals offer solutions to the various challenges faced by higher education at the start of the new century – under-funding across the sector, the drive towards quality, student hardship.

One solution proposed by some vice-chancellors and academics (led by the vice-chancellor of Nottingham University, Sir Colin Campbell), would see tuition fees raised in certain institutions by up to £10,000 per year. Concerns about widening access would be addressed through a bursary scheme. The advantage is clear on a financial level: institutions will be able to raise significant funds to compete with US institutions. However, this overlooks the social mission of universities. We do not believe that top-up fees can be part of a system of higher education where equality and widening access are the stated priorities. The very notion of high fees for the many and a bursary scheme for the brilliant, poor few must clash with the principle of equality of opportunity. Put simply, under top-up fees, if you are rich you have a great chance of attending an elite institution, if you are poor you have little chance of getting in.

Top-up fees are not a new idea. It is instructive to look at their impact elsewhere in the world. Top-up fees were introduced in Australia in 1996, with fees escalating quickly from 23 per cent (similar to current non-Scottish, UK levels) to an average of 45 per cent. Fees can vary from an average of 20 per cent for an agriculture student to over 80 per cent for a law student. Indeed many Australian universities now charge full cost fees for certain courses. The impact has, unsurprisingly, been a drop in applications – particularly from mature students.

In New Zealand, the impact of top-up fees has been similar. For example, if we look at the most expensive course in the country, dentistry, there has been a dramatic reduction in students who are able to take up places in the course. In 1995, not long after the introduction of top-up fees, 163 students refused an offer of a place in the dentistry course. Most of these said it was because of cost reasons. None of the places offered to students from ethnic minorities – Maori and Pacific island students – were accepted. All of them told the interviewing committee that they could not afford to pay the fees. In 1996 the intake for the course was made up of 61 per cent of students from overseas, most of whom indicated they will return to their country of origin upon graduating.

Supporters of top-up fees will quickly point to America to refute claims that top-up fees will harm access. Yet the system in America relies on an alumni culture of contributing to a former institution. This generates ample funds for bursaries for students in greatest need. There are two problems with this system: first, there is no culture of contribution among UK graduates to their former institution; second, a system of high fees for the many, bursaries for the brilliant few ends the principle of equity in higher education.

The other solution to the great funding problem hails from Scotland. Andrew Cubie, former Head of the CBI in Scotland, was asked to set up an inquiry into student finance to get the Scottish Lib–Lab coalition government out of a tight spot: Scottish Labour supported tuition fees, Scottish Liberal Democrats opposed them. The Inquiry came up in 1999 with a series of measures that managed to end up-front tuition fees, reintroduce maintenance bursaries for the poorest in society, and maintain the graduate contribution. These three cornerstones of no up-front charges, cash for the most needy and contributions from those who benefit, are the key ingredients to a real compact on student funding.

Cubie's report offers students a series of measures, targeted on tackling hardship among students from the lowest socioeconomic groups:

* up to £4,100 in targeted maintenance bursaries;
* more maintenance support in total;
* an end to the current system of tuition fees;
* an end to the fourth year anomaly;
* an employment strategy for students who work;
* a 10-hour week;
* a £1,500 childcare allowance;
* proposals to provide better support for Scottish students with disabilities;
* significant new funds for FE students;
* moves towards a more level playing field between further and higher education.

Cubie offers genuine fairness. During the passage of the Teaching and Higher Education Act (1998), Rt Hon. David Blunkett MP, Secretary of State for Education and Employment, stated that the government's funding scheme for students would offer, 'money at the point when they need it, and that they repay it when they can afford to do so'. Cubie picked up those words and ran with them.

To implement Cubie would be costly – around £600 million for its full implementation throughout the UK. Cubie himself described this as, 'a high cost, but not a high price.' However, Cubie's graduate contribution system asks students to repay a total of £3,075 once they are earning £25,000 per year, on an income contingent basis. The Graduate Endowment Scheme proposed by Cubie offers the opportunity to go much further: why wait for students to be earning £25,000 per year? Why stop collecting once £3,075 has been paid off? Why not have people contribute, on a decreasing scale if necessary, throughout their working lives? Cash for higher education when you need it; a fair contribution to higher education when you can afford it. The sums raised for Treasury coffers would be enormous in the medium term; the DfEE's next fight would be to ensure that such funds are maintained in the tertiary education sector.

The idea of a graduate contribution scheme is not a new one. What is new is that Cubie has offered a mechanism for implementing such a scheme. This precedent is useful, and can be developed into a significant step towards bridging the funding gap. The main argument against such a contribution scheme is that it is too slow in bringing in money from graduates; that depends largely on the method of collection. The one significant gain for students is that the notion of debt is removed. The significant gain for the higher education sector is that such a system will eventually generate significant funds for the sector. If successful, it may be possible to extend the contribution scheme across the lifelong learning agenda.

The elitist vision of top-up fees is horribly unattractive to students. The question of where it would leave institutions in post-devolution Scotland is mind boggling. The compact offered by Cubie offers students cash when they need it and fair repayments when they can afford it. We have a golden opportunity to offer a radical and progressive solution to this thorny political problem. What price Andrew Cubie to chair 'Dearing II'?

13 The Rise of the Student-Worker

GLENN RIKOWSKI

Introduction

This chapter explores the rise of the student-worker within the context of British higher education (HE). The term 'student-worker' refers to those full-time HE students who have part-time or weekend jobs in term time. They may also work in vacations too. Finally, such full-time students may undertake casual work (i.e. work not done on a regular basis) or agency work (when they are called up intermittently by a job agency to work on an irregular basis). The key point is that the student-worker is a full-time student. These students may be following complex work patterns: combining term-time, with vacation and forms of casual/agency work.

These students are not to be confused with worker-students: people with full-time jobs, but studying part-time in HE. Nor confused with *flexiwork students*, those working part-time or on a casual basis whilst studying on part-time, distance or open learning HE provision.

In relation to a Compact for Higher Education (Dearing, 1997), the experience of student-workers in HE raises key questions. First, how does Dearing's (1997) call for more work experience for HE students tally with the fact that increasing numbers of students are getting experience of the world of work through their part-time and vacation jobs anyway? Should, and can, HE student-workers' labour be accredited in some way (in terms of the skills and other attributes developed whilst at work) – so that education and work meet up? What are the implications for the existence of student-workers in increasing numbers for the notion of a compact (*pace* Dearing) for HE? These questions are addressed later on in this chapter.

The first section of the chapter outlines the forces making for an increase in research and writing on student labour over the last 10 years. This is followed by a discussion of research that points to the rise of the student-worker (in the context of HE) over a slightly longer time period. Data pinpointing the volume of HE student-worker employment and the types of jobs they do is highlighted too.

The third section of the paper – 'Risk, Stress and Role Conflict' – explores some of the tensions created in the lives of student-workers. For those students who have to work to get through their HE courses, the levels of risk, stress and role conflict can be severe.

As Rosemary Lucas (1996) has noted, whilst research, writing and media interest in working students has burgeoned in recent years, the field remains under-theorised. Lucas herself (1997, 1996) has started to remedy this situation through locating student labour within a labour process perspective based on Harry Braverman's *Labor and Monopoly Capital* (1974). However, as I noted in a series of research papers written 20 years ago (whilst a research student), a focus on the labour process in theorising education-economy relations tends to lapse into forms of functionalism. This approach invariably rests upon attempting to understand in what ways schools, colleges and universities do, can and are able, to produce forms of labour designed to slot into labour process positions (occupations). Bowles and Gintis' (1976) *Schooling in Capitalist America* illustrates that this line of enquiry terminates in attempts to theorise education-economy relations in terms of some kind of 'correspondence' (between education/economy). There is no point addressing how and why this line of enquiry leads to a *functionalist* form of explanation regarding education-economy relations, and what is theoretically debilitating about this approach, in this chapter. The critique of functionalism in educational theory in general (and Marxist educational theory in particular) has been explored at length in Rikowski (1990, 1996 and 1997).

The alternative I developed was an exploration of *labour-power* (the capacity to labour), the commodity upon which the whole capitalist system rests (Rikowski, 1999), as the basis for understanding economy-education relations (Rikowski, 1990). This work was developed further in Rikowski (1999), and aspects of labour-power theory will also be presented in a forthcoming paper (Rikowski, 2000). Thus the fourth section of the chapter – 'Contradiction at Work' – offers another modest development of this work through theorising student labour as incorporating contradictions between the *social production of labour-power in capitalism* and two phases of labour-power *re*-production.

The final section of the chapter discusses aspects of the analysis in terms of 'A New Compact for Higher Education' (from Dearing, 1997). This last section argues that the notion of a 'compact' as set out in the Dearing's (1997) *Higher Education in the Learning Society* requires modification. Higher education is an element in the social production of labour-power. Contradictions (experienced by students in their everyday lives) flowing from the clash between the social production of labour-power and forms of labour-power *re*-production are being *intensified* in, and by, contemporary British HE. Any form of 'HE compact' needs to recognise this.

Research and Writing on Student Labour

Research and writing on student labour within a British context burgeoned in the 1990s, and in the last five years in particular. A number of factors have contributed to this surge of interest in exploring the work patterns and experiences of full-time post-compulsory education students with part-time jobs in term time, Saturday/Sunday jobs and/or vacation employment.

First, by the mid-1990s, centres of expertise within academia on issues pertinent to student labour in Britain had started to form. The work of Rosemary Lucas and colleagues at Manchester Metropolitan University on working college and university students is the prime example (see Lucas and Lammont, 1998; Lucas, 1997; Lucas and Ralston, 1997; Lucas, 1996; Lucas and Ralston, 1996; Lucas and Ralston, 1995a, b, c). Work undertaken at the University of Central England's Centre for Research into Quality has also developed a research profile on student labour (see Moon and Bowes, 1998).

Secondly, the Trades Union Congress (TUC) has taken a keen interest in child and student employment, especially since the early 1990s, and some trade unions have researched and campaigned on these issues. The General Municipal and Boilermakers Union (GMB) in particular has carried out significant research (sometimes with the National Union of Students) into student labour (GMB, 1996 and 1995). In December 1998, the National Association of Teachers in Further and Higher Education (NATFHE), the national Union of Students (NUS) and *The Times Higher Education Supplement* held a day conference on 'Working Students'. NATFHE has also highlighted the issue in its newspaper, *The Lecturer* (e.g. Kirsch, 1998; Moon and Bowes, 1998). Finally, the NUS has also carried out research into working students with the GMB (Thomson, 1996). More recently, the NUS has published its *NUS Students at Work Survey – 1999* (NUS, 1999), in partnership with the Labour Research Department (LRD). The NUS is also currently undertaking research with the University of Warwick's Centre for Educational Development, Appraisal and Research (CEDAR) on student lifestyles. This research has generated data showing that 'financial survival is at the very forefront of student concerns' (Parker, 2000, p. 3). This research by trade unions and the NUS has kept the issue of working students in the public eye.

Thirdly, the issue of student debt and hardship has generated significant research. The decision by the New Labour government to introduce student fees and to abolish student grants – in part a result of the Dearing Report's (1997) recommendations on student finance – has boosted research on student finance and debt. However, research on the role that student employment can play in minimising student debt was well underway before the Dearing Report and New Labour's HE fees/grants abolition strategy. There was significant expansion of student numbers in the late-1980s and early 1990s (Ainley, 1999). This, together with the progressive devaluation of the student grant under Conservative administrations of that time (and the enhancement of student loans as the favoured form of student finance for HE study), generated significant research and writing outputs on these issues – (e.g. Gokulsing and DaCosta, 1998; Gold, 1998; Wilson, 1998; Thomson, 1998; Wagner, 1998; Eaglesham, 1997; McCarthy and Humphrey, 1995; Woods, 1995; Sorenson and Winn, 1993; Farrell and Tapper, 1992; Ghosh and Mallier, 1992; McGuire, 1991; Woodhall, 1989; Ball, 1988 – as a micro-fragment of the literature on student debt and finance). New Labour's student fees/grants abolition policy has generated a huge amount of mainstream, educational and Left press comment (e.g. Carvel, 1997; O'Connor, 1997; Shoesmith, 1997; The Daily Telegraph, 1997; Tysome, 1997; *Socialist Worker*, 1999, 2000 – the peak of a huge mountain of press comment and analysis).

The following section focuses on the research underpinning the 'rise of the student-worker' in Britain. It takes a longer historical view of the phenomenon.

The Rise of the Student-Worker

Although there has been less research into working full-time HE students than on working schoolchildren (Rikowski and Neary, 1997; Rikowski, 1993), the actual data available for the former is of better quality. Researchers have used official statistics – principally the Labour Force Survey (LFS), the 1991 Census data and the Family Expenditure Survey (FES) – to good effect for exploring employment patterns amongst post-compulsory education student-workers. However, as with the research on working schoolchildren, sixth-form college and further education (FE) students, research on working HE students has tended to incorporate different definitions of 'work' (sometimes in/excluding vacation jobs, mostly excluding – but not always – casual and intermittent forms of labour). Furthermore, different studies use a range of age-groupings. Finally, some studies amalgamate data for FE and HE students, focusing on the *age* of students rather than the sector they are studying in.

Despite these problems, all the studies undertaken show a marked upward trend for employment amongst full-time HE students. These studies indicate *the rise of the student-worker* in Britain. Micklewright, Rajah and Smith's (1994) work with pooled data from the FES over the period 1961–91 shows that: during 1968–71 around 40 per cent of 16–18 year olds in full-time education 'had some sort of income from employment' (p. 73). For the period 1988–91, the equivalent finding was 59 per cent (ibid.). Furthermore, 15 per cent of 16–18 year olds who worked whilst in full-time education contributed 'at least one tenth of the total income in the households in which they lived' (ibid.). Micklewright, Rajah and Smith conclude that: 'Our data show that their numbers have been rising over the last 20 years, despite the overall poor showing of the youth labour market during this period' (1994, p. 84). Thus, although the traditional youth labour market, where young people leave school and then enter work, had declined drastically during the period under survey, these researchers had found that, to some extent, it had been *replaced*, *recomposed* and redefined as a *student* labour market. Of course, whilst the time-span of the data is impressive, for our purposes, it fails to distinguish adequately between full-time FE and HE students. Some of the 18 year olds would be HE students, others FE. The failure to tease out the data by FE/HE sector is regrettable.

Recent work by Hatchett (a researcher at Income Data Services), using LFS data, shows an almost steady rise (with a small downturn during the recession of the early 1990s) in the numbers of full-time students aged 16–24 in employment (Hatchett, 1998). Again, some of these would be FE students, but these data show the upward rise of the HE student-worker with greater solidity than Micklewright, Rajah and Smith's (1994) data. Further work by Hatchett (1999), again based on LFS data, notes that: 'The number of full-time students who are working part-time in their college terms has been steadily increasing over the past decade or more' (1999, p. 10).

Hatchett argues that with the introduction of student fees 'we can anticipate an even larger number of students will be working' (ibid.). He notes that the expansion of shopping hours at weekends and in the evenings calls for a pool of flexible labour on relatively low rates of pay to work at times when individuals in other categories of labour might be unwilling to work. Hatchett concludes that the work of students is: *'no longer casual but has become structural'* (ibid., my emphasis). Well-known companies seek student-workers. Student labour has increased to the extent that it is now a significant structural element within the overall British labour market.

Hatchett notes that in 1984, 319,000 16–24 year olds in full-time education in Britain had a part-time job. By early 1998, this had risen to 893,000 (on LFS data). Hatchett produced a graph that shows how the rise of the student-worker has been particularly rapid since 1995 (ibid.). He notes that the main areas of work are in retail, wholesale and garage work, then hotels and restaurants, and then in 'other community, social and personal services'. Many of these enterprises are in areas where trade unions are either nonexistent or have been historically weak. Hatchett goes on to give some fascinating data (ibid., pp. 10–11):

- Sainsbury's employed 30,000 full-time students in 1999 (mainly to cover peak periods and weekends) – when in 1989 they employed only 6,000 students;
- Tesco employs 16,000 full-time students (just over 10 per cent of its total workforce);
- KwikSave employs a total of 20,500 workers: 8,330 of these are students;
- Pizza Hut (60 per cent), KwikSave (40 per cent) and Waitrose (35 per cent) have particularly high proportions of workers who are also full-time students, 16-24 years of age.

Hatchett pointed to variations in status and pay for student-workers. Sainsbury's and Tesco give students (and all part-time staff) *pro rata* terms and conditions, as do Asda, Safeway and some others (ibid., p. 11). On the other hand, student-workers at Waitrose do not take on the 'partner' status enjoyed by other mainstream worker categories, and hence forgo 'partnership bonuses'. For some companies, student-workers miss out on pension rights, company sick pay and profit-share schemes.

Lucas and Lammont (1997) point towards a Central Statistical Office study (CSO, 1995) that indicates that the participation rate in employment for 16–25 year old full-time students more than doubled over the 1985–95 period, to reach 19 per cent by the end date (p. 2). Participation in employment was highest amongst 16–17 year olds, at 58 per cent (ibid.). In another article, Lucas and Lammont (1998) quote LFS data that shows that 'between Spring 1984 and Spring 1996 the proportion of students under age 25 in full-time education *and* employment rose from 23 per cent to 37 per cent' (p. 41, their emphasis).

Recent work undertaken by the Government Statistical Service (GSS, 1997) also indicates an increase in the number of full-time 16–18 year old students in employment in England. In 1990, 19 per cent of such students were in employment according to the GSS. By 1996, the equivalent figure had reached 26 per cent (GSS, 1997:2).

What all these studies show – though they work with different age groupings, different time-spans and different definitions of 'work' – is that there has been an upward trend in the numbers of full-time FE/HE students employed. This has taken place within a radical recomposition of the youth labour market over the last twenty-five years. For HE students in contemporary Britain, participation in some form of paid labour whilst studying is becoming the norm. Student-workers flit in and out of the labour market; working less when exam pressures are on, and more when there is time to do steady work (vacations), thus cutting reliance on student loans and attempting to forestall horrific debt levels. On this last point, the NUS (NUS, 1999) has indicated that for full-time undergraduates, 17.6 per cent of students surveyed in a National Student Hardship Survey (of 1998) estimated their debt would be over £9,000 by the end of their course (p. 3). This same survey indicated that:

> In the workplace, students are poorly represented and many are working for low wages. The hours of work needed to sustain them financially is eating into student time, and increasing students' feelings of stress and tiredness (ibid.).

Even before New Labour's fees/grants abolition policy, John Monks, General Secretary of the TUC, had pointed towards 'a huge underclass of casualised student labour' in contemporary Britain (Labour Research, 1996, p. 14). The increasing 'Americanisation' of student life (Rikowski, 1993) where students 'work their way through college' appears to be taking an ever stronger grip on British HE student social existence. The incentive to find work during term-time for an increasing number of students facing poverty in the last few years, has been exacerbated by New Labour's strategy for HE student 'self-investment' (Marginson, 1997) in the development of their own labour-power (NUS, 1999). In a situation where the majority of young people either stay on at school or go into sixth-form college or FE college after compulsory schooling, and where just over a third of the cohort enter HE, this indicates a fundamental *recomposition* of the British youth labour market (Ainley, 1999). For Lucas and Lammont (1998, p. 43), 'students have become the privileged young because they have an extra slice of the cake of education *and* work.' These trends have established the rise of the student-worker, though whether they are as 'privileged' as Lucas and Lammont make out is open to some doubt – as the next section makes clear.

Risk, Stress and Role Conflict

The rise of the student-worker within the context of British HE has been attended by disturbing examples of students working in risky and unhealthy conditions. Furthermore, the 'poverty of student life' charted by research (e.g. NUS, 1999) has meant that some aspects of student poverty have *deepened*. Student life is becoming riskier. This is particularly so when we turn to some of the forms of 'employment' taken up by cashed-starved students.

There has been little systematic research into the riskier aspects of casual, semi-legal and illegal forms of HE student labour. Nevertheless, press reports map the territory. Some forms of student labour are mildly embarrassing: such as being a sperm donor (see Ryle, 1999). Others are more risky. Browne (1993) describes how students have increasingly become involved in the sex industry. She notes that the introduction of student loans in 1990 and the collapse of some forms of student employment in the early 1990s, meant that some turned to alternative areas of employment in order to make ends meet. Stripping, prostitution or marrying someone so that they can gain a British passport and charging a fee – are desperate forms of labour. Harrison (1993) describes how 'Vicky' – a philosophy student – has embraced the philosophical principle of 'I am poor, therefore I strip'. A more recent study sponsored by Barclays Bank found a disturbing number of students engaged in prostitution in order to combat the spectre of debt (Barrett, 1997). Barrett urges that 'Sir Ron Dearing should take note' (in his then-forthcoming report), and he points towards the personal safety and health risks being run by these students.

Drug dealing is another area that students have taken to pay their way through HE and fend of the debt syndrome. This illegal labour can be lucrative and develop into a way of life, with £1,000 a month not impossible (Baty, 1998). As Goddard (1996) shows, it was the advent of student loans in 1990 that gave a boost to this risky business. As 'Brian', a student dealer, explained: if he had a 'normal job' then he would have had less time for study (ibid.)

As well as risk, student poverty (or the shadow of debt) can lead to stress. The *Socialist Worker* (1997) reported on a Scottish Low Pay Unit report that showed how, if students did not succumb to the direct effects of poverty, that in some cases it was the stress (sometimes leading to depression) that caused them to give up their studies. Lago (2000) notes the rise in HE student drop-out, and also research that indicates increasing numbers of students turning to overloaded student counselling services now that the average HE student debt level has reached £5,000. Humphrey and McCarthy's (1998) large-scale survey on student stress found those university students experiencing above-average stress levels. They conclude that the old stereotype of students engaging in enjoyable, intellectual, sporting and other activities in a carefree manner has been put to rest (ibid., p. 238),

However, if students take on jobs in term-time, and also in vacations, then this can bring its own form of stress in terms of *role conflict*. The key conflict as student-worker is between being a 'student' and being a 'worker' – where role expectations may have to be managed, but never finally resolved (until graduation – but even then the loan debt lingers). The main danger is that working starts to affect academic performance. A number of studies and press reports (e.g. Shoesmith, 1997; Hugill, 1996; Richards, 1995) provide some evidence that student-workers risk lowering HE course grades and exam scores, if they have to work to survive as students. Research carried out at the University of Central England's Centre for Research into Quality (CRQ) found that students who had part-time jobs were more likely to think that financial problems were affecting their studies (Richards, 1995). Gold (1998) has indicated that up to 100,000 students are ignoring university guidelines on not working more than 15 hours per week in term-time. Tysome (1999) points to other activities suffering – such as student volunteer and charity work – as students spend more time in term-time jobs.

The role conflict caused by the rise of the student-worker can be severe. It is, however, an aspect of deeper structural contradictions, contradictions that have been intensified by New Labour's fees/grants abolition policy.

Contradictions at Work

Labour-power (the capacity to labour) is the foundation of capitalist society. It is a social force (Rikowski, 1999) that is transformed into labour within the labour process through acts of will and self-organisation on the part of individual labourers and labour collectivities. This creates commodities (which may be 'hard' commodities like bricks, or immaterial commodities like financial transactions) that incorporate *value* and eventually *surplus-value* – value over-and-above that represented by the labourer's wage. In turn, value is the source of profit, state, money and all the other social forms of *capital*. Value is the substance of the social universe of capital, but labour-power and labour generate and regenerate this social substance.

Higher education is an element within the *social production of labour-power*; the production of this strange living commodity. The drive to make students increasingly pay for the costs of the social production of their labour-power, through New Labour's fees/grants abolition policy and student loans, intensifies the contradiction between this social process and the social *re-production* of labour-power. This latter refers to the labour that enters into an initial phase of 'reproduction of the labourer' on a daily, weekly basis. This is the value necessary for the labourer's survival expressed in money-form as the wage. Traditionally, for British students, this money has mostly come from state revenue plus some parental contribution, and then some additional top-up by students working in vacations. In the last 10–15 years, but especially since the introduction of HE student loans and then abolition of grants and institution of fees post-New Labour, students have been forced to enter the labour market (in its legal or illegal forms) in increasing numbers to ensure their own social *re*production.

There is a second phase of social reproduction. This involves value that is expressed as an element of the wage that subsidises bringing up the next generation. Traditionally, the parental contribution to student grants can be viewed as being an aspect of this (whilst simultaneously subsidising the *social production* of labour-power). However, for increasing numbers of students, the advent of fees/grants abolition has led them to stay at home in order to lower the costs of the first phase of their own social *re*production. Parents are picking up the tab, directly (food and other reproduction costs) and indirectly (heating, lighting costs etc.) (Hodges, 1996).

There are, then, structural contradictions between the social production of labour-power and both phases of its social *re*production. These contradictions have been intensified in recent years. Students *live through* these contradictions in their daily existence. They *feel* their intensity. These contradictions pose a severe challenge to any future compact for higher education.

Regarding the practical questions raised in the Introduction to this chapter, the answers, given the analysis in this section in particular, must be necessarily cautious. On the question of how Dearing's call for more work experience for HE students, it would seem that on the data and analysis provided in previous sections, that such work experience was superfluous. Students seem to be getting plenty experience of 'the world of work' anyway. As Rikowski's (1993) study of working full-time FE students showed, many are getting first hand experience of working before they arrive in HE. Furthermore, many also work as schoolchildren (Rikowski and Neary, 1997). What might be useful, however, is targeted work experience that takes the HE student into types of enterprise (by size, product range and so on) that they have not previously encountered – to *expand* their experience. Secondly, work experience could attain an *educational* focus if it offered possibilities for the *critical* analysis of work, organisations and practice (e.g. marketing strategy, equal opportunities policies, environmental impact and so on) as part of the student's course, which could be accredited. But there is no point advocating more work experience in general if students are already getting a taste of *real* work. Rikowski's (1992) study of apprentice recruitment indicated that recruiters gave more importance to 'real' (paid) work than they did work experience schemes in the recruitment process. It may well be the same for graduate recruitment (though research on this issue is required).

On the question of accreditation of student's paid work in term time, it would seem that this may well intensify the tension between social production of labour power (education) and its social reproduction (first phase: work for own reproduction through the wage). However, several questions remain. First, would students find the tensions created by accrediting their paid work too great? Would they find it a useful exercise, say in terms of their own CVs, personal development or as aid to employment after graduation? Finally, would employers take the accreditation of the skills, development of personal and social attributes and qualities as significant within the context of recruitment professional and degree-level jobs after students have graduated? These are questions that require further research and investigation. A compact for HE (*if* it were to attain an organisational form) could be a vehicle for addressing the issues and sponsoring pertinent research.

Student-Workers and A New Compact for Higher Education

A compact for higher education, as outlined in Dearing (1997), attempts to reconcile the diverse interests involved in HE. The costs and benefits of HE for society, students/graduates, institutions, HE staff employers and parents/families are summarised in Table 18.1 (Dearing, 1997, p. 283). For Dearing, the summation of these various interests, on the basis of perceived costs/benefits, is the foundation for a new compact for higher education.

Inevitably, whatever organisational form a future HE compact assumes, the phenomenon of the student-worker will pose a significant reference point. The compact will need to address the issues of risk, stress and role conflict generated by the social existence of the HE student-labourer. It will also need to address the deeper structural contradictions inhering within labour-power re/production in contemporary society. These contradictions are likely to intensify.

There is a need for a National HE Student-Workers' Forum (NHESWF) as part of the Compact's institutional life. Representatives from the student body (NUS), employers, HE institutions and parents/families need to engage in dialogue and start to address the issues discussed in the previous three sections of this chapter. A useful starting point for this dialogic enterprise might be the National Union of Students' *Students at Work Survey – 1999* (NUS, 1999) – which provides data on the key issues.

It is up to all of those within the Compact to ensure that contemporary student-workers, and the student-workers of the future, have adequate time and resources to successfully undertake the *study* element in the dual mode of their social existence. Without vision and organisation provided by a Compact, incorporating a constituent NHESWF, risk, stress and role conflict will increasingly haunt student life.

References

Ainley, P. (1999), *Learning Policy: Towards the certified society*, London: Macmillan.

Ball, R. (1988), 'Student Vacation Workers and the Labour Market', *Youth and Policy*, No. 23, pp. 30–5.

Barrett, D. (1997), 'Students on the Game', *The Times Higher Education Supplement*, 18 July, p. 14.

Baty, P. (1998), 'A Degree in Dealing', *The Times Higher Education Supplement*, 9 January, p. 1.

Browne, S. (1993), 'Slump and Grind', *Time Out*, 24–31 March, p. 14.

Bowles, S. and Gintis, H. (1976), *Schooling in Capitalist America: Educational reform and the contradictions of economic life*, London: Routledge & Kegan Paul.

Braverman, H. (1974), *Labor and Monopoly Capital*, New York: Monthly Review Press.

Budge, D. (1998), 'Public Pain, student Gain?', *Times Educational Supplement*, 22 May, p. 23.

Carvel, J. (1997), 'Study Now, Pay Later Revolution', *The Guardian*, 24 July, p. 1.

CSO (1995), 'Labour Market Structure and Educational Status of Young People', *Labour Market Trends*, s.83, December, London: Central Statistical Office.

Eaglesham, J. (1997), 'Third of Students "live with permanent debts"', *Financial Times*, 18 July, p. 5.

Farrell, S. and Tapper, E. (1992), 'Student Loans: The failure to consolidate an emerging political consensus', *Higher Education Quarterly*, Vol. 46, No. 3, pp. 269–85.

GMB (1995), *Part-time Work Amongst School Pupils and College Students under age 19*, an investigation carried out by the Labour Research Department for the GMB, August 1995, London: General and Municipal Boilermakers Union.

GMB (1996), *Students at Work: A report on the economic conditions of students in employment*, an investigation by the Labour Research Department for the GMB and the NUS, London: General and Municipal Boilermakers Union.

Ghosh, D. and Mallier, T. (1992), 'Student Finance: The contribution of the long vacation', *Higher Education Review*, Vol. 25, No. 1, pp. 45–56.

Goddard, C. (1996), 'Student by Day, Dealer by Night', *The Independent (Section Two)*, 12 September, p. 11.

Gokulsing, M. and DaCosta, C. (1998), 'The Twilight of Certitudes: Changing discourses and practices in English university education', *The Social Science Teacher*, Vol. 27, No. 3, pp. 7–10.

Gold, K. (1998), '15-hour Guide Flouted', *The Times Higher Education Supplement (Your Students Extra)*, 4 December, p. 1.

GSS (1997), 'Education and Labour Market Status of Young people Aged 16–18 in England, 1990–1996', prepared by the Government Statistical Service for the *DfEE Statistical Bulletin*, Issue No.9/97, October, London: Department for Education and Employment.

Harrison, D. (1993), 'Reality of Student Life: I'm poor, therefore I strip', *The Observer*, 11 April, p. 6.

Hatchett, A. (1998), 'From Casual to Structural: Student employment and pay – why? where? when?', paper presented at the NATFHE, NUS and *Times Higher Education Supplement* Conference on *Student Employment*, 8 December 1998, Britannia Street Conference Centre, London.

Hatchett, A. (1999), 'Students in Employment: From casual to structural – students working through the college term', *IDS Report* No. 776, January, pp. 10–11.

Hodges, L. (1996), 'Comforts Keep Students at Home', *The Independent (UCAS Listings)*, 21 August, p. 1.

Humphrey, R. and McCarthy, P. (1998), 'Stress and the Contemporary Student', *Higher Education Quarterly*, Vol. 52 No. 2, pp. 221–41.

Hugill, B. (1996), 'Hard-up Students Skip Class to Work in Sweatshops', *The Observer*, 24 March, p. 3.

Kirsch, B. (1998), 'Earning, Learning, Spending, Fending', *The Lecturer*, December, pp. 12–13.

Labour Research (1996), 'Education Meets Exploitation', *Labour Research*, July, pp. 13–14.

Lago, C. (2000), 'Higher Degrees of Disturbance', *The Times Higher Education Supplement*, 3 March, p. 40.

Lucas, R. (1996), 'Youth, Gender and Part-time Employment: Implications in the labour process', paper presented at the *Fourteenth Annual International Labour Process Conference*, Aston University, 27–29 March.

Lucas, R. (1997), 'Youth, Gender and Part-time Work – students in the labour process', *Work, Employment & Society*, Vol. 11, No. 4, pp. 595–614.

Lucas, R. and Lammont, N. (1997), 'Combining Work and Study: An empirical study of full-time students in school, college and university', paper presented at the ILM Conference, *Understanding the School-to-Work Transition*, 16-17 June, University of Aberdeen.

Lucas, R. and Lammont, N. (1998), 'Combining Work and Study: An empirical study of full-time students in school, college and university', *Journal of Education and Work*, Vol. 11, No. 1, pp. 41–56.

Lucas, R. and Ralston, L. (1995a), 'Part-time Student Labour in the Hospitality Industry: Strategic choices or pragmatic response?', paper presented to the Hospitality Industries *Strategies for the Future* conference on the Internet, MCB Press, September/October.

Lucas, R. and Ralston, L. (1995b), 'Part-time Employment: Hospitality undergraduates and sixth form students', paper presented to the 4th CHME Conference, Hotel School, City College, Norwich, April.

Lucas, R. and Ralston, L. (1995c), 'Part-time Youth Employment in the Hospitality Industry and Elsewhere: Pilot study findings in Greater Manchester,' paper presented to the Human Resource Management in the Hospitality Industry conference, London, February.

Lucas, R. and Ralston, L. (1996), 'Part-time Student Labour in the Hospitality Industry: Strategic choice or pragmatic response?', *International Journal of Contemporary Hospitality Management*, Vol. 8, No. 2, pp. 21–4.

Lucas, R. and Ralston, L. (1997), 'Youth, Gender and Part-time Employment: A preliminary appraisal of student employment', *Employee Relations*, Vol. 19, No. 1, pp. 51–66.

McCarthy, P. and Humphrey, R. (1995), 'Debt: The reality of student life', *Higher Education Quarterly*, Vol. 49, No. 1, pp. 78–86.

McGuire, P. (1991), 'The Cost of Living for Students: A case study of Leeds Polytechnic', *Higher Education Review*, Vol. 24, No. 1, pp. 35–49.

Marginson, S. (1997), 'Investment in the Self: The government of student financing in Australia', *Studies in Higher Education*, Vol. 22, No. 2, pp. 119–31.

Micklewright, J., Rajah, N. and Smith, S. (1994), 'Labouring and Learning: Part-time work and full-time education', *National Institute Economic Review*, May, pp. 73–85.

Moon, S. and Bowes, L. (1998), 'Benefits and Pitfalls', *The Lecturer*, December, p. 12.

National Committee of Inquiry into Higher Education (Dearing Report) (1997), *Higher Education in the Learning Society*, London: HMSO.

NUS (1999), *NUS Students at Work Survey – 1999*, London: National Union of Students.

O'Connor, M. (1997), 'The British Degree Goes on Sale', *The Independent (Education+)*, 14 August, pp. 2–3.

Parker, A. (2000), 'Student Lives and Lifestyles', *CEDAR Newsletter*, No. 11, January, pp. 2–3.

Richards, H. (1995), 'Student Money Problems Affect Performance', *The Times Higher Education Supplement*, 2 June, p. 5.

Rikowski, G. (1990), *The Recruitment Process and Labour Power*, unpublished paper, Division of Humanities and Modern Languages, Epping Forest College, Loughton, Essex.

Rikowski, G. (1992), 'Work Experience and Part-time Jobs in a Recruitment Context', *British Journal of Education and Work*, Vol. 5, No. 1, pp. 19–46.

Rikowski, G. (1993), *Working for Leisure? Part-time and Temporary Working Amongst A-level and BTEC National Students at Epping Forest College*, Epping Forest College, Loughton, Essex.

Rikowski, G. (1996), 'Left Alone: End time for Marxist educational theory?', *British Journal of Sociology of Education*, Vol. 17, No. 4, pp. 415–51.

Rikowski, G. (1997), 'Scorched Earth: Prelude to rebuilding Marxist educational theory', *British Journal of Sociology of Education*, Vol. 18, No. 4, pp. 551–74.

Rikowski, G. (1999), 'Education, Capital and the Transhuman', in Hill, D., McLaren, P., Cole, M. and Rikowski, G. (eds), *Postmodernism in Educational Theory: Education and the Politics of Human Resistance*, London: Tufnell Press.

Rikowski, G. (2000), 'Why Employers Can't Ever Get What They Want. In fact, they can't even get what they need', paper presented at the School of PCET Seminar, University of Greenwich, Queen Anne's Palace, 30 Park Row, Greenwich, 27 March.

Rikowski, G. and Neary, M. (1997), 'Working Schoolchildren in Britain Today', *Capital & Class*, No. 63, pp. 25–35.

Ryle, S. (1999), 'Skint Students Scheme to Survive', *The Observer*, 29 September, p. 9.

Shoesmith, I. (1997), 'I Promise to Pay ...', *The Guardian (Higher Education)*, 16 September, p. vi.

Socialist Worker (1997), 'New Report on Student Poverty: Forced to work for slave labour pay', *Socialist Worker*, 18 October, p. 2.

Socialist Worker (1999), '20,000 Students on Fees Protest', *Socialist Worker*, 4 December, p. 15.

Socialist Worker (2000), 'Fees Fight Gains Pace', *Socialist Worker*, 5 February, p. 16.
Sorenson, L. and Winn, S. (1993), 'Student Loans: A case study', *Higher Education Review*, Vol. 25, No. 3, pp. 48–65.
The Daily Telegraph (1997), 'Earning and Learning' (editorial), *The Daily Telegraph*, 23 July, p. 17.
Thomson, A. (1998), 'College Student Hardship Revealed', *Times Educational Supplement*, 4 December 1998, p. 4.
Tysome, T. (1999), 'Decline in Student Volunteers', *The Times Higher Education Supplement*, 10 December, p. 4.
Tysome, T. (1997), 'Student Loans to be Means-tested', *The Times Higher Education Supplement*, 18 July, p. 1.
Wagner, L. (1998), 'Dearing is Dead – Blunkett is Born? The Future Funding of Higher Education', *Higher Education Quarterly*, Vol. 52, No. 1, pp. 64–76.
Wilson, T. (1998), 'Help the Workers', *The Times Higher Education Supplement*, 4 December, p. 20.
Woodhall, M. (1989), 'Loans for Learning: The loans versus grants debate in international perspective', *Higher Education Quarterly*, Vol. 43, No. 1, pp. 76–87.
Woods, R. (1995), 'Student Debt Explodes', *Workers' Liberty*, No. 24, September, p. 8.

14 Higher Education: Strategy and Perspectives. The contribution of the National Association of Teachers in Further and Higher Education (NATFHE) to a Compact

TOM WILSON

It is a boring truism that universities cannot function without their staff. More than any other organisation their success or failure depends on their employees' commitment. No amount of top down managerialism will ever be able to force staff to work at their best. Higher education institutions, almost by definition, rely on the creativity, enthusiasm and ability of their staff.

Yet it is amazing how often this truism appears to be forgotten in practice. Time and again NATFHE has to step in to sort out a mess caused by elementary management failure to consult, listen, negotiate – in short to work in partnership with staff. That partnership principle (between staff, students and management) lies at the heart of the notion of a compact. It is not always easy. A compact demands that staff, and their union NATFHE, behave professionally and responsibly. That culture can take time to develop. After years of autocratic management, if staff professionalism and commitment are ignored then it will hardly be surprising if sometimes they too begin to take a narrower view, seeking to defend just their department, their students or their own interests. The wonder is that happens so rarely.

Things are getting better. The advent of a Labour government in May 1997 put the concept of partnership centre stage. Better, more open, management is spreading in higher education (HE). Funding pressures have eased very slightly though remain acute. Adversarial industrial relations are slowly giving way, in most HE institutions, to a more partnership approach. The idea of a compact, which might well have been ridiculed in the early 1990s now makes a bit more sense. A more collegiate professional academic culture is slowly being allowed to emerge in the new HE institutions, (the HE colleges and ex-polytechnics) as staff begin to achieve recognition for their teaching excellence (particularly with non traditional students and innovative learning methods) and begin to have slightly more time and money for research and scholarship.

These changes are long overdue. It is another truism that the HE sector is being transformed and will continue to change rapidly but enduring change must involve the active commitment of staff. Similar transformations are taking place around the world as previously elite HE systems grow into mass systems with all the allied changes in funding, students, curriculum, organisation and therefore the nature of academic work. The most successful countries will be those which have managed to create a partnership culture.

Within the UK there are now developing variants from the English model in Scotland, Wales and Northern Ireland. Their systems may become more divergent but all are likely to continue to be dominated by the following key issues:

- funding and fees;
- quality – measurement, reward and enhancement;
- teaching – accreditation and support;
- research: selectivity and scholarship;
- staffing – work and workload, pay, conditions, discrimination;
- diversity, institutional autonomy, state or self-regulation;
- vocationalism – training versus wider education;

These are large, overlapping and complex questions. This short chapter briefly outlines NATFHE's approach to them, how NATFHE is arguing and campaigning for change, and NATFHE's contribution to a compact.

The Purpose of a University

All HE institutions serve a mix of different purposes: producing employees ('human capital'), developing critical and reflective citizens, developing individuals' full potential and searching disinterestedly for the truth are some of the commonly agreed aims. But there is a danger that human capital considerations are becoming dominant. The value of higher education cannot and should not be measured solely by its contribution to the economy.

NATFHE will argue strongly for expansion to continue (properly funded – see below) but for wider social and cultural purposes as well as for economic reasons. The current government has recognised the importance of opening up HE to those previously denied access – described as social inclusion – which is welcome and long overdue. However there is also a tendency to focus almost exclusively on meeting employer needs, for example in the 1999 Welsh Office Strategy Paper, which would inevitably result in a narrowing of the curriculum and loss of university independence. NATFHE will continue to argue and campaign strongly against too much emphasis on serving the needs of the economy which in any case often requires a broader view: most employers prefer critical, creative, reflective graduates. For that they know university independence is crucial.

The purpose of a university should not be to act as a bastion of privilege but as an engine of redistribution, offering opportunities to all, regardless of background. Of course universities should provide the training and education students seek but they must also remain islands of independent thought, teaching students to challenge received wisdom and think for themselves. Universities must argue for and embody the values of rationality, argument and evidence, however difficult for the state or employers. For those reasons universities must always remain independent, accountable for their public funding but upholding best standards of self-regulation.

Within that global view, the 'new' universities and HE colleges have a particular place and needs which NATFHE will champion. They now comprise well over half the number of UK HE institutions, teach over half UK HE students and employ over half UK HE lecturers. Yet they continue to be underfunded relative to the 'old' universities while their teaching and access mission is often seen as less important than excellence in research. NATFHE will fight to uphold the equal importance of teaching, the need for fairness in funding and an end to the unspoken snobbery which views the ex-polytechnics as 'second class'. That snobbery takes many forms, from those who offensively claim (without a shred of evidence) that expansion has caused a 'dumbing down'; those who argue that 'old' HE institutions need less regulation or quality auditing than the new, or that a broader (more expensive) education should be confined to the 'old' while the new concentrate just on narrow vocational courses. Of course the HE sector should be diverse, but very different institutions, with different purposes, should still have equal funding and equal status. The 'old' universities do not provide the best yardstick to measure the vastly different, modernised and expanding system of the new millennium!

Funding

The previous government created an internal market in HE and this has largely been continued by the current government. Funding therefore does not relate to the real cost of teaching any given subject but is simply based on previous costs plus a 1 or 2 per cent 'efficiency gain'. Higher education institutions are encouraged to compete for more places at lower cost with the inevitable driving down of working standards and threat to quality. Meanwhile the introduction of student fees and removal of grants has forced most students into substantial term-time paid work, reducing the quality of their academic learning experience.

NATFHE continues to believe that fees are wrong and will fight the growing threat of top-up and differentiated fees which would compound their deterrence and inequality effects. The 1999 Cubie Committee Report to the Scottish Parliament was a welcome opportunity to review the impact of and argue against, fees. NATFHE will fight for a similar enquiry in Wales. Cubie heard clear evidence that fees are a deterrent. That fees have now been abolished in Scotland (for Scottish full-time undergraduates) is a signpost to the rest of the UK. Cubie's proposed bursary system for the poorest, allied to a graduate tax but only above a higher income threshold, is plainly fairer. It is perhaps no accident that Scotland has always had both a strong commitment to HE (participation rate some 10 per cent higher than England) and a more partnership approach, involving all sections of the HE system and the community. Cubie was itself a Compact in practice with student and staff union representatives sitting on the committee alongside HE management representatives.

NATFHE will also campaign strongly for substantially increased government funding. The 1999 Bett report into HE pay and conditions identified £450m which should be seen as the absolute minimum for wholesale reform. That would add about 9 per cent to government HE funding – less than a third of the 30 per cent cut in funding per student over the past decade so hardly unrealistic. Funding channels should also be simplified and made more transparent. It is plainly wrong, for example, that Teacher Education is funded by the Teacher Training Agency, according to a different formula from Higher Education Funding Council for England (HEFCE) funding. There should be a single funding channel which would help ensure equality. Funding systems should also be made much fairer and more transparent. It is equally wrong that HEFCE's funding model results in some universities like Oxford or Imperial College receive some £12,000 per student while others, like Luton or Derby, receive only some £3,000. Subject cost differences can account for only a small part of that grossly inequitable discrepancy. All students pay the same fee and should receive broadly the same funding for comparable courses. Stakeholders will not support a compact which is unclear and unfair.

The current labour government does provide some opportunities. Ministers are much more open than their predecessors to Trade Union views, the limiting of the 'efficiency gain' (i.e. cut in real government funding per student) to only 1 per cent was at least a step in the right direction and the emphasis on continuing HE expansion and social inclusion is welcome. There is also growing recognition by the government and funding councils that teaching deserves greater attention, as compared to research, and that access courses may need greater funding than mainstream courses. So far, the government has also firmly rebuffed the attempts by some vice-chancellors to introduce top-up fees which would be highly divisive – the opposite of a partnership approach. The communication channels are open, NATFHE (nationally, regionally and locally) will use them to argue strongly for adequate funding. In particular the next 12 months will see an intensive campaign to argue for funding for Bett as the government draws up the next three-year HE spending plans to run from 2001/2002.

Pay, Conditions and Contracts

The Bett Report is far from perfect but it does set an agenda for wholesale and long overdue reform. NATFHE welcomes Bett's recognition that entry and senior level salaries need to be substantially raised but will argue for similar increases for those at the top of the existing senior lecturer grade. NATFHE is sceptical but prepared to negotiate a system of job evaluation provided that it was able to recognise the contribution of all staff (i.e. including Senior Lecturers) in moving to any new pay and grading structure and provided it established equal pay for work of equal value and thus overcame the widespread existing sex discrimination.

NATFHE is firmly opposed to performance pay, even at the relatively minimal level suggested by Bett. This important principle is based on professional not monetary arguments: for example the teamwork inherent in good practice, the difficulty of measuring and defining 'good performance' and the experience of performance pay elsewhere (e.g. the civil service) which is that it can often discriminate against e.g. women and ethnic minority staff. Performance pay can individualise rather than encourage the kind of collegiality which should underpin a successful compact.

Pay negotiating systems should be reformed along the lines Bett suggests. NATFHE agrees with Bett that a pay review body is not a realistic aim and that national collective bargaining for all staff is the way forward. The new single overarching National Joint Council and two sub-councils (for academic and non-academic staff) should all be set up together as quickly as possible. They will help to overcome outdated divisions between staff and encourage much more joint work, for example between academic and support staff.

Perhaps the most crucial issue is workloads. The national contract in the 'new' HE sector provides only limited protection against the grossly overloaded teaching and related administrative workloads and thus limited time for scholarship and research experienced by the majority of lecturers. Bett's recognition that the national contract must not be changed without negotiation and agreement is welcome. Change is certainly needed but the national contract should be reformed and updated, not watered down. It is itself a kind of national compact, balancing the competing pressures of localism and national consistency; funding and quality; managerialism and professional autonomy.

Bett's criticisms of universities' over-reliance on fixed term or part-time contracts are also welcome. Already, over half all 'new' lecturers work part-time and almost all research staff are fixed term. NATFHE commissioned research showed this casualisation inevitably threatens the quality of teaching and research. Of course short term funding is a problem, but other industries and economic sectors have far less assured funding yet still offer permanent jobs. Of course some teaching jobs are part-time to bring in staff with up to date working expertise outside higher education but that would only explain a fraction of the current part-time numbers. Fundamentally, casualisation is a product of short term, ad hoc university management. NATFHE welcomes Bett's recommendations aimed at strengthening the quality of management and extending good practice. Staff development is needed from top to bottom. NATFHE's part-time pack (launched early October 1999) will help branches recruit and organise part-time staff and improve their conditions and contracts. Nationally, NATFHE will fight to ensure the post-Bett negotiations include radical reforms aimed at reducing the extent of casualisation and improving the conditions of part-time and fixed term staff.

Teaching

NATFHE critically supports the Institute for Learning and Teaching (ILT). The accreditation of HE teachers is long overdue and the ILT will also provide support, access to research and new ideas, and a professional network. But NATFHE will continue to argue for the absolute minimum of bureaucracy and employer control. The ILT must be owned by and accountable to the profession.

The ILT should also provide an opportunity to argue for adequate resources. Time (and therefore funding) will be needed to prepare and update portfolios, develop new teaching methods and materials or review existing methods. Employers should recognise that time must be found and, with NATFHE, argue to government and funding councils for the necessary resources, without which the ILT risks becoming seen as yet another pointless administrative burden.

NATFHE will also continue to argue strongly that higher education level teaching must involve adequate time for scholarship – teaching, attending and contributing to conferences and seminars, discussing work with colleagues and so forth. This is distinct from time for HEFCE's Research Assessment Exercise (RAE) publications and distinct from pedagogical development. This self-managed scholarly activity time is in constant danger of being squeezed out by teaching and administrative demands. It is recognised in the higher education contract and NATFHE will fight to ensure it is funded and preserved.

There are some opportunities within the current climate to advance these policies. The £90m HEFCE fund to reward and encourage good teaching is welcome and should be expanded. More employers are recognising teaching expertise in promotions. The QAA's possible move to a 'lighter touch', relying on a description of teaching quality rather than a crude numerical rating is also welcome. It recognises diversity and prevents false numerical comparisons. The new Quality Assurance Agency approach should be extended to cover teacher education which should not be covered by a wholly separate body (Office For Standards in Education, OFSTED) with quite a different approach and criteria. Crude links between quality assessments and funding should also be abolished.

NATFHE will continue to work within the ILT and lobby government, funding councils, the Universities and Colleges Employers Association (UCEA), QAA and individual institutions. The post-Bett negotiating period will provide a major opportunity to improve the organisation of teaching, its funding and quality assurance.

Discrimination

Universities ought to exemplify tolerance, openness and multiculturalisation. At the very least the mix of staff should broadly represent the mix of students.

Instead they perpetuate staggering levels of sex and race discrimination with equally staggering complacency. No compact can survive while there is clear discrimination (even if mostly unintentional) against many stakeholders. Figures compiled for Bett showed women lecturers earned around £3,000 p.a. less than men, were over-represented in low paid jobs and under-represented in high paid jobs. Research (Modood, Fenton and Carter 1999, available from NATFHE) jointly commissioned by the Committee of Vice Chancellors and Principals (CVCP), NATFHE and other HE unions showed that very few ethnic minority staff were in senior grades and over half felt there were high levels of institutional discrimination.

The Commission on University Career Opportunity (CUCO) has been working for eight years but, so far, sadly, has changed little. It is true that the proportion of professors and vice-chancellors who are women has increased from some 3 per cent in 1990 to around 9 per cent in 2000 but it is still far too low and there has been little improvement elsewhere. Racial under-representation within university staff has been largely ignored, 'though some institutions have recognised the problem. NATFHE evidence of the £2,400 average pay gap between men and women academics helped persuade the Secretary of State for Education to instruct HEFCE, in November 1999, to ensure that every HE institution had an Equal Opportunities policy and was accountable for its implementation. NATFHE, with the other HE unions, discussed this with HEFCE and the UCEA throughout late 1999 and early 2000. The resultant HEFCE proposals to set up a new Equal Opportunities Directorate, massively strengthening CUCO while retaining the partnership or compact approach, are very welcome. NATFHE local branches will help ensure the new national impetus is reflected in similar local partnerships to push for long overdue action on Equal Opportunities.

NATFHE is determined to tackle discrimination. In the wake of the Stephen Lawrence murder enquiry report (which had many recommendations for the education system) NATFHE hosted a national further and higher education conference on race discrimination at the end of November 1999. NATFHE is also working closely with the Commission for Racial Equality and Trades Union Congress urging institutions to tackle racism and seeking more discrimination cases, lobbying CVCP and CUCO to issue clear national guidance, lobbying the funding councils to include proportions of ethnic staff within performance indicators and thoroughly reviewing NATFHE's own structure (see below).

On sex discrimination, NATFHE has taken many leading cases (e.g. Allonby) and is strongly encouraging members to take more equal value and other sex discrimination claims. The post-Bett negotiations will have to focus on the need for shorter scales, clear promotion criteria and more transparency. NATFHE's internal equal opportunities resources and organisation are also being reviewed and will be strengthened as soon as possible.

NATFHE Organisation

The new system for handling legal and other casework will improve service to members and allow greater monitoring and transparency. Support to branches through training programmes, delivered if necessary and desired, within the branch (or adjacent branches) will be increased and new guidance publications issued to branches on handling race discrimination issues, the new Employment Relations Act (ERA), disability as well as advice to part-time workers. The ERA, in particular, could offer major opportunities to extend recognition, representation and organisation, despite the attempts by some employers to interpret it in a minimalist way.

The NATFHE website (www.NATFHE.org.UK) will be further developed to become a first point of reference on all HE issues. Everything published in print format will also be available on the website, plus a great deal of other news, advice, general material and more detailed information on topics such as the progress of the post-Bett negotiations.

In addition, web-based discussion groups will be set up, some already exist in prototype form. These will help develop networks among, e.g. Black and ethnic minority members, part-time and fixed term staff, those with interests in issues such as disability or sexual orientation; and among certain professional groups such as teacher education, senior managers and professors.

The branch is the bedrock of NATFHE organisation and branch support is the priority for all regional offices. Branches will be encouraged to set membership targets well above the 50 per cent recognition threshold required by the ERA and, in particular, among part-time staff.

Regional organisation is also important and should be strengthened, or revived where HE Regional Committees have become poorly attended. Liaison with Association of University Teachers (AUT – the other major academic union for staff in the old universities) regional bodies (encouraged by NATFHE and AUT) should also be developed and joint regional liaison committees to support and develop the work of the national AUT/NATFHE Liaison Committee should be set up. Informal meetings will help exchange ideas and knowledge, underpin national bargaining solidarity and develop useful personal networks.

Equally important are good relations with UNISON (the biggest trade union for non academic staff) and other unions representing non-academic staff. NATFHE will continue to play its full part in the national meetings of all unions and continue to support the most low paid and poorly treated staff who have for too long, been seen as second class citizens.

There are many opportunities to develop branch and regional organisation which NATFHE will use: the improved recognition and representation rights in the Employment Relations Act; new rights for part-time staff arising from the Part-Time Working Directive; new rights deriving from the Working Time Directive; new negotiated rights which will implement the Bett recommendations and above all the potential for a new climate of genuine partnership (partly due to the new Labour government) in which institutional management know they must recognise, negotiate and reach agreement with NATFHE.

Summary

1   The UK HE system is changing fast and will continue to do so. But successful change involves the active support of staff and, their union, NATFHE, in a professional partnership. Enduring reforms cannot be imposed. NATFHE has a clear view of an expanded, improved and independent HE sector, together with a clear programme of action to improve the quality of lecturers' working lives and students learning experience.

2   A partnership approach, as the above has shown, is not an easy option. Yet it is essential. A successful compact in HE, whether national or local, must involve robust and honest acceptance of different stakeholders views, and the legitimacy of their views. That means dialogue, transparency, mutual respect and a shared commitment to the idea of inclusive higher education.

3   The idea of an HE compact is, right now, a tender plant. With care it will grow and flourish. Most of the conditions are certainly in place.

15 Higher Education in the Knowledge Age

RICHARD BROWN

As we move ever more inexorably into the knowledge age where international competitiveness will be determined by the application of knowledge, so the role of higher education assumes ever greater importance.

Universities are in this knowledge business. How effectively they develop, disseminate and apply knowledge and how far they inspire individuals in all walks of life to engage in lifelong learning will determine our international competitiveness. All organisations need individuals who can contribute ideas and play their part in constructively questioning whether things could be done better. They need individuals who can work in multidisciplinary and often cross-cultural teams to develop new products, processes and ways of tackling new problems. This applies to organisations in the private, public and not-for-profit sectors. Developing the powers of the mind, the power of analysis, articulation, communication and persuasion have always been central to higher education. We need more individuals to have these qualities, more critical and reflective doers that can help transform organisations. In short, in a compact for higher education we need more people to engage in higher education throughout their lives.

But in this compact, it is not just organisations that need what higher education has to offer. In a knowledge age more individuals will want to start and develop their own businesses, to be entrepreneurial and innovative. Higher education institutions should be able to play a central role in the development of a more enterprise driven culture of the type that characterises so much of the USA. While it will take a concerted effort to change the culture of risk aversion and inculcate a spirit of entrepreneurialism across society, higher education can play its part by offering the environment, the support services, the advice and the inspiration to encourage entrepreneurs to flourish. It can give more individuals exposure to the realities of running their own business, advice on how to prepare business plans, seek start-up finance, minimise risk, protect intellectual property and how to exit with minimum loss if things go wrong. Higher education should help take the fear out of being innovative and entrepreneurial.

Higher education is also central to the creation of a more just and caring society. Helping everyone to realise their potential is fundamental to social as well as economic progress. The two are dependent on each other. Gone are the days when an elite could lead and expect others to follow. A modern knowledge society and economy needs to tap the resources and release the potential of everyone. Higher education can raise the confidence of those that can all too easily be trapped in a culture of low expectations and under-achievement. It can reach out into the communities where they are located and be beacons of inspiration for everyone. It can impart in all students a sense of community and citizenship.

Given the shortening half-life of knowledge, higher education has an important role in inspiring individuals with the desire to go on learning throughout life. We have to get away from the notion that learning is something to be engaged in when young and then forgotten about. In a compact with every citizen, it should remain a fundamental purpose of higher education to offer learning that excites, that is not just focused on producing more employable graduates but offers art, the humanities and those subjects that have for centuries been available to learners of all ages. Society would be the poorer if individuals did not pursue knowledge for its inherent pleasure and fascination rather than utilitarian value.

Equally higher education needs to continue to value the vocational as a mainstream form of academic learning. The so-called creative industries of media, fashion, design and entertainment contribute more than most sectors of the economy and are growing twice as fast. They are worthy of academic study and debate. Vocational learning can also appeal and make learning available to those who may for whatever reason have missed out and perhaps been alienated by formal 'compulsory' learning. Higher education has a role in making learning accessible, relevant and attractive for everyone. New courses and new approaches will always be necessary. A mass higher education system cannot deliver the curriculum of an elite system.

Higher education is increasingly recognising the external forces that limit the life of so much knowledge and drive an ever-increasing pace of change. The need to think globally, the convergence of information and communication technologies and the expanding boundaries of knowledge require individuals to be able to transfer and apply learning in different and changing circumstances. These forces require us all to have high-level transferable attributes and skills. These are necessary for success not just in business but also in life. The ability to work in multi-cultural and disciplinary teams, to be able to communicate effectively, identify and address problems to which there may be no single or simple 'academic' answer, to have an appreciation of the key points from a mass of data and assess risks. These are some of the high-level skills which higher education can impart and develop but which are not always explicit in the curriculum.

A knowledge of the way organisations operate is also increasingly important. Work for The Council for Industry and Higher Education (CIHE) notably by Professor Lee Harvey has confirmed the view of employers that they now look to higher education not only to develop the powers of the mind, impart basic subject knowledge and skills and develop high level transformative skills, but also give students exposure to the way business operates. Companies do not have the luxury of training staff in the basics of business as perhaps they used to. That is even truer of small companies, the major graduate recruiters of the future if not of the present. They need individuals that have broad high-level skills and the expertise to respond flexibly to an uncertain future. They need to have had an experience of the workplace that has enabled them to get under the skin of an organisation. This is most likely to occur where they have been involved in project work. That work can also add value to companies since students on placements can develop business opportunities and solve business problems. So there is mutual benefit. Larger companies need to spread this message through their supply chains and encourage more smaller companies to appreciate the business benefits of taking a student on a placement.

CIHE's subsidiary, the government-funded National Centre for Work Experience (NCWE), has suggested the criteria that should govern best practice in work experience in a compact between academia, organisation and students.

Higher education has been very adept at responding to the challenges facing it. It has widened the courses available, widened access, generally maintained standards despite a rapidly reducing unit of resource and expanded its partnerships with the business and other communities. But the pace of change is accelerating and the increasing and sometimes divergent demands of students and businesses suggest that the higher education system will have to change still further and faster if it is to meet the expectations of the knowledge age.

There is a danger that a chapter trying to address the issue as to what business expects from a compact for higher education ends up with some impossible wish list; like a job advert that lists the attributes of some superhuman being. It is in reality impossible to expect a single answer because the nature of employment and the jobs that graduates perform are as diverse as the economy itself. To expect a single employer specification is naive and those who criticise employers for not providing one have not thought through the implications. Graduates might be nuclear physicists, nurses, charity or National Health Service (NHS) administrators or self-employed designers and workers in glass or metal. They might be school leavers, single parents with family and financial commitments, women returners or third age pensioners.

How can higher education hope to cater for such a diverse range of customers?

To define the issue is partly to suggest the answer. For students are indeed customers – and increasingly paying customers. They will want to know what they are going to get for their money and why they should enrol with one institution rather that another. They will want to know how one institution performs against another, the attributes that are likely to be developed and their chances of improved employment. They will want to be assured that certain threshold levels of learning can be guaranteed. They will want quality education and career guidance and advice so that more informed decision can be made. They will want to know how the learning will be delivered and whether it can be accessed easily from work, home, the local FE college or *learndirect* centre. They will want it in ways and at times that suit them not the academic or the institution.

The diversity of the customer base and its different needs and aspirations can only be met from an equally diverse and responsive system of higher education. A society with higher education participation levels for 18–30 year olds approaching 35 per cent (and a declared government intention to see this rise to 50 per cent by 2010) cannot operate like an elite system. Watered down versions of an approach that may have been satisfactory 20 years ago are entirely inappropriate today. Even the undiluted approach would be inappropriate if individuals are to be equipped with the life skills needed to face today's rapidly changing world.

Diversity of institutional mission is fundamental if the diverse needs of society, the economy and individuals are to be realised. Diversity remains one of the strengths of the UK higher education system. The specialist colleges are as valued by employers as the international brand names. But that diversity is under threat. The Research Assessment Exercise distorts the missions of institutions, reinforces a traditional research culture, the basis of promotion and esteem of so many academics and threatens to devalue the other forms of equally valid excellence that exist. The British have a habit of turning any diverse system into a hierarchy. Nowhere is this truer than in education. Quality regimes and government priorities also threaten to bring about a more homogenous system. If experimentation, risk and fun is taken out of higher education, how can it excite, inspire and help generate a more entrepreneurial and innovative society?

Others must help. The funding councils currently offer inadequate rewards for teaching excellence or for reaching out into the business and local community. The quality regime's preoccupation with thresholds has to be balanced by the light touch that is promised but not too apparent. There are few incentives to innovate and experiment. Even the Institute for Learning and Teaching is apparently showing little interest in how the system can adapt and develop the different modes of learning and teaching appropriate to different learning needs.

If there are indeed many forms of intelligence (as Howard Gardner (1993) and others have suggested) then maybe there are as many forms of learning style. Equally the maturer learner will bring a maturity and experiences very different to the school leaver's. To imagine that all can be 'taught' in the same way seems highly unlikely. Not everyone learns best from lectures. Some learners may indeed have as much to offer their peers as the 'teacher'. Indeed if today's lifelong learners need above all the ability to learn from experience, to find, sift, evaluate and present information, then their learning experiences need to reflect that. To use US terminology, the 'guide on the side' may be more significant than the 'sage on the stage'. This has fundamental and not entirely comfortable implications for academics. It also implies far greater involvement by businesspeople to support the development and delivery of learning.

The need to work in teams and across conventional disciplinary boundaries will also not come easily to people trained in the specialism of one discipline and in the paradigm of the researcher whose own publications are the basis for competitive career success and peer recognition. Group-based project work is increasingly needed to reflect the way organisations address problems. Student decisions on how to tackle problems, on data access and analysis and on team review should reflect business realities. Equally the projects will need to relate to the concerns of the business world, to become the raw material for learning where theory is derived from practice and not just the other way round. All this implies regular contact with businesspeople and a much more permeable world between what is learned in institutions and what is learned in the workplace, community or other arenas.

The integration of work based learning with institutional based learning (a feature of some North American institutions) remains less common this side of the pond while the accreditation of prior learning can still present theological problems for some. Yet in a world of lifelong learning where so much learning occurs through interaction with workmates and is in the important softer areas of interpersonal relations and interactions (see the work of Michael Eraut (1991 and 1999)) such learning is no less valuable. More innovation and experimentation should be encouraged and the current examples and lessons learned better disseminated. Perhaps the subject centres of excellence will perform this service.

We need to know much more about how different individuals learn, the appropriateness of different learning styles and approaches and how work-based learning can be better integrated with institutional based (but not necessarily delivered) learning. If small companies and more individuals are to be encouraged into higher education, we will also need to develop alternative funding regimes and clearer and easier routes of progression through learning pathways. Maybe credit based funding allied to more bite-sized learning will be needed to encourage those in smaller companies in particular to dip in and out of learning and gain credit as a result (rather than as at present both learner and university or college being branded as failures because a conventional three-year degree has not been completed).

In an age which places greater emphasis on innovation, entrepreneurship and the application of knowledge, more individuals will need the inspiration and support to start their own business. Unfortunately few institutions currently offer all their students the opportunity to acquire the knowledge, skills and experience needed to achieve this. The more vocational courses may offer this and there are some specific courses in entrepreneurship. But what about the engineer or chemist with a bright idea? Where can that person learn how to write a business plan, access venture capital or protect intellectual property rights (IPR)? What would be the case if the student were at MIT, Stanford or Berkeley? Could our higher education institutions do more to develop and facilitate a more innovative and entrepreneurial economy? Businesses also increasingly want 'intrepreneurs' (entrepreneurs within their organisations) and higher education will want to encourage that spirit of enterprise. If the curriculum can only slowly adapt to the changing needs in some areas, then how might institutions lay on optional seminars, workshops and other learning events including in the evenings and weekends when outside experts and advisers might offer their guidance to students, academics and those from the local community? HEIs could be centres of learning for the community and not just for their students as part of a mission to raise the knowledge and wealth creating performance of their communities.

At least one Vice-Chancellor has gone further and asked how far our institutions of learning are themselves learning institutions. How far are the discipline-based silos still dominant? How far do institutions learn from peer and private sector best practice and cooperate in its dissemination? How far do they really analyse their strengths, the nature of their competitive advantage and invest in those strengths? How far do they buy in the courses where they are not world class and join together with others that have similar missions to develop joint courses? Creating, marketing and delivering world-class curriculum material is expensive. Unless it can be shared across consortia the economies of scale will not be achieved. Private sector companies are adept at competing and cooperating at the same time (sometimes with the same players). Maybe to be truly world-class academic institutions will have to think as globally and as businesslike as their private sector peers.

UK business wants and needs a higher education system that is pre-eminent. It needs the highest quality from all institutions as they pursue through partnerships their own distinctive missions. So what contributions then can industry make in a compact with higher education?

In research the UK has strengths in depth and has a long and successful history of partnerships and international cooperation. With continued funding from the government and industry, a focus of resources on centres of international excellence and a continuation of the partnership approach, HE institutions can continue to underpin the knowledge economy. But more has to be done if the dissemination and application of that knowledge is to permeate the economy. Even more change is necessary if individuals are to have the attributes and experience necessary for a fast changing world.

Higher education will continue to respond and meet these challenges. But others must continue to play their part. The government must encourage the diversity needed and the experimentation that is part of that diversity. Its agents such as the funding and quality councils need to share and facilitate the delivery of that agenda. Neither can business stand idly by. If organisations want graduates with more employability skills that can better hit the ground running, then they need to engage more with institutions. They need to invest time and resources in the development of joint curricula that take real life current business problems into the syllabus. They need to develop jointly with academics both business case studies and simulations. They need to offer more quality work experience and persuade the smaller companies in their supply chains to offer that experience. Smaller companies will want to better appreciate what universities and colleges have to offer and the skills and knowledge available in today's modern graduates. Organisations of all types need to work with institutions on clarifying output measures, on an improved· and more coherent system of career guidance spanning lifelong learning, on the analysis of institutional strengths and how they might restructure to ensure their international excellence. Constant restructuring has been the life of many businesses and there is much experience that can be passed on.

If business feels that higher education is not fully responsive to its needs, then it should ask whether it has communicated its ideas clearly and consistently enough. It will not want to tell higher education its business, but rather should seek to articulate as best it can its view of the future, the needs as it sees them and then work in partnership to help ensure 'applied learning' is developed and delivered. A dialogue rather than a wish list is likely to be more productive. A more informed dialogue should benefit both parties and enable both to appreciate the strengths of the other and where partnerships could usefully be developed. Organisations are not always best at thinking of their long-term rather than short-term needs and a dialogue with academia (that tends to have the opposite trait!) can be particularly useful.

Businesses should ask themselves whether they have truly appreciated what our centres of learning can offer before they go to the private sector providers that have so far in the UK (though interestingly not always elsewhere) captured the lion's share of the continuing professional development (CPD) market. Before they establish more coιρorate universities they might consider where they might partner with universities and feed off the expertise on their doorstep. If they are concerned about the quality of some of our business schools, what are they doing about it? Do business leaders themselves aim to be the most informed in the world and drive an appropriate system of learning and briefing on the issues that will determine the international competitiveness of their operations? Or do they get what they deserve? How can a compact help?

The concept of a compact between higher education and other stakeholders is central to the achievement of these aims. It is only through a partnership of equals between all the various stakeholders that higher education can hope to respond to and even anticipate the needs of customers. Institutions will not be learning organisations unless they can reach out, embrace and respond to changing needs. But when they do reach out they need to be met with positive responses. Communities will not benefit from the local learning and knowledge powerhouses in their midst unless all work in partnership to develop, disseminate, access and apply that knowledge at times, in places and in a form suitable to the needs of different individuals and organisations. Supporting learning in the evenings, at weekends, in companies, libraries, FE colleges, schools, via the Internet to multinational organisations in different time zones is not just a job for HEIs. It requires willing and active partners. Neither can it be achieved by a cottage industry approach. Achieving the economies of scale needed to offer world class learning products to a hungry worldwide English speaking market requires enormous investment and hence a willingness on the part of institutions and private sector providers and customers to enter into long term partnerships where there are mutual benefits. A compact only works where all sides both bring something to the table and benefit from the results.

The Council for Industry and Higher Education has been at the forefront of those advocating and practising partnership for the last 13 years. We now believe that we need to be even more proactive and use our neutrality and convening power to help stimulate the consortia both real and virtual that can develop and deliver the world-class learning that is now needed. UK business wants and needs a higher education system that is pre-eminent in the world. It must help bring that about.

Business excellence in all its various forms is partly about building relationships and using networks. The same is true in the business of higher education. Higher education is moving from an era of competition to one not just of cooperation but also of complementarity. It needs encouragement and support in that process. It deserves the active participation of businesses and other organisations across society that have an interest in ensuring that the UK has a diverse system of higher education that is internationally pre-eminent.

References

Eraut, M. (ed.) (1991), *Education and the Information Society,* London: Cassell.
Gardner, H. (1993), *Multiple Intelligences: The theory in practice*, New York: Basic Books.

Conclusion

K. MOTI GOKULSING AND CORNEL DaCOSTA

In this concluding chapter, we review some of the insights provided by the various contributions to this volume and highlight some issues that deserve closer attention by all the stakeholders if a compact for higher education is to be achieved.

The contributors reflect a general groundswell of support for the idea of a compact. However, when we originally asked our contributors to address this notion of a compact for higher education in their respective fields, they asked us to define what we meant by a compact. Since there is no precise definition, we referred them to the Dearing Report (1997) and to Watson and Taylor's (see our introduction p. 1) interpretation of a compact as used in the Dearing Report.

Chapter 1 explored comprehensively the many facets of a compact. This was all the more important since the notion of a compact as used in the Dearing Report (1997) has a very short pedigree in higher education and indeed has been relatively unaddressed by academics. Many contributors, then, probed the Dearing Report's (1997) idea of a compact and argued that a compact for higher education was likely to offer a basis for transparency and a more systematic approach in the light of financial constraints and rapid technological developments. Indeed, with some exceptions, the contributors believe that a compact will establish a clear foundation for sound partnerships as opposed to the proliferation of ad hoc ones. But will it? In the rest of this final chapter, we try to answer this question by addressing two issues: What is the nature of this compact? What needs to be in place for the compact to be more than a paper exercise?

The Nature of a Compact for Higher Education

As argued by Craig et al. (1999, p. 28), the present interest in compacts reflects changing views of governance which emphasise an increasing interest in partnerships and 'the role of government as an enabler'. How can the different stakeholders in higher education best work together?

A fundamental issue is not if higher education has a future, but rather what sort of education the future holds in store for it. Higher education, like so many other social institutions, relies on traditions. As Giddens (1999, p. 45) has observed:

> Everyone in the academic world works within traditions. Even academic disciplines as a whole, like economics, sociology or philosophy, have traditions. The reason is that no one could work in a wholly eclectic fashion. Without intellectual traditions, ideas would have no focus or tradition.

Yet higher education is being shaken by strong winds of change that apparently threaten to uproot it, forcing academics to work in an eclectic fashion. In such a situation, it is crucial for academics to avoid reminiscing about the past as the golden age of higher education. Higher education is being stripped of its esoteric existence and of the glamour and status it used to confer on its graduates: it is being de-traditionalised. An important consequence of the de-traditionalisation of higher education is that it has to re-invent itself – hence the frequent reference in recent years to the phrase 'crisis in higher education'. For example, when Baroness Blackstone took office in 1997 as Minister for Higher Education, she described higher education as 'somewhere between a shambles and a crisis' (Willis, 1999, p. 14). However, higher education can only re-invent itself if it does a deal with other stakeholders. This is the framework advocated in this book; hence the notion of a compact as a central issue of higher education at the beginning of a new millennium.

The contributors' accounts fall into different categories of the framework used in this book and, in order to make sense of their contributions, it would be useful to comment on the various sections of this book. In Part 1, both the idea and the vision of a compact for higher education were explored from two different perspectives. One scenario argued that since the university was dead, unless we had mutual respect, understanding and agreements among the stakeholders for a new idea of the university, the realisation of a compact was problematic. The other scenario expressed scepticism about a compact in this informal sense and argued rather for a formal compact in the nature of contracts. But, who will resource this compact? Will employers as well as students pay? Are we now following the USA model of higher education? Or will the compact be a 'fudge', so characteristic of British governments' interventions?

In Part 2, contributors discussed the constituents of a compact from the providers' perspectives and dealt mainly with the economic, political and technological consequences of such a compact. The quality agenda is here to stay and, at present, benchmark information on subject threshold standards is being circulated to universities for consultative purposes. Once established, national criteria, agreed by the government, the QAA, HEIs, industry and students will mark a significant improvement in higher education, particularly in relation to the argument that quality audits can represent a form of consumer empowerment. Equally important is the argument that the involvement of HEIs as well as of FECs (Further Education Colleges) is crucial to the needs of regional economic regeneration and community organisations.

The last chapter in Part 2 on 'The Virtual University' and the first chapter of Part 3, 'What Kind of a Place is This?', theorised the future of a compact for higher education. In suggesting new paradigms for a future university, the authors introduced a debate and a set of probing and controversial questions.

It is difficult to predict the consequences of such paradigm shifts, but one clear implication of virtuality is that HEIs may be minor players in the creation of knowledge in cyberspace. According to Weber (1999), they will no longer be privileged and self-contained spaces for the acquisition and transmission of knowledge in the face of the delocalising effects of new technologies. Likewise, if, as the literature on globalisation suggests, Asia and the Far East will increasingly be key players in the world economy, then the arguments for HEIs to be more multicultural are likely to be powerful. A whole new mindset would then be needed to make sense of this ever changing map of higher education.

The chapters in the rest of Part 3 filled in some missing parts of a compact in practice, from social and sociological perspectives. The government's call for widening participation has been met by the new universities in particular, but in return they are being named and shamed. As Alan Smithers (1999, p. 2) states:

> We thus have the absurd situation of the University of East London being celebrated for widening access, but shamed for massive drop-out, while Cambridge is berated for apparently showing social class and school bias, but applauded for its high completion rate.

It is here that it is difficult to make sense of the government's rhetoric. Criteria used by 'elite' universities are not wholly applicable to institutions of mass higher education. For example, the 'elite' universities control quality at the point of entry and, through a high threshold, are 'able to educate students to a high standard in a short period of time with few drop-outs. This system worked wonderfully well for those chosen, but failed the other 90 per cent' (ibid.). Thus, the chapters in Part 3 draw attention to a significant proportion of the 90 per cent largely ignored by HEIs until three decades ago – disabled students and those from the lower socioeconomic strata. It is wrong to assume, as the government do with their insistence on league tables, that the academic success of these disadvantaged groups in higher education can be achieved by merely 'scaling up a system designed for a selected few' (ibid.).

Part 4 is devoted mainly to contributions from the consumers' perspectives. The term consumers is often equated with that of clients and customers, but all these labels are problematic when applied to education. The root idea of a customer, in Kiloh's (1998, p. 46) words, 'is of someone who exercises a choice of purchase and enters into a form a contract with the supplier'. The term client would appear to be wider than that of customer. In Kiloh's (1998, p. 47) view, the confusion in the ordinary use of these terms as applied to higher education 'arises from the imposition of the commercial paradigm on organisations for which it is largely inappropriate'. As Kiloh (ibid.) perceptively put it:

> The Nolan Committee has introduced some good sense into the argument [of imposing the commercial paradigm on universities], referring to the essential point that universities and colleges cannot be treated as businesses pure and simple, and that staff members and students are not merely employees and customers, but participants in a collegiate body with rights as well as duties.

Indeed, while the student who is buying fish and chips in the university refectory is a customer and a consumer, the same principle cannot be applied to what the student 'purchases' academically. Again, in the words of Kiloh (ibid.):

> The output of academic effort by the supplier may be *teaching*, but teaching is only one ingredient in the aim of the university, which is to increase learning (and to 'change' the customer) ... Learning is something you do for yourself.

Hence, in the first chapter of Part 4 the question 'What is the purpose of (my) learning?' is pertinent. But perhaps the fundamental question to ask is what are the ends of learning to which higher education institutions are the means? An answer to this question, deeply rooted in the consciousness of all learners, should, as suggested in the chapter, help initiate thinking towards a compact. For far too long students have been seen as 'abstractions rather than as persons in higher education'. In a recent editorial, Gareth Williams (2000, p. 2) remarked (quoting Watson) that 'sadly students and their interests are conspicuous by their absence'! This is regrettably true of much that is written about higher education. While students must learn to adapt, as the NUS contributors argue in this book, academic staff too, according to the Council for Industry and Higher Education, must learn to be adaptable and flexible. The unions' role is not only to protect pay and conditions of work, but also to be concerned about the structure and curriculum matters in higher education, particularly as the increasing number of student workers pose new problems for the organisation of higher education institutions. Work, but mainly work experience, is part of industry's call for the academic curriculum to be more vocational, but higher education's contributions to the knowledge age are substantial and closer links between industry and education are to their mutual benefit and that of society.

All the above insights and comments, however, do not guarantee the realisation of a compact. It is our firm belief that for a compact for higher education to materialise, the following participants/stakeholders need to be more serious and realistic in their objectives if the compact is to be more than a paper exercise.

What Needs to be Done?

We start with the government, since they are the main contributors for any compact to materialise. As far as higher education is concerned, there is a mismatch between the rhetoric and realities of government policies. A number of significant policy shifts over the past three decades have created a complicated and confused picture of higher education. For example, is higher education a stage in lifelong learning and what are actually the relationships between higher education and the University for Industry, let alone those between HE and FE under the Learning and Skills Council and in relation to Regional Development Agencies? The recent 'U-turn' on student loans following the Cubie Report (1999) is also an example of the confused picture of New Labour government's role for funding higher education. Indeed, the government, in the view of Alan Ryan (2000, p. 2), have lost the propaganda war by describing their new funding system as a system of loans: 'Nobody in their right mind lends money at a zero real interest rate for an indefinite length of time. To all intents and purposes that is a grant now and a graduate tax later.'

All the indications of the New Labour government's policies are that we are moving in the direction of the American model of higher education but without the generosity and endowments of American businesses and foundations for higher education.

Consequently, we are likely to see the following scenario: the Russell Group of universities – the elite – similar to the Ivy League in the USA will continue to attract the best brains, particularly from overseas. They will also capture an even greater proportion of the research funding than they already enjoy. The second group – the pre-1992 universities – will also attract research funding and a number of highly qualified students, especially to their better rated departments. The third group – the new universities, i.e. the ex-polytechnics, which became universities in 1992 – pale in comparison with the first two groups and will be further marginalised as far as funding is concerned as a result of the recent announcement of the government to invest more in further education (FE) than in HEIs for the development of the two year foundation degrees.

The consequences that follow from this scenario for higher education reflect the continuing confused picture of higher education mentioned above. For example, with regard to the proposal for the two year foundation degrees, lessons have not been learnt by the New Labour government, as John Pratt (2000, p. 16) has argued in a recent article. This scheme, under another label, has been tried before but it failed because of a lack of parity of esteem and under funding. Concern, too, about the government plan to expand higher education through two year foundation degrees is being raised by both employers and funding councils according to Goddard and Tysome (2000, p. 1). In principle, however, two years should be adequate for a degree; indeed, the independent University of Buckingham has been running such a degree for a number of years. However, the intake of the University of Buckingham consists largely of highly motivated and well-qualified overseas students who are attracted to the economy afforded by a degree course of four terms per year, over two calendar years. The proposed foundation degrees are intended primarily for those not currently participating in higher education. But, by redirecting funding to FE for higher education, the plight of universities, specially that of new ones, could be dire. The core problem then is resources.

It is now quite clear that complete dependence on government funding is no longer an option for HEIs. While governments cannot afford to resource mass higher education at a level which will enable HEIs to maintain themselves effectively, their policy of funding some parts of the education system at the expense of others creates a very uneven playing field. The subtext of government policies is of course to move higher education in the direction of privatisation, market forces, closer links with industry and meeting the needs of students conceived as customers. In this new situation, the government have been helped by the widespread and increasingly vociferous demand by the consumers –whether employers or students or trade unions – for their voices to be heard in policy making.

Indeed, what the government actually want is for universities to prove their worth. Sir Graham Hills (2000, p. 10) echoes the government's intention when he says that until the economic basis of higher education is clear – the economic cost of a university education as determined by its value in the market place – its attempts to move the heart of Treasury are doomed to fail. Herein lies part of the dilemma for a proper compact for higher education. For the still unanswered question arising from the policies and reports prior to and since the Dearing Report (1997) is how to manage the higher education sector in terms of the new imperatives – 'by government direction or through the market' (Robertson, 1998, p. 222). In line with what Daniels and Garner (1999, p. 10) suggest for inclusive education, we have tried in this book to broaden the debate about higher education from 'its somewhat parochial stance and to redefine the terms of reference from a point beginning with those most pivotal to and affected' by a compact.

But what is actually needed is a mechanism for the implementation of such a compact – ' a compact which in certain respects could with advantage be made explicit' – to echo Lord Dearing's (Dearing Report, 1997, p. 127) suggestion. At present, there are two possibilities. The fledgeling Institute for Learning and Teaching could provide a forum for stakeholders to participate in the decision-making process of a compact for higher education. Another possibility, suggested to us by Lord Dearing (and reinforced in chapter 1 of this book), might be the Council for Industry and Higher Education (CIHE). Over a number of years, the CIHE has been very active in promoting mutual understanding and cooperation between Industry, the government and Higher Education. With its links with the business community, academics, policy-makers and, if student and union representatives could be included, the CIHE could be an ideal forum for the deliberations of the stakeholders. A consensus could emerge from these deliberations leading to a workable compact and obviating the need for the government of the day to impose their centralising power or, to use the current metaphor – governmental steering.

For, despite the differences and the variety of views expressed in this volume, all the stakeholders believe that higher education will continue to perform a valuable task. This consists of 'preserving, refining and transmitting critical, independent inquiry into questions for which there may be no effective economic demand from any consumer at any one time, but which may well be of the very greatest value in the long term' (Rock, 2000, p. 19). Higher education institutions are supremely equipped for this task. Both Lord Dearing and the government are publicly committed to this belief. Indeed, in the words of the Minister for Higher Education, Baroness Blackstone (1999, p. 14):

> It is scarcely possible to imagine a democracy in which academics did not have the freedom to challenge prevailing orthodoxy and to pursue innovative and untested ideas. Without higher education our society would be incapable of functioning as a healthy democracy. Nor would our economy stand any chance of survival.

In many ways, a compact for higher education is an innovative and untested idea whose time has come. This book has been a contribution to the debate for its serious consideration and application.

References

Blackstone, T. (1999), 'Twin Forces of Change Set to Meet the millennium', *THES*, 15 January.
Craig, G., Taylor, M., Szanto, C. and Wilkinson, N. (1999), *Developing Local Compacts*, York: York Publishing Services Ltd.
Cubie Report (1999), *The Independent Committee of Inquiry into Student Finance*, London: HMSO.
Daniels, H. and Garner, P. (eds) (1999), *Inclusive Education*, London: Kogan Page.
Giddens, A. (1999), *Runaway World*, London: Profile Books Ltd.
Goddard, A. and Tysome, T. (2000), 'Industry Wary of Sub-degrees', *THES*, 14 April.
Hills, Sir Graham (2000), 'Universities Must Prove their Worth', *The Times*, 5 January.
Kiloh, G. (1998), 'Customers, Clients and Consumers', *Perspectives*, Vol. 2, No. 2, pp. 46–8.
Pratt, J. (2000), 'The Uncertain Future of Foundation Degrees', *THES*, 3 March.
Robertson, D. (1998), 'The Emerging Political Economy of Higher Education', *Studies in Higher Education* (review essay), Vol. 23, No. 2, pp. 221–8.
Rock, P. (2000), letter, *The Times*, 10 January.
Ryan, A. (2000), comment, *The Independent*, 2 March.
Smithers, A. (1999), comment, *The Independent*, 9 December.
Watson, D. and Taylor, R. (1998), *Lifelong Learning and the University A Post Dearing Agenda*, London: Falmer Press.
Weber, S. (1999), 'The Future Campus: Destiny in a virtual world', *Journal of Higher Education Policy and Management*, Vol. 21, No. 2, pp 151–64.
Williams, G. (2000), editorial, *Higher Education Quarterly*, Vol. 54, No. 1, January.
Willis, P. (1999), 'From a Shambles to a Crisis', *THES*, 24 December.

Index

academic freedom 70, 72, 116, 143, 154, 233
academic review 60, 100
academic standards and values 52, 58–9
Academy of Learned Societies for the Social Sciences 96–7
access to higher education 39, 41, 92, 105, 130, 135, 158–64, 181
    for disabled students 141–7, 150–1
accountability 48–53, 66–7, 75, 91–2, 150, 161, 209
accreditation
    of higher education teachers 212
    of students' paid work 202
    of students' prior learning 118, 222
added value 76, 108
adult learning 173–4
Anglia University 92
annotated bibliographies 100
applied research 86, 90
Aronowitz, S. 178
Asda 197
Assessment of Prior Learning (APL) 118
Association of University Teachers 215
Atkins, M. 5
audit 60, 67–76, 150, 228
Aune, B. 146
Australia 149–50, 189

Baker, Kenneth 37
Ball, S.J. 71, 73
Barclays Bank 199
Barnes, John 38
Barr, Nicholas 38
Bett Report (1999) 210–16
Blackstone, Baroness 3–4, 7, 227, 233
Blunkett, David 2–3, 139, 141, 190
Borland, J. 151
Bourdieu, P. 66
Bourke, A. 148–9
Bowles, S. 193

Braverman, Harry 193
Brown, Gordon 8
Brown, R. 72
Browne, S. 199
Burgess, T. 170
bursaries for students 164, 185, 188–9, 210
business, needs of 223–5
business schools 224
Butler, J. 69
Byers, Stephen 173

Campaign for Free Education 171
Campbell, Sir Colin 188
Campbell, J. 140
Canada 10
capillary notion of power 72
casualisation of employment in higher education 212
Catalonian Open University 111
Cazenave, P. 10
Charter for Higher Education 51
childcare allowances 188
Christie, I. 142
Clark, G. 91
code of practice for assurance of quality and standards 58–60
Cohen, P. 93
collegiality 208, 211, 229
Commission for Racial Equality 214
Commission on University Career Opportunity (CUCO) 214
Committee of Vice-Chancellors and Principals (CVCP) 4, 68, 159, 214
communications and information technology (ICT) 105–11, 115–18, 183
    adaptation and application of 109
    advantages for learning 117
    for visually disabled students 151–2
communities of practice 134–5
community education 173

234

For Product Safety Concerns and Information please contact our EU
representative GPSR@taylorandfrancis.com Taylor & Francis Verlag GmbH,
Kaufingerstraße 24, 80331 München, Germany

Printed and bound by CPI Group (UK) Ltd, Croydon, CR0 4YY

08/06/2025
01896999-0007